Bhakti
The Yoga of Love

Bhakti
The Yoga of Love

Gregor Maehle

Kaivalya Publications

2024

By the same author:

Ashtanga Yoga: Practice and Philosophy

Ashtanga Yoga: The Intermediate Series

Pranayama The Breath of Yoga

Yoga Meditation: Through Mantra, Chakras and Kundalini to Spiritual Freedom

Samadhi The Great Freedom

How To Find Your Life's Divine Purpose – Brain Software For A New Civilization

Chakras, Drugs and Evolution – A Map of Transformative States

Mudras: Seals of Yoga

Published by Kaivalya Publications PO Box 181
Crabbes Creek, NSW 2483 Australia

© Gregor Maehle 2024

This book is copyrighted. Except for fair dealing for private study, research, criticism, or review, as permitted under the Copyright Act, no part may be reproduced by any process without the written permission of the author.

First published 2024

Maehle, Gregor
Bhakti: The Yoga of Love/by Gregor Maehle;

ISBN (pbk.): 978-0-6488932-8-8

Includes bibliographical references

Bhakti yoga

Every effort was made to contact the copyright holders of quoted material, but this was not possible in every case.

A catalogue record for this book is available from the National Library of Australia

Cover image: Radha and Krishna, Bharat Kala Bhavan, Varanasi

Dedication

To the ancient sages of India who revealed the mysteries of life in the *Vedas* and *Upanishads*.

Acknowledgements

I am grateful to Shri T. Krishnamacharya for his lifelong dedication to teaching many extremely helpful yoga techniques.

To Shri Ramakrishna for showing that there is a common truth behind all religions that cannot be reduced to one single type of mystical experience.

To Shri Ramanujacharya for presenting an accurate theology based on the *Upanishads*, *Bhagavad Gita* and *Brahma Sutra*.

To Shri Aurobindo, who showed that *Jnana*, *Karma* and *Bhakti* Yoga are parts of an integrated whole.

To Alfred North Whitehead, who demonstrated that the same can be possible for mathematics, Western Science, Western Philosophy and Christianity.

Concise Table of Contents

List of Shastras quoted in this text: xvii
Introduction 1

Chapter 1: Who and what is the Divine? 23
Chapter 2: Who are we? 77
Chapter 3: What is our Relationship with the Divine? 95
Chapter 4: Bhakti, what it is 123
Chapter 5: Karma Yoga and its Importance for Bhakti 167
Chapter 6: Jnana Yoga and its Importance for Bhakti 213
Chapter 7: Raja Yoga and its Importance for Bhakti 237
Chapter 8: Role of Ethics in Bhakti 253
Chapter 9: Metaphysical Errors and what the Divine is not 263
Chapter 10: Clarification of Terms 293

Epilogue 323
Bibliography 327
Author Information 335

xi

Comprehensive Table of Contents

List of Shastras quoted in this text: xvii

Introduction 1
- My Encounter with *Bhakti* 2
- What is an *Ishtadevata*? 5
- Names of the Divine 8
- What is Human Love? 9
- The Difference Between Human and Divine Love 12
- What is Divine Love? 16

Chapter 1: Who and what is the Divine? 23
- The Divine as the Self 24
- Deities and Divine Forms 33
- God as the Universe 42
- *Vijnana*, God-Realization 48
- Transcendent and Immanent, Father and Mother
  Father and Mother, *Nirguna* and *Saguna* 59
- The Mystery of the Supreme Being 68
- Stages of God-Realisation 71

Chapter 2: Who are we? 77
- *Jiva*, the Individual Spirit Entangled in Rebirth 81
- *Purusha*, the Embodied Consciousness 88
- *Atman*, the Unembodied Self And aure Consciousness 92

Chapter 3: What is our Relationship with the Divine? 95
- The Egolessness of the Divine 96
- Why is this Relationship so Important for the Divine? 103

xiii

- How to See and Worship the Divine 111
- How not to Worship the Divine 115

Chapter 4: *Bhakti*, what it is 123
- Definition of *Bhakti* 127
- Qualities and Attitudes Supportive of *Bhakti* 130
- Types and Forms of *Bhakti* 138
- Consecration 145
- God-Realisations and the Intellectual Love of God 148
- Pure Love and Ecstasy 153
- Effects of *Bhakti* 155
- The Essence of *Bhakti* 162

Chapter 5: Karma Yoga and its Importance for *Bhakti* 167
- The Law of *Karma* 167
- *Karma* as Work 175
- What is *Karma* Yoga? 178
- The Deep Meaning of *Yajna* 179
- Why Karma Yoga is Important? 184
- Self-Contemplation (*Svabhava*), or Law of Being 189
- Self-duty (*Svadharma*) or Law of Becoming 196
- *Varna* or Caste and why it Matters for *Bhakti* 201
- *Yajna* – More on Offering and Giving 205

Chapter 6: Jnana Yoga and its Importance for *Bhakti* 213
- What is *Jnana* Yoga? 213
- *Vijnana* (God-realization) 217
- *Jnana* and *Bhakti* 218
- How to Practice *Jnana* Yoga 220
- Effects of *Jnana* 231

COMPREHENSIVE TABLE OF CONTENTS

Chapter 7: *Raja* Yoga and its Importance for *Bhakti* 237
   – What is *Raja* Yoga 237
   – Why *Raja* Yoga 241
   – Methods of *Raja* Yoga 245
   – Practical Tips for Integrating *Bhakti* into *Raja* Yoga Practice .. 248
   – Summary 251

Chapter 8: Role of Ethics in *Bhakti* 253

Chapter 9: Metaphysical Errors and what the Divine is not 263
   – The Unmoved Mover 264
   – God not a Giant Human in Heaven 267
   – The World not an Illusion 273
   – Consciousness not all that Exists 277
   – *Karma* Yoga not an Inferior Discipline of Yoga 281
   – *Bhakti* Yoga not the Only Way of approaching the Divine 283
   – Individual Self and Divine Self not One and the Same 286

Chapter 10: Clarification of Terms 293
   – Mind 293
   – Avatarhood 303
   – *Shraddha* 306
   – *Shastra* (scripture) 311
   – *Yugas* (world ages) 314
   – Castes and *Varnas* - Additional Notes and References 318

Epilogue 323

Bibliography 327

Author Information 335

List of Shastras quoted in this text:

Yoga Sutra,
Gheranda Samhita,
Hatha Tatva Kaumudi,
Bhagavad Gita,
Chandogya Upanishad,
Bhagavata Purana,
Mundaka Upanishad,
Brhad Aranyaka Upanishad,
Aitareya Upanishad,
Hatha Yoga Pradipika,
Taittiriya Upanishad,
Mandukya Upanishad,
Mandukya Karika,
Ramanuja's Vedanta Sara,
Ramanuja's Shri Bhashya,
Mahabharata,
Narada Bhakti Sutras

Introduction

In 14th-century Shiraz in Persia, a 20-year-old baker walked past the balcony of an upper class woman and, upon seeing her beauty, fell hopelessly in love with her. The baker was poor, of low class birth, and not considered handsome. To the degree that it dawned upon him that his desire for the woman, who later became the king's wife, could never be consummated, his obsession with her only increased. His infatuation went to the extent that he eventually could hardly eat or sleep anymore. Through various twists and turns, the young man eventually became the student of a Sufi master who advised him to turn his human love god-wards. Hafiz, as he came to be known, recorded his entire mystical journey in his poetry, which is today the finest in the Persian language. Although not a *bhakta*[1] in the narrower sense of the word, Hafiz's work nevertheless gives us a clear road map of what it means to turn human love into divine love. Notably, even in Hafiz's case, cutting and polishing the heart's raw sentiment took 40 years of practice to turn into the precious gem of divine realisation.

While I do not possess Hafiz's gift of poetry, also my entry onto the path of *bhakti* was not through the front door. I was attracted to *Jnana* Yoga when I was young, which is the path of realising the formless Absolute or infinite consciousness through reflection on scriptural

---

1 A practitioner of Bhakti Yoga, the path of devotion

passages. I also practised the *Raja* Yoga of the *Yoga Sutra*, which consists of various meditation and concentration exercises to make the mind sharp like a laser so that it may cut through ignorance and delusion. *Bhakti* Yoga, though, always made me uncomfortable. It reminded me of the religious indoctrination of my childhood, where I was told I had to have faith in a giant, bearded, white man in the sky, who upon my refusal, would send floods, locusts, plagues, etc., or send me to eternal damnation in hell.

MY ENCOUNTER WITH BHAKTI

When I arrived in India, I was the same age as Hafiz when he saw Shakh-e-Nabat on that balcony. Here was a land where nobody cared whether my God was the formless Absolute, *the nirvana*, a blue-skinned flute player, or indeed a naked, black woman wearing garlands of skulls. In my luggage to India was a recent experience, which I had placed into the too-hard-to-integrate basket, as it was irreconcilable with my atheist-agnostic tendencies. After I had, for an extensive period, meditated, fasted, maintained isolation, and studied the *Upanishads*, I came to the solution that I was incapable of reaching what I was aiming for: *moksha*, spiritual liberation. In a rare moment of surrender, I lay down on the forest floor and raised my eyes to the night-time sky. I thought, "Help, show me who I am, " although according to my professed agnosticism, there was no entity out there that I could have addressed.

At that moment, it was as if a giant zipper was pulled across the sky, and the fabric that veiled reality was being removed. Behind it appeared an infinite and eternal beingness, whose body was the total of all universes. Before my inner eye, this beingness brought forth an endless stream of universes and reabsorbed others, which had run their course. At the same time, the entity radiated out an infinity of sentient beings, microbes, plants, fungi, animals, humans, and divine forms, which all were computations and emanations of Itself, and by doing so, It became Itself. At the same time, an aspect of Itself, Its eternal essence, was completely unaffected by these transformations. I watched this revelation before my mind's eye for about 45 minutes. I then reflected on it for over a year before concluding that it did not fit into my view of life and, therefore, had to go into the too-hard basket. What I had seen was all too alive for me, too much of a being; it entailed too much process, evolution, and multiplicity. I only wanted oneness, nothingness, emptiness, non-existence, awareness, consciousness, and silence. I certainly didn't know what to do with God and love.

Equipped with such preconceptions, I arrived in India during the early 80s, where I first settled for various instant enlightenment-peddling sects and cults before embarking on a multi-decade training in classical yoga. This training involved *asana*, *pranayama*, *chakra*-Kundalini meditation, *samadhi*, Sanskrit, and *shastra* (scripture) study. About 20 years into this training, and without thinking much, I almost accidentally started to perform *Trataka* (gazing) on various divine images and symbols during long breath retentions (*kumbhakas*). I wanted to determine whether such focus would help keep the mind luminous (*sattvic*) during the retentions. What I got was much more than what I had bargained for. I learned that inspired divine images are akin to spiritual archetypes that can reveal knowledge if the meditator's mind is empty and receptive. During long yogic breath retentions, if executed correctly, the mind will become empty and receptive more or less automatically.

While initially focussing on Hindu divine images combined with Sanskrit *mantras*, I later learned that Buddhist, Islamic, Christian, and Jewish images, combined with Pali, Arabic, or Hebrew incantations, work just as well. The Indian mystic Shri Ramakrishna, who embarked on all these paths sequentially, had already confirmed as much. Later, I experimented with animistic, indigenous, and nature-based sacred symbols such as animal and plant spirits, holy mountains and rivers, etc., whose value and capacity to instruct the meditator also proved their value. Although I continue my *Raja* Yoga to this day, these experiences ultimately turned me from being a technique-based *Raja* Yogi into a devotion-based *Bhakti* Yogi. I hope this text on *Bhakti* Yoga may support anyone interested in delving deeper into their spirituality and associated experiences.

You can practice *Bhakti* Yoga whether or not you are a member of a spiritual denomination. What I found extremely important is that authentic spiritual experiences and knowledge ultimately replace that belief. Somebody who only believes knows they are on an insecure footing and therefore tends to dogmatically defend their position against those with different beliefs. Demonstrating certainty regarding one's religious and spiritual beliefs

INTRODUCTION

is often displayed to the extent to which internal doubt and questioning rise. This paradox of outer certainty and internal doubt has contributed much to our history of holy wars, which are attempts to convert by the sword those to our fold who hold different beliefs, which we deem threatening. When we have attained knowledge, whether or not somebody else believes we are correct becomes irrelevant.

For example, you would not feel threatened if somebody told you you do not have eyes. The fact that you can see tells you that you have eyes. Alternatively, you can look into the mirror to confirm that you have eyes. The case is similar if somebody says they don't believe in gravitation. You can stand on your feet and feel gravitation pressing your feet into the ground. Even if you sit on a lounge, you will feel gravitation pressing your body onto the soft surface. If somebody tells you they don't believe you have eyes or don't believe in gravitation, you will likely consider them odd but certainly no threat to your primary system of values. Different is the situation with religious beliefs. If we have yet to attain knowledge, the fact that somebody else may follow different beliefs may make us insecure about whether our beliefs are wrong. We may compensate for this insecurity through aggression. This insecurity and the aggression it fosters become obsolete once we obtain mystical knowledge.

WHAT IS AN ISHTADEVATA?

All of this changes once we know the one nameless Divine known under a thousand names. Such knowledge leads to

5

devotion and service to the One, the ancient source of all religions, spiritual paths, and mystical schools, all equally valid. The *Yoga Sutra* states that studying sacred treatises reveals one's appropriate deity (*ishtadevata*).[2] The concept of *ishtadevata* implies that there are many different types of personalities, each divine form representing a different frequency, assumed by the one Divine to communicate with us individually. While the Divine is not a person nor a giant human in the sky, it is personal to each of us. This is so because all of us are permutations of the one Divine, through which It embodies Its unlimited creativity. In its seventh chapter, the *Gheranda Samhita*, a medieval Hatha Yoga text, teaches six avenues to reach *samadhi* (absorptive ecstasy and revelation). One of these six avenues is *bhakti samadhi*, which consists of visualising one's *ishtadevata* (the for a particular individual appropriate divine form) in our heart until we shed tears of happiness.[3] It seems baffling that the simple visualisation of a divine form should lead to the shedding of tears of happiness, but context is everything. This particular stanza occurs in the final chapter of a treatise that gives endless lists of occult practices, such as *asanas, kriyas, mudras, pranayama,* meditations, etc., to prepare for *samadhi*. Even when arriving at this concluding subject, the *Gheranda Samhita* does not insist on *bhakti* but only lists it as one of six possible approaches.

However, the critical hint in the stanza that makes *bhakti* so powerful is the term *ishtadevata*. The important connotation included in this term is that you must choose a

---

2 *Yoga Sutra* II.24

3 *Gheranda Samhita* VII.14-15

INTRODUCTION

representation of the Divine as appropriate for you and not impressed on you by somebody else. A form suitable for me might be entirely inappropriate for anybody else. Such a situation should not make us insecure but cause us to celebrate our diversity. For example, a situation in which you were the only person alive on Earth to meditate on a particular *ishtadevata* would not devalue this *ishtadevata*, nor would it devalue your experience in any way. It means that currently, you are the only person on Earth of that particular spiritual personality type, that's all.

Ultimately, especially if our meditation and communion with our *ishtadevata* is profound, we may come to the point where we have plumbed the depth of what this particular *ishtadevata* can reveal to us. Note that this is not a limitation of the Divine but of our spiritual personality type. We may then choose to meditate on another divine form and then yet another, as Shri Ramakrishna has demonstrated. Shri Aurobindo said that an accomplished *bhakta* would ultimately meditate on all available *ishtadevatas*. However, we should not let this statement lead us to some form of rat race from divine form to divine form. Still, Aurobindo pointed out a fact that will become extremely important for a future global spiritual community. When you enter an unfamiliar culture, prepare yourself by meditating on the divine forms used by that culture. By such meditation, you will immerse yourself in another culture from the inside. By understanding the divine forms of that culture and gaining their *darshana*[4], you will enter another culture, like a fish entering the water.

---

4 *Darshana* directly translated means view. During a deep view, we gain revelation.

7

NAMES OF THE DIVINE

To express universality, I will use the following terms for the Divine in this text: the Supreme Being, Purushottama (Sanskrit for Supreme Being), the One, and God. This latter term is especially loaded since almost everybody has a clear opinion on what it denotes, whether favourable or unfavourable. I found it very important to reclaim this term. This book's first and most significant chapter deals with what the Divine is and is not. Fishes apparently have no awareness of the ocean they swim in, as it is everything they have ever experienced. The Divine is like that. Our situation regarding the Divine is akin to the situation of a fish regarding the ocean. We define something by demarking its boundaries against something that it is not. Our definition of good achieves meaning by demarcating it against wrong, and so does our concept of hot, which arises by separating it from what is cold.

Similarly, blue was the last colour to be named in most languages. This is because the vast part of the world, the sky and the oceans, is blue. For this reason, we did not see it as a colour for an extended part of our history but took it as what the world looks like. This is precisely the case with the Divine, and that's why we have a hard time seeing It. The Divine is not only the backdrop on which everything takes place, but all the actors on that screen are the Divine, too.

I will base this text on scripture, the testimony of ground-breaking mystics, and my own experience. By and large, everything written in this book is based on all three. The authoritative scriptures that I have quoted at

INTRODUCTION

every twist and turn are the *Bhagavad Gita*, the *Bhagavata Purana* (in both of which the main speaker is the Vishnu-*avatar* Krishna), and Narada's *Bhakti Sutra*. I will also quote from the *Bible* and various yoga texts, particularly the *Yoga Sutra*. Additionally, I have quoted the Indian theologian Ramanujacharya (1077-1157CE), the Indian mystics and philosophers Shri Ramakrishna (19th century) and Shri Aurobindo (20th century), the British mathematician and philosopher Alfred North Whitehead (20th century) and various contemporary Indian scholars, including Swami Tapasyananda and Swami Tyagisananda. When it first occurs, I address these authorities with the honorific Shri, commonly used in India. Due to the mass of quotations and so as not to be too repetitive, I will leave out the title further down the track. I do not mean this disrespectful, and I hope nobody takes offence.

WHAT IS HUMAN LOVE?

The medieval *Hatha Tatva Kaumudi* asks what the use of Hatha Yoga without *bhakti* is.[5] It then describes *bhakti* as the process during which a yogi gets drenched in tears of intense bliss, provoked by love through communion with the Divine. The text further states that *bhakti* is experiencing eternal love upon plunging into the ocean of divine love. It is apparent from the choice of words that the concept of love here significantly differs from contemporary ideas about love currently used in modern society. Today, we use the term mainly in the context of romantic love. Romantic love subscribes to the myth that we are somehow incomplete

---

5 *Hatha Tatva Kaumudi*, p.629

and that there is precisely the right person out there to make us whole and complete if only we can find them.[6] Modern people, therefore, tend to enter romantic relationships saddled with enormous expectations, under which weight they tend to collapse quickly. Most people cannot live up to the expectation that it is their responsibility to make their partner whole and happy, and why should they? We then believe that we chose the wrong person, go our way, and continue to look for Mr or Mrs Right.

One of the problems with human love is the always-present element of projection. Freud pointed out how our relationships with our primary carer(s), usually our parents, leave certain psychological wounds, in yoga called *samskaras* (subconscious imprints). Based on such early imprints, we select our partner(s) later in adulthood based on their capacity to re-inflict those same wounds simply because they confirm our existing biases. Thus, our partners become the receiving screen for projecting our subconscious biases. I will refer to them simply by the term projections.

These biases may involve beliefs such as that life is painful or complex, that we are worthless or unworthy, that men are interested only in sex, that women are in it only for money and security, and many more. Our subconscious has distilled such beliefs from our life experiences for the purpose of survival, and many of them during early childhood by emulating our primary carers. We developed such beliefs as a response to coming to terms

---

6 Robert A. Johnson, *We: Understanding the Psychology of Romantic Love*, Harper One, 2009.

with the behaviour of our primary carers and all others we encountered. Unless we engage in transformative work, such subconscious biases and beliefs are usually not examined in adult life simply because they worked in the past. For this reason, in yoga, we refer to the totality of these beliefs as robotic programming.

We tend to select our partners not based on who they truly are as individuals but based on their suitability to receive our projection. The point at which we wake up from projecting subconscious needs on our partner is often the point at which the romantic relationship breaks down. At this point, we usually scout for a new partner to become our projection's next recipient. Alternatively, when we consciously decide to love our partner without projecting on them, our love may take on a spiritual quality. In this case, the relationship's focus will switch from receiving what we need from our partner to what we are ready to give. This is the point of departure where human love begins to turn towards and into divine love. Ultimately, divine love asks us to see and experience everybody as an embodiment of God. For many of us, starting with one's partner is a natural starting point on this journey.

A similar source for projection may be our love for our children. Modern people who don't follow a particular religion or spiritual path often harbour the subconscious hope or belief to attain some form of immortality by continuing to live on in their children. As a child, I was struggling with my mother's sometimes obsessive form of identifying with me. When I approached my father with the request for advice on how to handle this situation, he said that I needed to understand that my mother was an atheist. Like all atheists, so my father said, she saw her children as a continuation of herself and her ticket to immortality. Such unconscious and unexamined beliefs may surface in statements as simple as "I don't want my children to suffer the same deprivation or difficulties that I did", or "I always wanted to do this or that but never could. Now I make sure that my children can." Alternatively, we may have wished to become a doctor, successful singer, or athlete, but it never worked out. We may now attempt to achieve this success through our children by manoeuvring them into a position where we can enjoy and consummate their success per extension. Such an attitude is present to the degree to which we try to push our children in a particular direction.

Of course, also, here, an evolution can take place. This is especially clear when we start loving our children not for who they can be for us but simply for who they presently are, even if that is not necessarily the person we bargained for. Especially if our child has what we could call a problematic fate, and we still love and support them selflessly or possibly gradually learn to do so, then our love is beginning to evolve towards the ideal of *bhakti*, divine love.

THE DIFFERENCE BETWEEN HUMAN AND DIVINE LOVE

Human love is love in which our focus is on receiving a hormonal high when being together with the loved one. Once our love has matured to the point where the focus is on our ability to love, independent of the qualities of the object of love, we are already practising a pre-state of *bhakti*. The vital difference is the shift from wanting to receive love to wanting to give love. The more mature this love is, the more independent it is from the actual behaviour of the recipient. This is clear in our image of the ideal motherly love, in which the mother loves her child unconditionally, even as the child continues to display unfortunate behaviour and choices.

Therefore, it is not untrue to say that our families offer the first training ground for exercising *bhakti*. If we develop a mature quality of love towards our spouse, children, and parents, we can extend this love to all children of God, human and otherwise. This is a massive step as our family often functions as an extension of our ego. While mature love towards one's family members is a significant step forward, it cannot be said to be true *bhakti* unless directed towards the whole of existence. This is so because the whole of existence is the crystallised body of the Divine. The Divine is not a bearded white man in the sky. On the contrary, the Divine consists of:

- a transcendental aspect (variously called the formless Absolute, infinite consciousness, the Dao, the Father, *nirguna* Brahman, etc.),
- an immanent aspect (called cosmic intelligence, divine creative force, Shakti, the Mother, Shekhinah, etc.),
- all matter as the body of the Divine,
- an infinity of beings into which the divine enters by becoming Itself as them,
- and an infinity of objects, which the Divine enters by giving them their characteristics.

You don't need to memorise the list above; I will repeat it frequently in this text. It forms the key to genuine *bhakti*. The *Bhagavata Purana* states that we need to meditate on each aspect of the Divine individually and then on all parts together.[7]

When we genuinely want to love God, we must love every being and atom in this universe and everything beyond. The first chapter of this text is devoted to this subject because a true understanding of what the Divine is forms the foundation of *bhakti*. Seeing everything as God does not mean that we accept everything as perfect or that the world that humanity has created for itself is perfect. It is everything but. It means, however, that we need to become agents of change, not from a position of frustration, anger, or fear at the fact that things are the way they are, but from a position of love.

Bhakti is sometimes called the yoga of emotions or the act of turning one's emotions God-wards. Neither of these statements is wrong, but they require explanation. These statements do not mean we should be emotional or that emotions are closer to the Divine than thoughts. Emotions are feelings based on past imprints. If I am emoting, I'm reacting based on past conditions. An easy way to understand this is if we look at our response to something our spouse does. If it triggers a response based on the present moment, our response can only be said to provoke in us a feeling. For example, we could be sad, concerned, or fearful about something our partner says or does. In either case, we would be capable of pointing out our feelings

---

7 *Bhagavata Purana* III.33.22

without much emotional charge in our voices. We could communicate that it would be helpful for us if our partner could adjust their behaviour for such and such reasons.

The situation would be much different in the case of an emotion. Here, we would not respond to our partner based on feelings arising in the moment. Rather than that, we would react based on emotions related to the past. These emotions are often linked to similar situations we have experienced with a parent or primary carer. As children, we are usually powerless to respond adequately at the moment; hence, an emotional charge, such as one related to humiliation, will gradually build up over time. These charges may then become triggered decades later, and we may display an emotional outburst that is seemingly out of proportion to what our partner has just communicated. An emotion is, hence, an accumulated feeling based on past experiences, reactions, and imprints.

If we then call *bhakti* the yoga of emotions, or when talking of turning one's emotions God-wards, what we really mean is that *bhakti* deals with purifying one's emotions by turning them God-wards. Let's look, for example, at the emotions of fear and hatred. It is impossible to love God and hate any of Her children. To hate anybody amounts to hating God. In this case, turning one's emotions God-wards means having to let go of hatred, as hatred for anybody would amount to hatred of God. About fear, Shri Krishna states in the *Bhagavad Gita* that His devotees are those who fear nobody and who cause fear in nobody.[8] They do so because they see everything as a manifestation

---

8 *Bhagavad Gita* XII.15

of God. Of course, it would be foolish to say that *bhakti* will prevent any feeling of fear. For example, if we are crossing a street and a large truck careens towards us at high speed, feeling fear is healthy. Fear will mobilise adrenaline, which helps us to lurch with incredible velocity toward the safety of the food path. But *bhakti* will help us overcome the more or less permanent state of unconscious anxiety that many experience today. Notice here again the difference between a feeling related to the present moment and a long-accumulated emotion. Therefore, we can generalise that emotions can only continue to exist in the absence of divine love. In the presence of divine love, they will melt away, and only feelings related to the present will remain.

WHAT IS DIVINE LOVE?

Writing or theorising about divine love is difficult because it silences the mind whenever one feels it. For this reason, it is also called the voice of the heart. But writing about it, I must because divine love, *bhakti*, is a spiritual discipline. It does not come automatically or spontaneously, but it is a learned response, a spiritual practice, a *sadhana*, as we have seen in the example of Hafiz and many others. Studying and practising it can bring more love into the world. We can also help God, the Divine, to come through us more than presently is possible.

Divine love is pure love. Pure love is love purified from our emotionality, from our needs, and from our need to being needed. Love is the central radiance of our being. It is what shines from our core, from our *atman*, our consciousness, our soul, outward towards our surface personality. The *bhakta* attempts to make the surface personality translucent like a crystal or diamond so that the radiant love at the core of our being can shine out.

The metaphorical use of a crystal or diamond is constructive because both need polishing and cutting to reveal their radiance and luminosity. A diamond may be concealed inside a stone, and little from it may be visible at the surface. Work and expertise in polishing and cutting are required to bring out its greatest potential. Similarly, the practice of *bhakti* requires work and expertise to bring out the radiance of our *atman*, the self, the consciousness.

Love is an aspect of our consciousness, the self, and the Divine. Similarly, as our consciousness is aware of everything without omitting anything, it also loves everything and everybody equally. The practice of *bhakti* is about bringing out this capacity. If we can bring out this quality, it will fulfil us. We can then go beyond needing to receive, take, and be needy. True *bhakti* must always involve degrees of self-knowledge, knowledge of the Divine, and readiness to carry one's love out into the world by serving the Divine and all beings. Shri Aurobindo says that love without knowledge can be passionate and intense but often blind, crude, and even dangerous. It is a great power but also a stumbling block.[9] Love, limited in knowledge [of the Divine and the self], condemns itself in its fervour to narrowness. Love combined with knowledge, so Aurobindo, is not inconsistent with, but instead throws itself with joy into divine works; for it loves God and is

---

9 Sri Aurobindo, *The Synthesis of Yoga*, Sri Aurobindo Ashram, Pondicherry, 1948, p. 548

one with Her in all Her beings. Working for the world means feeling and fulfilling one's love for God. We should, therefore, not be concerned that our practice of *bhakti* will lead us to become aloof, sectarian, or disinterested in the world. On the contrary, *bhakti* will allow us to act with great joy and compassion in service of the Divine and all beings.

Since the Divine is pure love, we cannot truly feel It unless we become pure love. Such becoming does not imply change but rather a letting go of destructive aspects of our surface personality. We cannot be pure love unless we surrender and let go of enmity, hatred, and adversarialism. This triad is representative of externalised inner conflict. Externalised inner conflict means that we reject aspects of ourselves that are too painful to look at and acknowledge. We are, therefore, suppressing these aspects into the depth of our unconscious and combat them by externalising them, i.e., recognising, fighting, and attempting to destroy them in others by projecting the suppressed conflict on them.

By developing the quality of pure, divine love, we can acknowledge harmful, destructive, and painful aspects of our psyche and surrender and let go of them to the Divine. Apart from acknowledging painful and destructive elements of our psyche, this process also entails forgiving ourselves for harbouring them. To the extent such forgiveness is enacted, it also extends to others for their shortcomings. This puts an end to inner conflict and its repression. With that, the externalisation of such conflict loses its necessity.

In other words, to truly feel God, we must ultimately end all conflict within ourselves and love and accept ourselves. When done correctly, the significant side effects of this process are letting go of negative attitudes and developing gratitude and forgiveness. We are hampering our evolution and holding us back by holding on to negative attitudes about life, the world, and others. We develop these attitudes to protect ourselves from adversity, but they impede the satisfaction and happiness we get out of life. These negative attitudes are usually based on painful, sometimes traumatic experiences in the past. By realising the Divine, understanding that the nature of the Divine is love, and placing ourselves in Its service, these painful experiences lose their purpose and can gradually be let go of.

Letting go of painful experiences is done by first becoming aware of the effort, and of visceral and neurological energy we invest in holding on to them. Once we create this awareness (and only then), we can let go of this energy and use it for more creative and life-affirmative purposes. In this context, the affirmations (*sankalpas*) and cultivation of thought patterns in alignment with the Divine (*bhavanas*) that I described and listed in my 2020 text, *How To Find Your Life's Divine Purpose,* are helpful and essential. With over 100 pages, the subject is too extensive to cover here.

A crucial subject related to this, also described in that book, is forgiveness practice. Also, here, the easiest way of forgiving is to realise that all beings are emanations and children of the Divine. They may be injured, distorted, and through their long, painful, and traumatic history of errors, may even commit evil and sadistic acts. Even then, in their own distorted way, they are on their journey to happiness, love, and freedom. They, too, will ultimately reach their destination, albeit probably in various roundabout ways. They will also reach the same destination of becoming knowers and lovers of the Divine. In the meantime, we need to forgive them and, if necessary, correct their behaviour compassionately without deriving any ego-aggrandisement for being right, better, or more virtuous.

Forgiveness does not mean we are letting somebody else off the hook, for their *karma* will catch up with them. Forgiveness is a purification practice for our own subconscious. Grudges that we hold on to are poisoning our subconscious. Our subconscious cannot distinguish whether we hold a grudge against somebody else or ourselves. That's why Jesus Christ said, "Judge not, for by the same metre with you judge, you yourself shall be judged."[10] To the degree to which we let go of negative attitudes and to which we forgive, the dominant theme of our life will become gratitude and love. Gratitude is one of the most healing sentiments we can have. Genuine gratitude that we are alive and that the Divine experiences Itself through us cannot exist in the same space as anxiety, depression, and trauma. Nor can they exist in the same space as genuine gratitude.

The most surprising thing to discover when diving deeper and deeper into *Bhakti* Yoga is that consciousness (*purusha, atman*, Brahman) is not just cool, detached, colourless awareness, but at its very centre, at its core, is of the nature of pure love. That's why it is correct to say

---

10 Matthew 7:1-2

INTRODUCTION

that God is love and that the practice of *bhakti*, on the one hand, can lead to knowledge, but also that, on the other hand, the practice of *Jnana* Yoga (the yoga of knowledge) can lead one to *bhakti*. Only together are they complete. In Sanskrit, the terms *hrt* and *hrdaya* both mean heart, core, and centre. The heart *chakra* is the central of the seven main *chakras*. The unstruck sound (*Anahata*) is heard in this *chakra*, which is the primordial syllable OM. From it, all other vibratory patterns emerged. That's why it is correct to call the OM Indian philosophy's equivalent of the Big Bang. In astrophysics, the Big Bang is the original wave, the first vibratory pattern from which everything emerges.

The *Chandogya Upanishad* says about the heart that in the centre of the chest is a small shrine with a small flame (the *atman*, the self). Inside of it miraculously is this entire vast universe with all its planets, stars, oceans, continents, mountain ranges, rivers, and beings.[11] This passage reflects a mystical state in which the seer cognised that the entire creation comes from the formless Absolute via the heart in a state of pure love. Consciousness reveals itself to yogis, who are centred at the heart, as being of the nature of pure love. We do this by focussing on the heart *chakra* while remaining in a state of pure consciousness, an advanced meditation technique. This experience then has the potential to radiate out and heal us and our attitude toward the world. We can take this state to the point that there is only pure love, nothing else. There is no sense of I, body, mind, or separation, and initially, there is also no perception of anything else but love—a profound state of

---

11 *Chandogya Upanishad* 8.1.1-3

beauty, freedom, peace, and expansion. We can then let this love radiate into the world, becoming a vehicle for this divine love.

For us to pass on this healing flame of divine love, the surface self (the egoic body-mind complex) has to be cleansed and transformed by the experience of pure love. This can only occur if we call off and let go of all conflict and struggle with ourselves. This conflict with ourselves at times seems ancient, almost eternal. For an eternity-like time, we have defined ourselves through the war we fought against ourselves, including adversarialism, antagonism, ambition, competition, degrees of domestic violence, and armed conflict between cultures. We can overcome these tendencies by rediscovering divine love. This love does not worry about receiving. It is so overflowing that it always wants to give, has to give.

Despite all the self-created adversities that humanity is encountering, we need to rediscover that we are crystallisations of divine love and that our essential nature is love. *Bhakti* Yoga's goal is that this internal quality of love shines through our being out into the world, providing healing for others and meaning for us. For this heart, there is only one purpose in life: to make a valid contribution to the lives of others.

Chapter 1
WHO AND WHAT IS THE DIVINE?

As with all yogas, *Bhakti* Yoga is ideally not practised alone but in conjunction with all other yogas. This way, it is much more effective. *Bhakti* Yoga is the yoga of divine love or surrender to the Divine. Before going into detail about the methods of *bhakti*, we need to understand what we are surrendering to or loving. Our love for the Divine will be compromised if, deep down, we believe that the Divine is anthropomorphic, i.e. a giant man in the sky.

God is not a man. Neither is God a human, nor does God have an ego from which to meter out punishment to some while withholding it from others, dearer to him. Imagine for a moment if God was a human. How would that impinge on evolution's drive to develop lifeforms more advanced than humanity? Or do we honestly want to hold on to the belief that humanity is the crown of creation and that evolution ends here? The last few centuries of human history, including humanity's almost permanent warfare against itself and nature, have shown that evolution is in dire need of upgrading to post-human biology.

I will explore how we may experience the Divine in the following pages. There is a certain sequentiality to this, although that does not mean that the aspects of the Divine have to be experienced in this order. However, the earlier aspects are generally more apparent and accessible than the later ones. Ultimately, a *bhakta* will aim to have all these views and possibly some that, due to ignorance, I failed to list.

THE DIVINE AS THE SELF

The *Bhagavad Gita* says in stanza VI.29 that a wise person sees the self residing in all beings and all beings as resting within the self. Seeing both is an experience we can have after some progress in meditation and yoga and is available to all. Please note that unless specified, I am using the term yoga to mean the totality of all spiritual disciplines, including physical, respiratory, mental and spiritual practices (*sadhanas*). When referring to the exclusive physical aspect of yoga, I will use the term *asana* (posture).

When beginning the process of yoga and meditation, we may start with the concept that we are the body, as that is what modern society teaches us. After some progress, we realise that the body and how we feel it (sometimes called the body-consciousness) constantly changes. One day, we feel tired; another day, we feel energetic. One day, we feel stiff and aching; another, fluid and strong. Ultimately, we notice how our bodies feel, changes daily and gradually over time. That means the body is not the self, as the self is a permanent state (I will explain that later in more detail). However, after some time, we find a more profound entity within us, watching and observing the body. This entity either stays the same or changes much slower so that we initially don't notice it. We then graduate in meditation

CHAPTER 1

to observe this entity, and we learn to isolate it from the body. Isolating means that we can at all times differentiate whether what we observe is a signal from the body or this new entity.

Those stemming from a Western-influenced society would call this new entity the mind. I will forgo at this point that somebody from a traditional Indian background may interpose between the body and the mind the so-called *pranic* self or *pranic* sheath, which Shri Aurobindo calls the vital self. Whether we interpose this layer or not will not change the functioning of the process in its entirety. After some period of observing the mind, we notice that it constantly changes not only from a day-to-day or even hour-to-hour perspective but also gradually, over time, how our mind feels changes. This also includes what the mind tells us about ourselves, our self-image or our identity.

There is what we could call a surface mind, which deals with day-to-day survival issues and chores, and a deeper mind that contains our sense of self, long-held values, and beliefs about who we are. In yoga, the surface or sensory mind is called *manas* (the English terms man, human and woman are derived from the Sanskrit *manas*). For simplicity, we may stick to the English shorthand 'mind'.

The deeper layer of the mind that contains our long-term sense of self, values, and beliefs in yoga is called *ahamkara* or *asmita*. These terms could translate as I-am-ness, sense-of-I, I-maker, or ego. Of those, the term ego is the most common, but we must remember that we are using the term without any value judgment. It does not

25

mean whether somebody has a large or pathological ego. It simply includes what forms and shapes our sense of self and identity on a deeper level.[12]

Once we have isolated the body from the mind and later the ego from the mind, we may eventually notice that even the ego feels different daily. Additionally, it will evolve gradually over a more extended period, although usually slower than the body and the surface mind. Having observed the changing ego over a more extended period, we eventually become aware of a deeper level in our awareness to which body, surface mind and ego changes arise. Some schools of yoga again interpose one or two more levels, but some accept that we can drop straight from our egos into what can be called pure awareness. Pure awareness here means that one is aware and conscious, independent of any contents of the awareness.

For example, we may feel shame, exultation, embarrassment, pain, envy or fear, but these are all just contents of awareness. In yoga and meditation, we train ourselves to become conscious of the very entity that is aware, utterly independent of the sensation that one is aware of. Being conscious of this entity is a compelling state. Of it, the *Bhagavad Gita* says, "he who is the same in glory and shame". Glory, shame, and other sensations try to carry us away, out from our centre and seem to force us into an immediate reaction. How do you react to this glory or shame? What's your position? What do you identify with? If we stay with the awareness, we may find a

---

12 An advanced discipline of yoga deals with reducing the ego to the pure I-thought. The *Yoga Sutra* lists this discipline under the term *asmita-samadhi*.

layer of our personality, our deep self, which is unchanged whatever may occur to our surface self.

The *Upanishads* usually call this deep self the *atman*. The *Yoga Sutra* calls it the *purusha* (consciousness), the Abrahamic religions call it the soul, and the *Bhagavad Gita* mostly calls it the *jiva* (individual spirit). In the next chapter, I will define each of these terms and explain their differences. They are all helpful in particular circumstances and less so in others. But let's return to the *Bhagavad Gita*'s statement that a wise one sees the self residing in all beings and all beings as resting within the self. When we meditate on pure awareness for long enough, we realise that it is contentless, meaning it can be aware of whatever we direct it towards, but the contents do not stick to it. The contents or objects of awareness pearl off consciousness like water. They are like mud that does not stick to a lotus leaf or, more profanely, cooking oil that does not stick to a non-stick pan. This awareness that we cognise deep within us is also infinite, which means it extends spatially in all directions, and eternal, which means it extends temporally into the past and future. Everybody can confirm both facts through long-term meditation and yoga practice.

But because this awareness, our deep self, is eternal and infinite, it is the same in all beings, wherever they are and whether they exist now, have existed in the past, or will exist in the future. That's why the *Gita* exhorts us to see "the one self residing in all beings". But the *Gita* does not stop there. It then claims that all beings reside in the self. How can that be? This second dictum requires us to dive much deeper into the experience of the self. If we manage to hold our focus on the self for extended periods, we eventually see with the *Chandogya Upanishad* that there within the space of the heart, in the self, is mysteriously this entire vast universe with all its celestial bodies, continents, oceans, mountain ranges, rivers, forests and beings.

Mysteriously, then, God is not only within the hearts of all of us but also collectively, this deep self contains all of us and the entire universe. To use a term from geometry and mathematics, the Divine is of fractal nature. That means whenever we zoom into minutiae (such as the self of the individual meditator), the nature of the whole is again revealed. It is this fractal nature of the mind to which the Buddha was pointing when he said that [the deepest layer of] mind contains the world and all beings.

The divine form which speaks to us through the *Gita*, Shri Krishna, says in stanza VI.30, who sees Me in all beings and all beings in Me, to him I'm never lost, nor is he to Me. Let's unpack this statement. Firstly, our deep self is identified with a conscious being that we can feel and communicate with and, in turn, can feel and speak to us. In upcoming sections on God-realisation (*vijnana*) and the Supreme Being (Purushottama), I will detail that. Let's note that seeing the Divine in all beings is suggested here as a form of practice. We are told to go beyond the point where we can see the Divine only in a moment of exultation, in an epiphany, a revelation, and turn it into a constant view. This continuous view becomes crucial, especially when we have a problematic relationship with somebody. It is then that our resolve must hold our ability to see the same self we know within us, also within them.

We may object, but why don't they behave like God if God is within them? But also, we don't always act like God, even if, in exulted moments, we have seen the Divine within. If somebody assails us with negativity, we must internally signal to the Divine, "You are doing a great job hiding in that person, but I've recognised you nevertheless". Please note that I do not advise communicating this realisation to our adversaries directly. If they can't see God within themselves, there is no point in us telling them that we can. However, we can change their behaviour by not being drawn into adversarialism. We cannot communicate this change in words, but it must become apparent from our peaceful and non-threatening stance. It must radiate out from the core and be visible in our actions and attitudes.

The *Gita* then continues with the advice that if we see the Divine Self in all beings and all beings in the Divine Self, then to us, the Divine is never lost, nor are we to the Divine. The picture here is similar to an individual cell's relationship with our body. Our consciousness includes this cell; on the other hand, the cell is included in our body. The *Gita* asks us to make this relationship conscious, meaning we realise on one hand that it is the entirety of the Divine that expresses Itself through our microscopic self (and trillions of other microscopic selves, too), while at the same time, we are conscious that we are playing a role in the larger game plan of an infinite entity. The art of life is to create a conscious feedback loop, an avenue of communication between the cosmic self and our own individual self, which is always within our sight.

Let's look now at some text references in the *Bhagavata Purana*, a text sometimes referred to as *Shrimad Bhagavata*. It is one of the 36 *Puranas*, meaning "Ancients", a group of *shastras* (scriptures) that primarily deals with mythological material. Of those, the *Bhagavata* is the most devotional *Purana*. In the *Bhagavata Purana*, the Divine states that Its presence in all beings should be recognised.[13] In Swami Tapasyananda's prologue to Vol.3 of the *Bhagavata Purana*, we find a detailed elaboration of worshipping the Divine in all beings and of the importance of the practice of *"vandana,"* i.e. the saluting of God in all beings and everything.[14] In a later passage, the *Bhagavata Purana* then asks us to realise the Supreme Being as lodged in the heart of all beings.[15] Why is the same injunction repeated ad nauseam in both the *Bhagavad Gita* and the *Bhagavata Purana*?

The answer is that many people gain a first glimpse of the Divine by witnessing consciousness at the core of their being. I use the term consciousness here in the sense of the *Yoga Sutra*, where it denotes what is conscious, i.e., the seat of awareness, rather than what we are conscious of (i.e., the contents of the mind). In the latter meaning, the word is today used in Western psychology. In yoga, it has the earlier meaning.

Once we have recognised the consciousness, the self, the witness, the awareness within us, it is a conceivable step to realise it in all other sentient beings as well. The *Gita* and the *Bhagavata Purana* always insist that the same self must be seen in all beings. This view must be gained because of the transformative power of this experience and view, which

---

13 *Bhagavata Purana* III.29.16

14 Swami Tapasyananda, *Srimad Bhagavata*, Sri Ramakrishna Math, Chennai, 1981, vol.3, p. 29

15 *Bhagavata Purana* XI.29.47

will change our ethics and interactions with all others. The very concept of other will cease to exist as all other beings are included in our sense of self once we realise our very self, the consciousness, in them, too. Especially in conflict situations, we must remind ourselves that the very same self, God, is looking out through all beings into the world.

In day-to-day life, we may assume that we can externalise demerit to "other" and, through that, avoid demerit ourselves. Once we realise the same self in all beings, we realise that in conflict situations, we need to negotiate so that everyone shares the demerit evenly. Through this understanding, we automatically defuse conflict. Ethical rules are fundamental until we have realised the same self in all beings. Once we have attained this realisation, it will be challenging for us to act unethically as we automatically feel the pain of all beings. The *Gita* supports this very fact by saying that the greatest of all yogis are those who feel the joy and suffering of others as if it was their own, due to recognising that all beings share the same *atman*.[16]

The *Gita* also repeatedly states that we must combine the realisation of the same self in all beings with the realisation of all beings held within the same self. This statement is sometimes in the *Upanishads* called the unity or identity of the pure consciousness (*atman*) and the cosmic self (Brahman). This can be seen and experienced in moments when we dissociate from our surface personality and identification with the egoic body-mind and drop into the deepest layer of our psyche, the consciousness, our awareness. To the extent that we can, through skill

---

16 *Bhagavad Gita* VI.32

in meditation and yoga, maintain dis-identity with our surface personality and egoic body-mind, we can remain absorbed in the deep self/consciousness. If we stay in this state for extended periods, it can broaden and deepen into the realisation of the Cosmic Self, the Brahman. This realisation is what the *Gita* calls "to see all beings in the self".

For the purpose of spiritual hygiene, I want to point out here already that should we, through grace, experience this state, we should not come out of it expounding, "I am the Brahman". We can experience the Brahman in a moment when identification with "I" and the body is surrendered, relinquished. When conscious of the egoic body-mind, identity with the Brahman is impossible. When leaving the *brahmic* state, a memory persists, and this memory is vital for spiritual integration. However, in the moment when we use our linguistic mind and voice box to intonate a phrase like, "I am the Brahman", the ego and body consciousness are necessary, and therefore, technically, the state of Brahman-ness is no longer present (apart from its memory). That's why yogic texts often say that when the Brahman appears, awareness of the world (and the body) disappears, and when awareness of the world (and the body) disappears, the Brahman appears. That's why the late Bengali mystic Shri Ramakrishna noted that after an experience of divine revelation, we should only ever say that we are a child of the Divine rather than claim an identity with the Divine. He noted that asserting identity and identifying with the Divine is incorrect as long as we are embodied. This delicate and essential differentiation is

CHAPTER 1

necessary to avoid developing a spiritual ego, which can be as problematic and prevalent as a materialistic ego.

DEITIES AND DIVINE FORMS

Another way many of us may initially find access to the Divine is through deities, forms of the Divine or *avatars*, embodiments of the Divine in humans, such as Jesus Christ or Shri Krishna. I will deal with *avatars* in a dedicated section in Chapter 10 and with deities here. The advantage of deities is that they can provide an avenue for the individual seeker through which they can access the Divine. The problem with deities is that once such access is made, it can easily lead to sectarianism. An example would be the belief that my deity is superior to yours simply because I can understand it, whereas I cannot understand yours.

Another example would be the belief that I am superior because I now have a hotline to the Divine. However, if we want to practice true *Bhakti* Yoga, we need to realise that no deity is superior to another and no devotee is superior to another just because they have a better deity. Comparison, competition, and jostling for advantage are common traits of humanity, but we need to throw them overboard when embarking on the path of *bhakti*, service to the Divine. This path means to serve the Divine through all beings and all divine forms. To make this clear, the *Bhagavata Purana* says, for example, that the worship of Vishnu is the worship of all beings.[17] This stanza reminds us that there is no point in worshipping the Divine if that does not translate into

---

17 *Bhagavata Purana* IV.31.14

humility, friendliness, and service toward all. Suppose we have difficulty recognising the Divine, the Brahman, in a particular deity or human being. We must admit that this is our own limitation and never theirs.

The *Bhagavad Gita* says that whichever aspect of the Divine we desire to worship with conviction, the Supreme Being will strengthen our conviction.[18] The idea here is that some form of worship is better than none, even to a limited aspect of the Divine. The reason for that is evident to those who have ever worshipped in their meditation the formless Absolute (in Sanskrit called the *nirguna* Brahman). Because the formless Absolute is formless, we cannot visualise it in any way nor represent It by auditory (sound, language, etc.) or visual symbology. However, the human mind can only think and make meaning with visual and auditory symbols. Practically speaking, the worship of or concentration on the formless Absolute, because there is no cognisable object, is a non-worship or non-concentration. This is a noble way of saying it's a waste of time unless somebody is very advanced in yoga. Krishna states this very fact in stanza XII.4 of the *Gita*.

In my own meditation practice, I use a large bandwidth of deities and divine forms to worship the Divine. But each time I do so, I remind myself that the divine form is only a pointer to an abstract principle behind it (the formless Absolute), which I could not otherwise represent. The relationship between the formless Absolute or the Supreme Being and a deity or divine symbol is similar to that of an icon on your desktop on one hand and a computer

---

18 *Bhagavad Gita* VII.21

application of several gigabytes on the other. The icon may only have 18kb, but it opens a comparatively colossal application if you click on it. The icon is only a pathway to the application. Similarly, we use divine forms and deities to access the Divine, the Supreme Being. To forget that the icon is not the Supreme Being will lead to fundamentalism and sectarianism.

The *Bhagavad Gita* says that if you worship a particular deity, you will obtain the results of such worship granted by the Supreme Being alone.[19] That's another way of saying that there is only one true God, and all deities and divine forms are dependent emanations and symbols radiating out from that Divine. But it also says they are all viable ways of accessing the one true Divine. This stanza then says that if that's where you are, the Supreme Being will happily meet you there and help you. But in the next stanza, the Divine says that whereas the fruits obtained by worshipping deities are finite, the fruits of worshipping the Supreme Beings directly are infinite (I should also hasten to point out that it's that much harder because we have to constantly admit to ourselves that we rarely completely comprehend what it is).[20] Thus, the Supreme Being here says that worshipping deities is acceptable for now, but if you are ever interested in truly understanding who I, the Supreme Being, am, research and probe further. This statement tells us that there are layers to understanding the depth of the Supreme Being. The more of them we can understand, experience and appreciate, the deeper

---

19 *Bhagavad Gita* VII.22
20 *Bhagavad Gita* VII.23

our practice will be. I will explore many of them in the upcoming sections.

One crucial result of broadly knowing and understanding the many aspects of the Divine is the continuation of such knowledge at the time of death. In a later stanza of the *Gita*, the Supreme Being states that those who have understood that It is the power sustaining all physical manifestations of the Divine and all deities will continue to know It as such, even at the time of death.[21] For that to occur, let's again go across to the *Bhagavata Purana*, where we find that the devotee needs to realise that deities are only emanations of the Supreme Brahman. That is, they have no power and independence of their own. If we realise and remember that when worshipping a deity, such worship becomes worship of the Brahman, the Infinite Consciousness, the Supreme Being. The *Purana* then goes on to state that the actual name of Brahman is Sat-Chit-Ananda. The Indian mystic Shri Aurobindo also uses this term to denote the name of God. Sat-Chit-Ananda is a compound often mentioned in the *Upanishads*, the ultimate source text for most mystical teachings coming out of India. *Sat* is a term translated as truth or existence, which is what truly exists. *Chit* means consciousness, and *ananda* means ecstasy. The term *sat* refers to the immanent aspect of the Divine, the element that is here with us and that we can observe, ultimately resulting in the view that everything is God. *Chit* as consciousness is the transcendental aspect of the Divine, transcendental because it is not cognisable to the senses. *Ananda* is the ecstasy that ensures in the interplay

---

21 *Bhagavad Gita* VII.30

of both. It is also the joy and ecstasy that the *bhakta* feels, who witnesses the interplay of both and becomes a conduit for it.

In the *Bhagavata Purana*, we find the enigmatic statement that God constituted of Sat-Chit-Ananda is the worship suitable for the *Krta Yuga* (Golden Age, often referred to as *Satya Yuga*, age of truth).[22] If you thought the previous paragraph about the ecstasy ensuing when the God Transcendent and the God Immanent meet was a bit of a stretch of the imagination, then you are not alone. The *Bhagavata Purana* says that while ultimately we all will want to get back to that level, it is a form of spirituality common and en vogue during an age long gone, the so-called Golden Age of the *Vedas*. Whether we believe in such a golden past or not, for most of us today, it is easier to start with more straightforward concepts of the Divine, such as the self or divine forms and deities, before working towards more complex ones. In a later section, I will explore the interplay of the transcendental and immanent aspects of the Divine, also called the Divine Father and the Divine Mother. For now, let's round up our discussion of divine forms by returning to the *Bhagavata Purana*, which says that adoration of the Divine is to take place through the adoration of all deities and of the whole universe.[23] Again, this is a complex statement. Shri Aurobindo said that a yogi should be able to worship all deities, but in the beginning, don't get overwhelmed and start with one or a few, and never let a sectarian tell you that you need to

---

22 *Bhagavata Purana* III.21.8
23 *Bhagavata Purana* IV.31.14

stick to the same one. As we all know now, they are all only representations of the one nameless Supreme Being.

How can we find out which deity works for us? The *Yoga Sutra* says that by reading sacred texts, we can find out which form of the Divine is suitable for us.[24] To simplify it, whenever you have an intensely positive reaction towards a description of the Divine, that one is worth investigating. Print an image of the form and then meditate on it by practising *Trataka* (yogic gazing) on it and possibly even during *kumbhaka* (yogic breath retention in the context of *pranayama*, yogic breathing).

Before finishing the section on divine forms, I want to discuss anthropomorphism briefly. While the scriptures state that the human form has been created in the image and likeness of the Divine, we have made many divine images in our own likeness. Without wanting to offend anybody's sensitivities, imagine for a moment if any other species had a religion; how would they imagine God to look like? Like a human? No, more likely, their God would look exactly like them but be blown up to giant proportions, suffused with omnipotence, and located in heaven. I am saying that imagining God to look like yourself is probably an evolutionary state a species goes through until we know better. It is a form of speciesism, the belief that your species is better than others, followed by actions of discrimination against them.

Believe it or not, there is in many cultures a long history of accusations of atheism against mystics who refused to describe the Divine in anthropomorphic terms. Meaning

---

24 *Yoga Sutra* II.44

that if you don't believe in the giant, white, bearded, air-born man (or insert any preferred appearance), then you are, by definition, an atheist. According to this view, the author of this book would, in the eyes of many, qualify as some form of crypto-atheist. I want to turn the whole argumentation around and suggest that the *Gita* and the *Bhagavata Purana* describe a complex, multi-layered Cosmic Being, which, because It is too difficult to comprehend for our limited human intellect, can, in the meantime, be worshipped in human form. This is only the more understandable if we consider that those who give witness to an advanced understanding of this nameless Supreme Being (yet at the same time all names pointing towards the Divine are It's) are always exclusively human. Hence, we have learned to worship them as *avatars*.

There seems to be a connection between the speciesist belief in human supremacy, the exclusive anthropomorphic depiction of the Divine as a giant man towering above the clouds, ruling it from heaven, and the destruction of our natural environment and abuse of animals, forests, oceans and the atmosphere. As I have described in my earlier book *How To Find Your Life's Divine Purpose*, the religious injunction of "make the Earth thy dominion" was unquestioningly absorbed into Western Science and today forms its philosophical bedrock. In its first 300 years of existence, Western Science was exclusively promoted by religious people, including Bacon, Copernicus, Newton, Galilei and Descartes, who believed in a supra-natural God who was essentially different from nature. Hence, nature was non-divine and could be exploited at will. I suggest here that the *Bhagavad Gita*, the *Bhagavata Purana*, and mystics like Ramakrishna and Aurobindo consider the world to be an integral aspect of God. These authorities point to the necessity of seeing matter, nature, and all beings as essential aspects of God. If we integrate this tenet into Science, we could develop a science that does not improve something at the expense of something else. In other words, I am taking a mystical approach to what the late biologist James Lovelock called the Gaia Theory, today called earth-systems sciences.[25] Here, we look at the world and everything included in it as a connected whole and possibly as a superorganism in which all individuals play roles like individual cells in a body. As a mystic, I focus on directly experiencing the intelligence and beingness of that superorganism. Such an experience, if robust and detailed enough (as there are layers to the experience, which will gradually emerge in this text), will stop us from acting unethically, exploitatively and in an ecologically unsound way. At this point in time, the ecological movement tries to intellectually convince us that it is in our self-interest to change our behaviour, with somewhat limited success. If, instead, we see the Supreme Being in Its entirety, as Aurobindo did, conflicted and detrimental behaviour is not possible anymore.

I will talk a lot about this later, but for now, let's go back to why anthropomorphic images are so popular: anthropomorphic images of the Divine, i.e. those having human characteristics, work, and I use them myself. They form a heuristic shortcut that we can and should

---

[25] James Lovelock, *Gaia: A New Look at Life on Earth*, Oxford University Press, 2016.

CHAPTER 1

use when it is not feasible to recall all the many aspects of the Supreme Being in their entirety. But ultimately, we have to realise that this is a stage in the evolution of our spirituality, and we have to, at last, open ourselves to non-human representations of the Divine. In a section called The Glories of the Divine, the *Bhagavad Gita* says, "Among deities, I am Krishna, among humans I am Arjuna, among bodies of water I am the ocean, among mountains I am the Himalayas, among trees I am the Peepal tree (*Ashvatta* or *ficus religiosa*, called *Bodhi* Tree by the Buddhists) and among animals I am the lion, etc.".[26] This section encourages us to see, recognise and worship the Divine everywhere and in everything. For example, the highest form of yogic *samadhi* is sometimes likened to oceanic ecstasy or simply the oceanic experience. From where I am typing this book, I have a sweeping view of the Pacific Ocean. Whenever my eyes tire or I need inspiration, I look up and become aware of this vast oceanic presence. There is something eternal, numinous, revelatory and awe-inspiring about the ocean. We can see God in the ocean if we are open to it. The same can and must be said about mountain ranges, holy mountains, lakes, rivers, forests, the sun and moon, the starry sky, sacred trees such as the *Peepal* or the *Banyan*, and, of course, animals. The question is not so much whether God is in them. God indeed is because there is nothing but God. The question is whether a particular object or form is suitable for you to see God in it. Then, use it on your path towards ultimately being capable of seeing

---

26 *Bhagavad Gita* stanzas X.19-41

God in everything. Although this ultimately requires a high degree of mastery, we must start somewhere.

GOD AS THE UNIVERSE

Another aspect of the Divine that many of us can understand and access is God as the universe. What I mean by this is not that God and the universe are identical (this view is called pantheism) but that the universe is the crystallised body of God (this view is called panentheism), similarly as my physical body is the humanoid form in which I am currently getting around. The view that the universe is part of the Divine but that the Divine is larger than the universe is stated in the *Bhagavad Gita*, where Krishna says, "All this universe is permeated by Me, the Transcendental Being. All objects are supported by Me, but I am not in them".[27] This statement clarifies that the Divine is in everything but that some aspects of the Divine are not part of the physical universe. Later, Krishna extends this thought further by stating, "With Me as the witnessing choreographer, the divine creative force projects forth this mighty universe of moving and unmoving parts and continues to revolve it."[28] The concept of the witnessing choreographer implies that the universe is not a random occurrence but a directed expression of the creativity of the Divine, i.e. its physical extension. We find the universe lawful because it expresses the Divine, and its lawfulness is the nature of the Divine.

To be able to see the Divine in everything is the bedrock for being able to lead a devotional life. If we have an abstract

---

27 *Bhagavad Gita* IX.4

28 *Bhagavad Gita* IX.10

idea of the Divine as some remote entity somewhere in far-away heaven or nothingness, then this is unlikely to change our behaviour here and now. But the concept of *Bhakti* Yoga is to see and recognise the Divine in everything we look at and subsequently to be able to acknowledge, praise and love the Divine in everything.

In Chapter 13 of the *Gita*, Krishna says that a true seer is one who recognises the Supreme Being everywhere and in everything.[29] The medieval Indian theologian Ramanuja developed this view clearly through the so-called *Visishtadvaita* philosophy, according to which the universe is the body of God and not separate from the Divine. Ramanuja was the great adversary of the *Advaita Vedanta* philosopher Shankara, who taught that the world is an illusion. That the world is an illusion is not the view of the Krishna of the *Bhagavad Gita*, and Shankara, in many ways, has to twist the meaning of Krishna's words to make them comply with his philosophy, a process referred to as eisegesis. I will write more on this later.

The universe is the body of God, and it must start with an intellectual understanding, but it cannot remain at that level. In the 11th chapter of the *Gita*, Arjuna tells Krishna that he has now intellectually understood Him but requires a mystical view of what Krishna stated earlier. When Krishna complies and reveals His universal form (*vishvarupa*), Arjuna sees a brilliance akin to that of a thousand suns blazing simultaneously in the sky.[30] But this is only an introduction to Arjuna seeing the whole

---

29 *Bhagavad Gita* XIII.27
30 *Bhagavad Gita* XI.12

universe as a multiplicity appearing unified as the body of the God of gods.[31] The wording of the stanza is essential. Firstly, it confirms that the universe is indeed the body of the Divine. Secondly, it develops the idea of multiplicity as unity. If we look at the physical universe and the evolution of life, we find both to be a race towards multiplicity and complexity. But behind this complexity, we can readily cognise the unifying intelligence that gives birth to it all but, importantly, expresses Itself creatively through this multiplicity. Both must be kept in view simultaneously to understand the Supreme Being.

The human mind desperately needs simplicity, an almost pathological need to reduce everything to the smallest, single denominator. As devotees of the Divine, we must realise that the Divine has an intellect of infinite firepower and, therefore, has no need to limit Itself to simplicity. The Divine is unity and endless multiplicity at the same time. That's why we often find ourselves wholly baffled when studying complex sciences such as history, economy or earth-systems sciences side-by-side. It all seems so complicated. Why can't it be simpler? Trust that the Divine is not baffled by these sciences but that this bafflement only reflects our insufficient intelligence.

Let's switch to the *Bhagavata Purana* to see what it says about the subject. *Skanda* II, Chapter 5 of the *Bhagavata*, deals with the universe as the outer form of the Divine and introduces a divinised concept of nature for meditation. A few pages later, the *Purana* suggests performing *dharana*

---

[31] *Bhagavad Gita* XI.13

(concentration) on this universe as the form of the Divine.[32] We will later discuss a section in chapter XII of the *Gita* where Krishna states that the formless Divine, often called the formless Absolute or *nirguna* Brahman, is much harder to concentrate on and understand. Seeing the universe as the form of the Divine (*saguna*) removes this difficulty. It makes it clear to us that we are, as the Bible would have it, living, moving and having our being in the Divine.[33] Similar to the *Bhagavad Gita*, also the *Bhagavata Purana* says in the above passage that the Supreme Being imbues this universal cosmic form [i.e. the universe] with its five elements.

A few stanzas later, the *Bhagavata Purana* advises the devotee to exclusively concentrate on the universe as the gross body of God, outside which there is nothing.[34] The phrase "outside which there is nothing" means that there is only God. There is nothing in the universe that is non-God, i.e., nothing which is not sacred, not to be revered, and nothing that should be desecrated, not worshipped or externalised from God. Our modern society is in constant need of toxic waste dumps, nuclear waste dumps, and places where we can sink obsolete oil rigs or burnt-out naval atomic reactors. In economics, we call this process externalisation of demerit, and we perform it to let somebody else pick up the tab and pay the bills so that our production facilities can remain profitable. Externalisation of demerit is a key process that makes our culture unsustainable.

---

32 *Bhagavata Purana* II.2.23ff
33 Acts 17:28
34 *Bhagavata Purana* II.2.38

In the teaching of *bhakti*, there are no places where we can externalise waste to because everything is God. Similarly, our society defines individuals or societal groups as personas non grata, a person or persons not welcome. This is done so that demerits can be externalised to them in an attempt to write the demerit and the personas non-grata off our balance sheets. Even in societies that have, to some extent, overcome racism, demerit is still often externalised to women (for example, through lower pay or by automatically expecting them to take care of older people) or other species by destroying their habitats to make space for agricultural exploitation and industrial facilities.

Early on in the *Bhagavata Purana*, we find that the entire universe is an expression of the creative thought of the Divine.[35] The fact that creative thought is the universe's origin should make us doubt the New Age's commonplace that most personal problems are due to the mind and that we could solve our problems by discontinuing thinking. How would one expect the Divine to have brought the world into existence? By rolling up the sleeves, picking up a shovel and starting building? No, the Divine is Cosmic Intelligence and Divine Law as two of its aspects. Because it is the one without a second with nothing to oppose it and because it is omnipotent, whatever it contemplates (i.e. thinks) will crystallise and condense into existence. It is, therefore, correct to say that the universe is an expression of the creative thought of the Divine or that the Divine has thought the world into existence. The *bhakta*'s aim is not to

---

35 *Bhagavata Purana* II.5.3 and 11

stop the mind entirely but to think in alignment with the Divine. I have explored this in my previous book, *How To Find Your Life's Divine Purpose*, but this concept will also be explored in this text in the section on *Karma* Yoga.

Early in Vol. 2 of the *Bhagavata Purana*, the entire universe is likened to a *yantra*.[36] A *yantra* represents sacred geometry that we meditate on to understand the principle behind it. The principle behind the universe is the Supreme Being. The universe is not separate from the Divine but Its gross form, meaning it is Its crystallised body. By meditating on the beauty, uniqueness, intelligence, and wisdom inherent in the universe, we develop a sense of wonder and awe that helps us understand the qualities of the beingness that gave rise to it. I am using here the term beingness instead of being because, in the English language, we use the term being to denote an entity separate from everything around it and limited in space and time. Even by placing supreme in front of being, it is still hard for some not to think of a giant, bearded male in the sky. Using the term beingness, however, helps us understand that we are talking about the principle at the base of all beings, that which expresses Itself through all beings and through this beautiful, miraculous universe in which we live. We are fractions (*amshas*) or sparks (*jivas*) of the Divine, living inside It, i.e. in the universe.

It is again important to point out that the realisation that the universe is divine is not an abstract or intellectual realisation that does not impact our lives. The late founder of process philosophy, Alfred North Whitehead, said that

---

36 Swami Tapasyananda, Srimad Bhagavata, vol.2, p. 2

we do not achieve peace by holding particular cognitive beliefs more or less intensely but by understanding our relation to the fact that the universe is divine.[37] Whitehead says that the universe is an expression of infinite creativity, freedom, and infinite possibilities, but that it is impotent to become real without the completed ideal harmony, which is God. This is important to understand because, without this understanding, we would fall back into pantheism, i.e. the belief that the universe in its totality is God and that there is nothing divine beyond the universe. I'm concerned that this is the philosophical base of the spiritual platitude "the universe takes care". This statement reduces the universe to a giant shopping mall that, for some reason, has to supply according to every whim our mind and ego may imagine. However, the *bhakta* meditates on the universe to understand the gargantuan intelligence that has contemplated it into existence, realising that the universe would be nothing without the Divine.

VIJNANA, GOD-REALIZATION

We have now completed our inquiries into the simple concepts or aspects of the Divine, those of the Divine as self, as deities and as the universe. These will generally appear to us first on the path of *bhakti* as they are easier to understand and comprehend. The following concepts are more advanced but are very important, and ultimately, the *bhakta* needs to integrate them all. Even if this takes time, the love of God is not complete until we understand God

---

[37] John B. Cobb, *A Christian Natural Theology*, Westminster John Knox Press, 2007, p. 62

as profoundly as possible, a process that the *Gita* calls *jnana yajna* - knowledge offering.

The first six chapters of the *Gita* are fairly introductory, with most advanced concepts introduced in the latter 12 chapters. Unfortunately many readers restrict themselves in their analysis to these first six introductory chapters. But the seventh chapter, at its outset, presents one of the most essential concepts of the *Gita*, juxtaposing the terms *jnana* and *vijnana*. The term *jnana* is generally identified as referring to knowledge of the self or self-realisation. The prefix *vi* in *vijnana* denotes enlargement or extension. Hence, it represents a form of super-knowledge, more comprehensive than just self-realisation. Shri Ramakrishna was the first to point out the importance of the term *vijnana*, and he taught that it meant God-realization, consisting of the combined realisation of the Divine with form (*saguna* Brahman) and the formless Absolute (*nirguna* Brahman).[38]

Shri Aurobindo picked up the baton from Ramakrishna and further developed the concept of *vijnana*. Aurobindo usually translates *vijnana* as supermind, i.e. the intelligence of the Divine.[39] Aurobindo also defines supermind as the Supreme Being knowing Itself dynamically as time.[40] To elaborate further, Aurobindo also described the supermind as the Supreme's creative knowledge–will aspect.[41] This

---

38 Sw. Tapasyananda, Shrimad Bhagavata, Vol 3, p.9

39 Debashish Banerji, *Seven Quartets of Becoming- A Transformative Yoga Psychology Based on the Diaries of Sri Aurobindo*, Nalanda International, Los Angeles, 2012, p. 157

40 Debashish Banerji, *Seven Quartets of Becoming*, p. 187

41 Debashish Banerji, *Seven Quartets of Becoming*, p. 277

is important to understand because Aurobindo's lifelong practice and endeavour was to align himself with the divine supermind, something he labelled as the "calling down of the supermind." It was important for Aurobindo to focus not just on the transcendental consciousness- stillness, emptiness, and nothingness aspects of the Divine but also on its creative and intelligent self-expression.

Aurobindo developed the terminology supermind in the early part of the 20th century, and today, more than 100 years later, the term sounds dated, as we more readily associate it with information technology and artificial intelligence (or more profanely with things such as Superman or supermarket). Instead, I suggest the terms God immanent or cosmic intelligence, and the connection between both is explored in the next section. I don't mean to be disrespectful when I appear here to improve Aurobindo's language. I consider Aurobindo the leading intellectual and mystical titan of the 20th century, and I am anything but. But the English language dates quickly, a fact that Aurobindo was only too aware of. Other than Sanskrit, in which the meaning of words is predefined in ancient texts on grammar, in English, definitions of words are derived through convention. Hence, they change if enough people change their minds about what they mean.

Let's look into the mysterious, often overlooked, and misinterpreted passage of the *Gita* that introduces the term *vijnana*. After Krishna, in the first six chapters of the *Bhagavad Gita*, has taught Arjuna *Karma*-, *Jnana* -, *Samkhya* -, *Buddhi* -, and *Raja* Yoga, he speaks the following powerful words, "I will now disseminate to you the essential knowledge (*jnana*, i.e. self-realisation) and the comprehensive knowledge (*vijnana*, i.e. God-realisation) after which all that is to be known is known".[42] Both Ramakrishna and Aurobindo believed this to be the pivotal stanza of the *Gita*. The term *jnana* generally refers to the realisation of pure consciousness/ awareness, the witness abiding in our depth, which Patanjali calls *purusha*, our own true nature, and the *Upanishads* label the *atman*, the deep self. This realisation usually involves us dropping into the core of our being and cognising there a presence which is infinite, eternal, unchangeable and un-conditioned, i.e. it does not change whatever we experience. Because this experience (depending on how long we sustain it) may lead to a disidentification and subsequent distance to the surface self, the egoic body-mind, it is often labelled self-realisation.

Many schools see this self-realisation as the goal and end of the spiritual path, and some argue that Patanjali's school of yoga, with its emphasis on objectless *samadhi*, the *samadhi* on pure consciousness, is among them. According to another view, Patanjali's yoga with its teaching of the *siddha* (immortal liberated beings who remain active) in the third chapter of the *Yoga Sutra* goes further, but it is beyond the scope of this book to discuss this vital subject. Krishna, however, teaches in the seventh chapter of the *Gita* that behind self-realisation, there is the larger opening of God-realization, consisting, as Ramakrishna taught, of the integrated realisation of both the *nirguna* and *saguna*

---

42 *Bhagavad Gita* VII.2

Brahman, the Divine with form and the formless Absolute, both of which are much vaster than the individual self.

A short excursion into Indian theology: The just stated view is, of course, irreconcilable with Shankara's teaching (the leading proponent of *Advaita Vedanta* and the view that the world is an illusion), but it does tally with Ramanuja's (Ramanuja was the great adversary of Shankara) identity-in-difference doctrine as we will have more time later on to explain. I will mention these things frequently because *Advaita Vedanta* dominates the Western impression of Indian philosophy so much that Westerners often seem to think that everybody in India believes the world is an illusion. The view espoused in chapter seven of the *Gita* also tallies with Shri Aurobindo's experiences in the Alipore jail, where he was incarcerated in the lead-up to being tried for sedition and organising the armed resistance against the British Raj in India. Making good use of his time in jail, Aurobindo experienced first the vast stillness and emptiness of the self, an experience he later referred to as freedom and *nirvana,* and later the realisation of the Cosmic Self, when everything around him, the cell walls, his blanket and bed, his guards and co-inmates, merged into the Divine, in this case, Krishna.

In the following few stanzas, Krishna Himself describes what He means with *vijnana*; although this is only the seventh chapter of the *Gita*, he also doesn't reveal everything here. He divulges even more profound facts in chapters 15 and 18. In stanza VII.4 of the *Gita*, He states that His lower nature (*apara prakriti*) is eight-fold, including the five elements, mind (*manas*), intelligence (*buddhi*) and I-am-ness (*ahamkara*). Let's look at the term *prakriti* first. The term is most readily translated as nature, procreativity or procreatress. Nature is, of course, the least cumbersome of those, but we must, in this context, understand nature as the force that brings forth everything.

In Patanjali's *Sutra*, the evolutes of *prakriti* are things that we need to dis-identify with to finally make the pure individual consciousness free, isolated, independent, and stand revealed in its own splendour. This latter expression sounds like a handful, but it describes precisely how it feels when the pure consciousness stands by itself unimpeded and is not let down by any identification with the surface self, the egoic body-mind. This fact is also beautifully expressed and confirmed in the story of the two birds in the *Mundaka Upanishad*.[43] Here, we learn of two birds, good friends, that sit on the same tree of life. The first bird, representing the surface self, bound up with *prakriti*, eats the fruits of the tree of life: pleasure and pain. Due to the constant rollercoaster ride, impermanence, and up-and-down of pleasure and pain, the first bird eventually becomes dejected and falls into despair. The *Mundaka* now advises that the first bird, the surface self, needs to turn away from the fruits of the tree of life and behold its friend, the second bird. The second bird is representative of the *purusha* of the *Yoga Sutra*, the pure consciousness abiding in objectless *samadhi* (rapture), standing free of *prakriti* and her many children of mental identification and sensory experience.

---

43 *Mundaka Upanishad* III.1

Although this is simplistic, we could reduce the advice given here to *purusha*/consciousness as to be abided in and *prakriti* and her evolutes as to be avoided. And this is precisely the view we may hold when exclusively practising *Jnana*- and *Raja* Yoga, which the *Gita* covered in the first six chapters. But Krishna now leads us further to *vijnana* by saying that the *prakriti* is His divine creative force. It is a term He will repeatedly use in the *Gita*, making the *prakriti*, His Shakti, His power. This contrasts Patanjali's yoga, which exhorts us to isolate ourselves from the *prakriti* (although it goes beyond that stance when introducing the egoless *siddha*).

Before going on to the next stanza, let me briefly comment on Shri Krishna's list of eight constituents of the lower *prakriti*, the five elements, mind, intelligence and ego. The complete list given in the *Samkhya Karika* is, of course, 23 evolutes, including the quantums or subtle elements (*tanmatras*), the five organs of action (*karmendriyas*) and the five sense organs (*jnanendriyas*). Krishna has, however, already exhaustedly spoken on *Samkhya* philosophy in the second chapter. The term *Samkhya* means enumeration and one of its chief features is the enumeration and listing of all categories of *prakriti*. Here in the *Gita*, Krishna gives only a shortlist of the essential categories because the point here is not how many categories of *prakriti* are there in total, but the fact is that the *prakriti* is the force by which He moves the world, rather than being a mechanical force acting independently by itself.

Another important point is that *prakriti* is twofold, a higher and a lower. In the *Gita*, Krishna exhorts us that

His higher nature, the *para prakriti*, is the origin of all *jivas*, individual spirits, and the support of the whole universe.[44] In a later chapter, I will isolate terms like *jiva* (individual spirit), *purusha* (consciousness), *atman* (deep self or sacred self), etc., from each other. They all have similar connotations, but they also have essential differences that must be understood. However, including the term *jiva* here necessitates a sneak preview of its meaning. The *jiva* is often called the surface self or individual self. It is called a spark of the fire of the Divine. As explained in more detail under the following subheading, the Divine has two main aspects: *saguna* (with form or God immanent) and *nirguna* (God transcendent, infinite consciousness, formless Absolute). The current passage does not deal with the transcendental aspect of the Divine, which is analysed in chapter 15 of the *Gita*, but here deals with the immanent aspect, i.e. the Divine that is here with us, that is perceptible. This God immanent Itself consists of the following main elements:

- cosmic intelligence that thinks and contemplates everything into existence according to divine law,
- the material universe, including all objects, which are the result of the lower *prakriti*
- all beings who are the result of the higher prakriti.

How can this be understood? Imagine the beingness aspect of the God immanent as an infinite being with infinite permutations, individuations, paths, and computations of what it could appear in the world. In the

---

44 *Bhagavad Gita* VII.5

aggregate, these represent its endless potential. However, it does not have an ego. The *Bhagavata Purana* confirms this egolessness.[45] Being without ego, the only way for the God immanent to individuate and embody the infinite aspects, personalities and individualities It potentially could be is to become all of them. Each of them is supplied with a body, a consciousness, a mind and, importantly, an ego. An ego is a psychological piece of software that binds consciousness, body, and mind together in an individual sense of self, i.e., it enables us to say that this is my body, mind, and consciousness. We take this for granted, but an exceedingly complex operation makes this possible. If our I-am-ness or sense-of-I becomes damaged through *karma*, mental illness (such as schizophrenia or multi-personality disorder) or the use of psychedelics, we may suddenly realise how precarious and tenuous the bond between deep self (consciousness) and surface self (egoic body-mind) is.

Because the Divine, being egoless, cannot become an individual, it must individuate through an infinite number of individual selves, us, to act on the level of the individual. The Divine is cosmic; it is everything and cannot be, therefore, the individual. It can only be the totality of all individual selves simultaneously. The Divine must individuate through us to act and experience on an individual level. An individual has an ego, and therefore, it can limit Itself in the space-time continuum, i.e. it can say I am here now and not elsewhere and at other times. Since the Divine has no ego, it cannot be an individual. Being free of individual persona and ego makes it possible

---

[45] *Bhagavata Purana* III.12.38

for the Divine to be simultaneously everywhere and at all times. Since the Divine has limitless potential, It contains an endless number of individual permutations. Hence, we see the multitude of beings across all timeframes and places. These are all sparks (*jivas*) and fractions (*amshas*) of the Divine, i.e. possible pathways that the Divine can take, limited in space and time through their egos.

Without utilising individual beings with egos limiting them in the space-time continuum, the Divine cannot individuate. The ego enables a being to be something or somebody with specific characteristics versus someone with other characteristics. The Divine has all characteristics simultaneously as long as they align with divine law, an essential aspect of the Divine.

Why did the Divine split into infinite divine sparks without its integrity and unity being affected? Without becoming an endless multiplicity of beings, the Divine transcendent, the infinite consciousness, would only be conscious of Itself as the Divine Immanent, cosmic intelligence and Its embodiment, the universe and all beings, in a general form, but not in particulars. Becoming a multiplicity of beings, the Divine can now experience Itself through the multiplicity of beings pursuing Its agenda. This agenda could be called *lila*, divine play. Another way of understanding it is because the divine immanent is infinite potential and creativity, and it is the One without a second, i.e., nothing impedes It from manifesting. This means that everything that can be must be.

Aurobindo described the agenda of the Divine as the billion-year-long process of lifting all matter and life to divine consciousness. The British mathematician and philosopher Alfred North Whitehead described the agenda of the Divine as one of novelty and intensity. I will explore this statement further later on. Krishna Himself spoke of it as His *yoga-maya*, His mysterious power. The use of the term mysterious power implies that we may not truly understand what He is up to. We must nevertheless give it our best shot if the pinnacle of *vijnana* is our goal.

It is crucial to not just lay these explorations aside as an albeit interesting but theoretical and ultimately futile explanation of the workings of the Divine. On the contrary, understanding and knowing the Divine is the secret of the successful *bhakta*. When we are in love with another human being, the more we understand and know them, the more our relationship will likely endure. And this is much more true in our relationship with the Divine. We must realise that we live inside the Divine in the form of the universe as the crystallised body of God. We are the sense organs with which the Divine, as the infinite consciousness (*nirguna* Brahman), experiences Itself as the divine creative force. This Shakti embodies Itself as all beings and the intelligence behind all that drives them. If the *bhakta* consciously sees all these aspects, she lives, moves and has her being in the Divine. And this realisation is the bedrock of a divine life, without which it isn't easy to conceive.

Krishna continues His elaboration of the comprehensive knowledge by revealing that He is the genesis and fountainhead of the universe and all beings[46] and he also promulgates that all universes are held on Him as beads are

---

46 *Bhagavad Gita* VII.6

strung on a thread.[47] Here is no talk of an unreal universe that cheats us like an illusionist. No mirage, imagination, or illusion is conjured up here, no mere figment of our mind. Instead, we are introduced to a real universe, which is the body of God, peopled by real beings, all aspects and permutations of the same unified Divine, which are here with a particular purpose, a role to play in the agenda of the Divine to express Itself through Its unlimited creativity.

We are playing these roles already, but in an unconscious way. *Bhakti* is an invitation to do so consciously, to participate in the creative play and opus magnum of the Divine, and to see it as such. *Vijnana* means that God has become the *jivas*, the individual spirits, the universe, expresses Herself in divine play and is yet the ocean of infinite consciousness, the immutable, formless Absolute, the God transcendent. This is why Shri Aurobindo, in *Essays On The Gita*, calls *vijnana* the direct spiritual awareness of the Supreme Being.[48]

TRANSCENDENT AND IMMANENT, FATHER AND MOTHER, FATHER AND MOTHER, NIRGUNA AND SAGUNA

On our quest to understand what the Divine is, we have now gone past initial realisations of God as the self, an anthropomorphic deity, and the totality of the cosmos. We now begin to comprehend that God-realization is not a single act or experience we are done with for once and all

---

47 *Bhagavad Gita* VII.7
48 Sri Aurobindo, *Essays on the Gita*, Sri Aurobindo Ashram Trust, Pondicherry, p. 266

but a multifaceted process. We will now follow up on Shri Ramakrishna's statement that *vijnana* (God-realisation) consists of the separate realisation of the Divine as both *saguna* (with form) and *nirguna* (formless). There is no meaningful way of approaching both experiences at the same time. They are so fundamentally different that it is impossible to have them both simultaneously. To give an example that may elucidate the matter, it is impossible to simultaneously scale a mountain and sail a boat on the ocean. But we can do both sequentially and afterwards maintain an awareness of both of them.

Similarly, the case is with experiencing God as immanent and as God as transcendent. So says Shri Aurobindo, we have to separate the experience of God's immanence within us from that of God's transcendence. It is clear here that he admits to a variety of spiritual experiences,[49] and in doing so, he also warns against oversimplifying by reducing all mystical experiences to only one type, the most profound pitfall on the mystical path. Yet, unless a mystic has both (the *saguna* and the *nirguna* and some others, too, as we shall see later), they remain bound to fall into certain traps.

In the *Bhagavad Gita*, Krishna says He is the father of all beings and their mother.[50] This is a fundamental statement to consider in our quest to comprehend the Divine. What did He mean? The terms father and mother are used in the same way tantrism uses the terms Shiva and Shakti. The father, in *tantrism*, is called Shiva and represents pure consciousness and awareness. In the *Upanishads*, the father

---

49 Sri Aurobindo, *Essays on the Gita*, p. 315
50 *Bhagavad Gita* XIV.4

is called *nirguna* Brahman (the formless Absolute), and in philosophy, we use the term God transcendent or the transcendental aspect of the Divine. Transcendental means beyond, i.e., the part of the Divine that is beyond sensory perception and direct experience. Transcendental denotes infinite consciousness, which means, in this context, the conscious entity rather than what we are conscious of. The latter is how the term is often used in modern psychology, where it is applied to the content of the mind. However, the meaning of the term used here is different. In the Old Testament, we find the beautiful sentence, "Be still and know that I Am God".[51] This sentence refers to the transcendental aspect of the Divine, i.e., the infinite consciousness. It cannot be seen when the mind is active. Thoughts cover consciousness like clouds cover the sky's blue on a rainy day. That's why the biblical Yahweh, the Father, charges us to "be still" lest we can behold Him. Let's keep that in mind whenever we use the term consciousness in the context of yoga.

Patanjali, the author of the *Yoga Sutra*, says, "Yoga is the stilling of the mind. Then (when the mind is still) consciousness abides in itself".[52] Note the similarities of the descriptions. It is also interesting that the biblical phrase states, "Know that I Am God". It is an accurate wording as, strictly speaking, the transcendental aspect of the Divine is beyond perception and experience. That's why Yahweh does not say, "Perceive and experience that I am God". This reverberates halfway around the world in the writings of

---

51 Psalm 46:10

52 Yoga Sutra I.2- I.3

the Indian philosopher Shankaracharya, who says in his *Brahma Sutra Bhashya* (commentary on the *Brahma Sutras*) that consciousness (Brahman) cannot be perceived and experienced; it is only known.

We find a similar focus on the transcendental aspect of the Divine in ancient China. In the *Tao Te King*, sage Lao-tzu says, "What can be said about the *Dao* (consciousness) is not the *Dao*". Notice again here that consciousness is beyond perception and description. Lao-tzu also states that the transcendental is beyond being described through language. The Indian prayer to the Nagaraj, the serpent of infinity, illustrates the same concept of the God transcendent. Here, consciousness is identified with a one-thousand-headed serpent, with all one-thousand heads emerging from the same trunk. The trunk itself is silent; it does not have a mouth to speak with. The trunk represents the Brahman, infinite consciousness. The one thousand heads growing out of the same trunk all speak different languages, representing differing systems of philosophy, science, and religion. But the ultimate truth is only in the trunk, which itself does not have a language, as absolute truth is beyond words. While each head may teach an internally consistent system that cannot be refuted when allowed to start from its own premises, the heads all contradict each other. Each head may offer a viable interpretation of the truth but never the truth itself, which is unspeakable.

Because everything we so far have heard about the transcendental is rather non-concrete, most traditions tend to anthropomorphise it (i.e., give it human characteristics), which can be helpful to a certain extent. For example, the God transcendent in the Old Testament is called Yahweh; in the New Testament, the Father, and in India, most often either Shiva or Vishnu. Both Yahweh and Shiva were thought to reside inactive on mountaintops, looking at the world from afar. This residence is, of course, to be understood as metaphorical. In India, for example, the mountain on which Shiva sits is called *Meru*, referring to Mt Kailash in the Himalayas. However, *Meru* is also used for the human spine and the world axis. The mystical meaning of the name Shiva is consciousness. According to yoga, consciousness is experienced when the life force is transported up the spine and held in the crown *chakra* at the top of the spine (*Meru*). From that vantage point, consciousness does not look like a blue-skinned, dreadlocked male, brandishing a trident while sitting on a tiger skin (such as the Lord Shiva). But it can be a helpful metaphor to visualise it as such during day-to-day life and for the practice of devotion, *bhakti*.

But what about the second aspect of the Divine, the Mother? She is conspicuously absent in the Abrahamic religions, or at least we have disempowered Her. This disempowerment is the result of thousands of years of patriarchy. Aurobindo says that the higher nature (*para prakriti*) of the Supreme Being represents its Shakti, the creative force that is the womb of the universe and all beings.[53] Aurobindo lamented that our concept of spirituality has created a separation between the active, dynamic aspect of the Divine, the Mother/ the God immanent/ the Shakti, and its passive, static side, the nirvanic and transcendent

---

53 Sri Aurobindo, *Essays on the Gita*, p. 268

formless Absolute, the Father.[54] To overcome this chasm, we must bring about what Aurobindo calls the voluntary integration of the God transcendent/ Father/ consciousness on the one hand and the God immanent/ Shakti/ Divine Mother on the other.[55] Unlike the *Yoga Sutra*, Aurobindo takes a *tantric* view and calls the *para prakriti*, the self-conscious Shakti of the Supreme Being, the Devi (Goddess), the Mother.[56]

Other than the transcendental aspect of the Divine, the Mother is immanent, meaning here-with-us, something that we can perceive, experience and touch. Unfortunately, religion was so obsessed with the transcendental aspect of the Divine that we have often ignored and forgotten the immanent and feminine element. There is an exciting passage in Shankara's *Brahma Sutra* Commentary that says, "Consciousness [the God transcendent], similar to a mirror, is of the quality of reflectiveness. If there was nothing to be reflected, consciousness could not bring about its quality of reflectiveness". What does that mean? Try to imagine a giant mirror floating in empty space. Nothing could ever be reflected in the mirror, as nothing else existed. This means the mirror could not reflect anything. But since the mirror is not a mirror outside of it being reflective, it would not be a mirror. That's important to understand, and the same is valid for consciousness. Consciousness (the seat of awareness) is only consciousness if there is a world to be conscious of.

---

54 Debashish Banerji, *Seven Quartets of Becoming*, p. 282-3
55 Debashish Banerji, *Seven Quartets of Becoming*, p. 116-7
56 Debashish Banerji, *Seven Quartets of Becoming*, p. 294

CHAPTER 1

What that means for us practically is that the transcendental aspect of the Divine, consciousness, is forever conscious of the immanent aspect. The immanent aspect is the cosmos, the world of matter and energy, the entire universe. All that you see, feel and perceive is God. The whole cosmos is nothing but a crystallisation of the Divine. There is no place, time, particle, energy, radiation, or wave pattern that is not God. The entire material world is the crystallised body of the Divine. That's why the Bible says, "In Him, we move, live and have our being".[57] You cannot live, move and have your being in anything else because there is nothing else.

We have been looking for the Divine everywhere without finding Her; in that way, we act like fish looking for the ocean. For a fish, there is nothing but the ocean; for us, there is nothing but God. Wherever you stand, you stand on God. Whatever you look at is God. You breathe nothing but God, and you think nothing but God. That's why in the *Gita*, Lord Krishna says, "All actions are performed by my *prakriti* only a fool believes to be the doer".[58] In this *Gita* phrase, Krishna implies, "You are not breathing yourself, but I breathe you through the divine creative force. It is not you beating your heart but the God immanent is beating it through you. Can you order your arm to rise? No, it is Me who thinks the thought, sends impulses through your neurons, and powers your muscles. Can you transform food into energy via your metabolism? No, it is Me as the God immanent who does so. Can you write your DNA, create

---

57 Acts 17:28

58 *Bhagavad Gita* III.27

proteins, power cells via mitochondria, harvest sunlight via photosynthesis and turn it into proteins?" No, all of these miraculous processes the God immanent performs through us without us having to do anything. That's why Krishna says, "only a fool believes to be the doer". Our foolishness consists of having appointed ourselves to be the doers, whereas these actions express themselves through us without our conscious input.

This leads me to the probably most important concept related to the God immanent, cosmic intelligence. Looking at the above paragraph, there is no denying that the cosmos itself is intelligent since it could produce something as miraculous as life, and exceptionally complex life at that. We have often looked at matter as dumb, dead and inert, but the entire material cosmos is an intelligent incubator of intelligent life designed to embody cosmic intelligence and co-create with it. This same intelligence has crystallised itself as matter, the cosmos and us. There is no difference between intelligence, spirit and God immanent on one hand and matter on the other. Matter is crystallised intelligence and spirit. Matter is the crystallised body of God. Matter is part of God. Whether present as waves, particles, or energy, matter is an essential aspect of the God immanent. The Dutch philosopher Spinoza was not wrong when stating that God is a substance although it could be argued that this statement leaves out the transcendental aspect of the Divine.

Aurobindo also identified the God transcendent and God immanent as being and becoming.[59] Conventional

---

[59] Debashish Banerji, *Seven Quartets of Becoming*, p. 172

spirituality and religion focus excessively on the being aspect of God (consciousness), leading to a static, solid-state spirituality. So is the ideal yogi often depicted as a lone male, sitting immovably on a mountaintop with mind and thoughts arrested, having shut out the entire world. He may as well already be dead, and in fact, some spiritual movements aim for something close to spiritual self-annihilation.

However, the Becoming aspect of the Divine will save us from this cul-de-sac. The Becoming aspect of the Divine is the aspect of God constantly evolving, growing, developing, and moving forward. It is what the British mathematician and philosopher Alfred North Whitehead called process. Nobody in the West understood the God immanent as deeply as Whitehead did. Whitehead taught that neither God nor the universe reach static completion, as both represent the creative advance into novelty.[60] Whitehead also adopted the Freudian term "Eros" (the creative urge and urge to create beauty) as the name for the primordial nature of God, which is the power in the universe urging toward the realisation of ideals. Don't mistake the term Eros here as reduced to eroticism. That's a minute aspect of it. Some scholars have noticed the convergence of Aurobindo's and Whitehead's ideas (and, for that matter, even of Ramanuja's and Whitehead's thoughts). Aurobindo believed that God's ideal and goal was the divinisation of all life and matter in the universe, and it is to support this goal that the *bhakta* must commit. Whitehead believed that the individual soul can establish

---

[60] Alfred North Whitehead, *Process and Reality*, Free Press, 1979, p. 349

with the Divine a peculiarly intense relationship.[61] This is also stated in the *Bhagavata Purana*. For example, in the *Bhagavata Purana*, Krishna declares that the devotee is His very heart and that He is indeed the devotee's heart.[62] He even goes as far as to declare Himself a slave of the devotee without any freedom. He then declares that His heart is in the grip of the *bhakta*, whose lover He is. Right here is the "peculiarly intense relationship" that Whitehead talked about. As *bhaktas*, we need not ask ourselves how to establish a loving relationship with God. We need to tune into the fact that God's heart is already in the grip of ours and that we only need to return the love directed at us. This return of love is, of course, challenging at first. Whitehead also speaks of God as the universal consciousness, which is individual in us, and God as the all-embracing, universal love, which is partial in us. We need to make the love that is partial in us all-embracing and universal, like the love that God extends to us. That means to love God in all and everything we see and in all of Her children.

THE MYSTERY OF THE SUPREME BEING

Having now comprehended that we need to place ourselves into the service of a Divine that has two significant aspects, the static, solid-state, transcendent, which is infinite consciousness (Shiva, the father, *nirguna* Brahman and being), and the dynamic, immanent, and fluid cosmic intelligence and divine creative force (Shakti, the mother, *saguna* Brahman and becoming), we are now

---

61 Alfred North Whitehead, *Adventure of Ideas*, Free Press, 1967, p.267
62 Swami Tapasyananda, Srimad Bhagavata, vol.4, p. 227

ready to behold the mystery of the Supreme Being (*purusha* + *uttama* = Purushottama). In the *Bhagavad Gita*, Krishna re-assesses *Samkhya's* and Yoga's teaching of the *purusha* (consciousness), of which both systems say that each individual has its own *purusha* and God has a separate one, different to all others in that it is eternally free.[63] Krishna teaches a single *purusha*, albeit with three different layers or stages. He initially only reveals that there are two stages of *purusha*, the perishable (*kshara*) and imperishable (*akshara*). The perishable includes all embodied *jivas* (individual spirits), identifying with their surface selves and living in a constantly changing world. The imperishable *purusha* consists of the community of the liberated *jivas*, unassailed by the ever-changing world (Patanjali would call them *siddhas*). This statement acknowledges that although consciousness is always conscious, when embodied and identified with the egoic body-mind, it will become coloured by this identification and act differently.

However, in the following two stanzas, Krishna reveals that there is yet another *purusha*, the Supreme Being (Purushottama), the highest of all forms of consciousness, who pervades all worlds and beings and sustains them.[64] He states that in this form of the Purushottama, He is superior to both the perishable (*kshara*) and the imperishable (*askshara*). This statement clearly rejects Shankara's view that the individual self and the Brahman (the cosmic self) are the same. The *Gita* is, however, in support of Ramanuja's identity-in-difference doctrine (*beda-abeda*),

---

63 *Bhagavad Gita* XV.16
64 Bhagavad Gita XV.17-18

which declares that we are identical with the Divine in that regard that we are *purusha* (consciousness), but we are different in that our powers, intelligence and bodies are limited, whereas the Divine's aren't. A sentient being can evolve from a perishable being to an imperishable being by recognising that it is not the egoic body-mind but instead identifying itself with the eternal, infinite and immutable consciousness within. But above both is and will always remain, as Krishna said, the Supreme Being, the Purushottama, on which all beings and worlds are strung like pearls.

The right attitude towards the Supreme Being is different from identification. We should not walk through the world proclaiming that we are one or identified with God (as, for example, Manjour al Hallaj did). But, as Krishna then states[65], if we understand the Divine as both immanent and transcendent, father and mother, being and becoming, as the entirety of the material universe, space and time, including in Itself all beings bound and liberated, and beyond even as a mysterious, super-intelligent and super-conscious entity, which sustains, nurtures and supports everything, surpassing in its vastness everything, then our attitude to this entity, the Purushottama, can only be one of love, adoration and service with all our being.

In the final stanza of this passage, we are told that this spiritual doctrine is the most profound of all sacred teachings.[66] If we comprehensively understand it, we cannot but reach total fulfilment. This is indeed so! At this

---

65 *Bhagavad Gita* XV.19

66 *Bhagavad Gita* XV.20

point, it is again tempting to reduce the Purushottama, the Supreme Being, to the formless Absolute, the *nirguna* Brahman, the *nirvana*. On the contrary, the formless Absolute and *nirvana* are only some of the Purushottama's integral aspects. The Purushottama is a mysterious entity that includes the formless Absolute, emptiness, nothingness, being and becoming, all sentient beings, all matter, and all universes, but It is more than even that. The Purushottama is in all beings and makes them live and real, but all things and beings are also in It and contained in It. The Purushottama also includes all deities and divine forms. But the Purushottama is more than even that! It is a living, feeling cosmic intelligence capable of responding to us, guiding us and having an intimate personal relationship with each and everyone of us.

Let's not mistake this capacity for God being an individual, for God is not a person but personal to us, not an individual, but all personal and individual existences are part of It.[67] This peculiar, intense, intimate, personal relationship that we can develop with the Supreme Being is the goal of the *bhakta* and the subject of this text.

STAGES OF GOD-REALISATION

It has by now become clear that there is no mystical experience that, once obtained, teaches us all about the Divine, rather than that there is a variety of mystical states. The more of those we attain, the more authentic and complete our surrender to the Divine, and hence our practice of *bhakti* can become. Already, Shri Ramakrishna

---

[67] Sri Aurobindo, *Essays on the Gita*, p. 573

taught that the Divine must be experienced in more than one way, and at the outset of the 7th chapter of the *Gita*, Krishna refers to attaining other views of the Divine rather than essential *jnana*, as *vijnana*, comprehensive knowledge. Shri Aurobindo wrote that the *Gita* outlines four different types of God-realisations:[68]

1. The transcendent, supra-cosmic aspect of the Divine, the Father, the formless Absolute, is everywhere but beyond everything manifest. The *Gita* stresses that this is the aspect of the Divine that we must always keep in our visors, even if we have already attained the other views.
2. The God immanent, the Shakti and *prakriti*, the Divine as the universe and active agent in everything. God as the space/time process, the intelligent, creative force that rolls out the universe and evolution to become embodied in it. Both Ramakrishna and Aurobindo taught that it is this aspect of the Divine that we must surrender to in our daily lives.
3. God as the in-dweller in all bodies, the self in the heart of all beings, the conscious *atman*. We need to realise the divine meaning of all living beings; we need to see that all their lives are spiritual expressions of God, i.e., that all express an aspect of the Divine and are, therefore, sacred.
4. Beyond that, we must also realise God in all things, objects, manifestations, and phenomena. This realisation refers to Krishna's many *vibhutis* (powers), such as "among mountains, I am the

---
[68] Sri Aurobindo, *Essays on the Gita*, p. 316-7

Himalayas, among receptacles the ocean, among animals I am the lion and among humans the king." This aspect of the Divine is worshipped in animism and shamanism as spirits and elements.

Aurobindo maintains that only by realising all these aspects of the Divine can we reach complete surrender, which Krishna repeatedly asks for.[69] All these aspects of God must be known and seen. Otherwise, our *bhakti* will be limited, and the mystery of the Purushottama will remain locked away. Ultimately, we are asked to see God in everything that we encounter and nothing but God. However, we must keep our eyes on the fact that there will always remain aspects of the Divine we cannot see, such as the transcendental aspect of the Divine. The more of God we can see, the more our actions will be informed by the Divine. This will make the Divine more tangible and concrete in our embodied existence and further the agenda of the Divine, which is lifting all life and matter to a greater level of divine consciousness than currently available.

Narada's *Bhakti Sutra* lists seven ways the Divine may be worshipped.[70] I have chosen the names of the sub-headings of this chapter so that they follow a trajectory that begins with the four aspects of the Supreme Being as taught by Krishna in the *Gita* and continues through the

---

69 Sri Aurobindo, *Essays on the Gita*, p. 333
70 Swami Tyagisananda, *Narada Bhakti Sutras*, Sri Ramakrishna Math, Chennai, 2001, p. 52

evolutionary stages described by Narada. Narada's seven forms of the Divine suitable for worship are:
1. A deity and personal form of the Divine such as Shiva, Vishnu, Shakti, etc. The teachers who functioned as my spiritual guides, T. Krishnamacharya, Ramakrishna and Aurobindo, extended this list to non-Hindu forms of the Divine and never attempted to convert anybody to their religion. On the contrary, they encouraged individuals to choose divine forms according to their best understanding. This is my view, too, as I do not believe in pushing my religion onto others, nor do I believe in the superiority of one system over another.
2. A material image of the Divine as per above for the purpose of ritualistic worship. For most people, a mere idea or concept of the Divine, even personal, is not enough to remind ourselves. A sacred image or statue representing the Divine is often more powerful.
3. An *avatar*, a physical embodiment of the Divine, such as Jesus, Krishna, Moses, the Prophet Muhammad or Buddha. For many of us, even a personal divine image is still too abstract, and we long for the God that has become flesh. This should be a historical figure beyond doubt and not some modern cult leader.
4. One's spiritual guide. This is risky in today's environment, as many charlatans invite us to see them as divine to manipulate us. I take Narada as a historical figure who lived thousands of years ago,

and I wonder if, had he lived today and witnessed the current spiritual industry, this point still would have made the list. This is, after all, the *Kali Yuga*. More on that later.

5. The whole of humanity and all of life. The latter is even more critical since the speciesistic tendency of humankind to lift itself above other lifeforms has led to severe damage to the biosphere. That God is all life is also stated in the *Bhagavata Purana*, a surprisingly cosmopolitan text.[71] We need to meditate on the whole collective of life forms on planet Earth as the only "son of God" (or possibly child of God to overcome gender specific language).
6. The whole universe as the crystallised body of God; all matter as divine. Again, this is also taught in the *Bhagavata Purana*, which again excels in its spiritual visionariness.[72]
7. One's own witnessing consciousness (*purusha*), the deep self or *atman*.

While it initially does not matter with which of these aspects and forms of the Divine we start, ultimately, in the spirit of Ramakrishna and Aurobindo, we want to gradually work through the list and embrace all of them to attain complete *vijnana*, God realisation and embrace the totality of the Purushottama.

---

[71] *Bhagavata Purana* III.29.21-34 and VII.14.34 -38
[72] *Bhagavata Purana* XI.2.41.

Chapter 2
WHO ARE WE?

In this chapter, I will attempt to clarify the various terms used in Indian *shastras* to denote the self, consciousness and spirit. The previous chapter established working knowledge of what the Divine is. In this chapter, we will carve out what the individual *bhakta* is. Based on this, we can then define the relationship between the two, which is the subject of the third chapter. Armed with this knowledge, we can then tackle the various methods of *bhakti* in the fourth chapter, which would make little sense without understanding the subject matter of the three previous chapters.

We have earlier established that through meditation, a yogi will experience various layers in the human psyche that are deeper than the body and more profound than bioelectrical and biochemical occurrences in the brain. In this view, yoga is at odds with Western medicine and neuroscience, which both hold that everything we call the mind is a mere result of precisely these bioelectrical and biochemical occurrences in the brain. Yoga, however, proposes not only a mind deeper than the body but also various layers that are even deeper than the mind (*manas*). In yoga, we call these deeper layers of the mind intelligence or intellect (*buddhi*), I-am-ness or ego (*ahamkara* or *asmita*), consciousness (*purusha*) or the deep self (*atman*). The term *jiva* (individual spirit) is a compound of several of the above categories, and so is the Abrahamic concept of soul.

I'm assuming that you, valued reader, have made some, even if only tentative, acquaintance with the eternal aspect of your soul or have an intuition that it exists. I'm concluding this as otherwise, you unlikely would have read up to this point. I have covered gaining a view of the deeper layers of the psyche in several of my books, including *Yoga Meditation, Samadhi The Great Freedom,* and *Chakras, Drugs and Evolution.* Hence, I will not delve into it here. At this point, I will go into some quotations of scripture that generally establish that there is an eternal aspect to us before going into its various categories.

In the second chapter of the *Bhagavad Gita*, Shri Krishna responds to Arjuna, who identifies the opponents he sees on the battlefield of *Kurukshetra* with their bodies.[73] Krishna states there was never a time when any of these people did not exist, nor shall they ever cease to be. Krishna reminds Arjuna not to look at people as bodies but as eternal, spiritual beings who currently have a physical experience. Erroneously, we look at life from the other side, believing ourselves to be physical beings looking for a spiritual experience.

Like many of us, Arjuna is baffled by the question: If the body is so temporary, how can the self be eternal? Krishna then explains that similarly as a person discards worn clothes into the laundry basket in the evening and chooses a fresh set after awakening in the morning, the deep self discards a worn-out body, which has exhausted its current

---

[73] *Bhagavad Gita* II.12

karma, at the dusk of our life, only to choose a new body at the dawn of the next.[74]

Arjuna now wonders how this so-called self might be different from the body, which is so changeable and fragile. The *avatar* then states that the self is eternal, infinite, immutable and unchangeable, as it cannot be burned by fire, drowned by water, or blown away by wind.[75] This stanza occurs almost identically in the *Yoga Sutra*, which adds that it cannot be pierced by thorns and cut by blades. The deep self is, therefore, indestructible and eternal, and it is in this knowledge that we want to be established as a result of our yoga, whether through *bhakti* or otherwise.

Arjuna now wonders how Krishna has all this detailed knowledge, whereas he seems to have no cognisance of these matters. Krishna clarifies that both of them (and everybody else, too) have gone through numerous embodiments spanning many world ages.[76] But, so Krishna, "I remember them all, but thou dost not". He exhorts Arjuna that just because he lost his memory of his previous births, they are nonetheless real. A comparison may help here. Our situation is akin to that of a perpetrator who, through suppression of conscious memory or inebriation, may claim to be innocent of a deed he has committed but cannot remember. A court of law will sentence him not according to his memory but based on established facts. During death and rebirth, we will lose most memories of previous births to focus on the *karma* associated with

---

74 *Bhagavad Gita* II.22

75 *Bhagavad Gita* II.24

76 *Bhagavad Gita* IV.4

our present body. Some memories can return in dreams or sudden glimpses, but we can also regain them through yoga methods (although it's worth questioning whether the effort appropriately rewards the outcome). They are, however, relatively irrelevant for yoga practice as there is not much difference between dwelling in the past of one's current life and dwelling in past lifetimes. Yoga aims to live in the present moment so that we can focus our energies on what needs to be done now to create a divine future.

Arjuna then questions the purpose of this strange setup, according to which beings repeatedly return to live numerous lifetimes. Krishna then explains that it is He who, through His divine creative force (Shakti or *prakriti*), projects forth all beings over and over again. These beings must undergo this process mechanically because subconscious forces control them.[77] This process has some degree of similarity with Sigmund Freud's understanding of relationships, although he, of course, only applies this to the present life. Freud saw that a person might have been negatively imprinted by a parent and then is re-creating such a negative relationship with their partner. They may then leave such a relationship as unfulfilling only to find the negative unconscious pattern to manifest in a future relationship. This process may repeat until the pattern is recognised and we become free of it. This repetition and potential resolve is precisely what Krishna teaches, only that his teaching applies these same Freudian patterns over many lifetimes and not just one. When we die with

---

[77] *Bhagavad Gita* IX.8

CHAPTER 2

an unconscious pattern unresolved, it will resurface in the next one, or any future one, until it is cleared.

Arjuna now wonders how to escape this mechanical repetition of unconscious patterns. Krishna responds that a wise person recognises the self as being present in all beings, but at the same time, this self is also mysteriously the container that contains the world and all beings.[78] Krishna repeats this statement and also emphasises the self repeatedly. Hence, this chapter focuses on establishing what the self really is.

When Krishna speaks of the individual's self, he uses different terms, which makes clear that the individual's psyche is not just a homogenous core; various forces are at play, which we need to understand. Krishna says, "Know me to be the eternal seed of everything that exists."[79] Shri Aurobindo points out that seeds can grow into very different plants depending on the quality of the ground, the amount of water, fertiliser, etc.[80] Aurobindo confirms that we are of divine origin, but Krishna's comparison with a seed emphasises that the import is on what we make of our potential.

JIVA, THE INDIVIDUAL SPIRIT ENTANGLED IN REBIRTH

Swami Tapasyananda, who produced high-class translations of both the *Bhavagad Gita* and the *Bhagavata Purana*, calls the *jivas* spiritual centres, sparks from the fire

---

78 *Bhagavad Gita* VI.29
79 *Bhagavad Gita* X.7
80 Sri Aurobindo, *Essays on the Gita*, p. 273

of the Divine.[81] The term *jiva* means spark. The idea here is that a spark has something of the nature of an entire fire (for example, its shine or luminosity) but to a much lesser extent. To explain what individual spiritual centres mean, we must resort to the image of the Divine as a vast ocean of consciousness. A drop within that ocean partakes of the nature of the sea in that it is water. But it is not the same as the ocean as it is not of oceanic expanse. The *jiva* can temporarily have an oceanic experience (*samadhi*) by letting go of its identification through suspending ego and mind. As long as the *jiva* exists as an individual spirit with a body, it must return to its identification as the limited individual spirit to function. However, the memory of the oceanic experience can change our outlook and ethics, and that's what Krishna asks us to do.

Further down in his commentary on the *Gita* Swami Tapasyananda makes the case that the *jiva* is a compound of the immortal self (depending on the school of thought called *purusha* or *atman*) and the subtle body (*sukshma sharira*)[82]. The yogic teaching talks of three bodies: the gross body (*sthula sharira*) of flesh and blood, the subtle body (*sukshma sharira*) of *nadis*, *chakras* and *prana*, and the causal body (*karana sharira*) of knowledge of our individual divine purpose. While Tapasyananda does not explicitly state so, the *karana sharira* must also be included in the *jiva*. Thus, we find that the term *jiva* excludes only the gross

---

81 Swami Tapasyananda, *Srimad Bhagavad Gita*, Sri Ramakrishna Math, Chennai, 1984, p. 6

82 Swami Tapasyananda, *Srimad Bhagavad Gita*, Sri Ramakrishna Math, Chennai, 1984, p. 74

body, which makes the *jiva* very similar to the Abrahamic concept of the soul, including the deep and surface self. Hence, the term individual spirit is apt. As we will discover later, the deep self (*atman, purusha*) does not in itself contain individuality. It consists only of content-less consciousness and awareness rather than information that makes us an individual, such as personality. That the *pranic*, subtle body (*sukshma sharira*) survives death is already affirmed in the *Brhad Aranyaka Upanishad*, which states that like a caterpillar, which upon reaching the end of a blade of grass reaches across and drags itself over onto the next blade, the subtle body migrates at the end of life from one gross body to the next.[83]

Let's go now forward to the *Gita* stanzas that define the *jiva*. In the passage that describes the *vijnana* or comprehensive knowledge of the Divine, Krishna introduces the fact that His is not only the lower nature (*apara prakriti*, which plays a crucial role in *Samkhya* philosophy and the *Yoga Sutra* of Patanjali) but also the higher nature (*para prakriti*), which is the origin of all *jivas* that form the support of the whole universe.[84] Firstly, this confirms that the *jiva* is not only consciousness (*atman, purusha*) but also *prakriti*, which we may, in this context, call material force. Secondly, the *jiva* or the collective of *jivas* is called an aspect of the Divine, which is the Divine partially expressing Itself through the multitude of individual beings. The fact that the collective of the *jivas* is a vital aspect of the Divine again shows that seeing the world and all beings as an illusion is far off

---

83 *Brhad Aranyaka Upanishad* IV.4.3
84 *Bhagavad Gita* VII.5

the mark. The picture painted here is that the collective of individual centres of consciousness is an intricate part of the creative self-expression of the Divine, a becoming-Itself of the Divine without which the Divine would not be complete. We can understand this making-complete of the Divine through the *jivas* through the fact that the *jivas* have indeed a material aspect (the higher or *para prakriti*), which is still inherently divine and is related to the material cosmos, the universe, which is also part of the divine play.

But what do we have to make of the statement that the *jivas* form the support of the material universe? We can understand this by resorting to quantum physics. Quantum physics found that when light was sent through a double-slit aperture in the absence of an observer, it depicted a wave pattern. When, on the other side, the light was projected onto a bromide plate in the presence of an observer, the light was colouring individual particles on the plate while it left others unchanged. Hence, this established that light in the absence of an observer has wave characteristics, whereas it has particle characteristics in the presence of an observer. This paradox implies that a conscious observer (*jiva*) moves whatever they observe from a mere potential or probability (wave) into a concrete actuality (particle). The Divine became a multitude of *jivas* so that It, as the material cosmos, could become an actuality rather than a potential.

This way, the Divine can witness this actuality as infinite consciousness experiencing the world through all *jivas*, permutations of the Divine. In its totality, this process is called the divine play (*lila*), its understanding is called *vijnana*, and the Divine as all three, the *jivas*, the universe and the infinite consciousness, comprises the mystery of the Purushottama (Supreme Being). Those who understand this will obtain happiness and freedom due to the importance this places on the individual *jiva* for God. This comprehensive understanding forms the bedrock of our personal and ecstatic relationship with the Divine.

One of the most critical stanzas of the *Bhagavad Gita* in total but specifically concerning the *jiva* is stanza VIII.3. Let's quickly recall that in chapter 15, Krishna talks of a triple or three-tiered consciousness (*purusha*), consisting of the bound beings (*kshara*), the unbound beings (*akshara*), and the Supreme Being (Purushottama). In VIII.3 now, Krishna says that the Supreme as *akshara* contemplates Itself (the term self-contemplation means *svabhava*, one of the essential concepts in the context of *bhakti* to understand) to bring forth the transmigrating, embodied *jivas* (individual spirits), which in turn bring all objects into being (by moving them from the wave-state to the particle state). This creative act (of bringing all things into being) is called *karma* (action).

I know this is a mouthful, but here we have the entire philosophy of the *Gita* in a nutshell. Although the above statement is complex, its understanding marks the unravelling of the mystery of life and our close relationship with God, which is the secret of *bhakti*. To simplify it, God consists of three tiers, of which the middle is called unbound consciousness - *akshara purusha*. This *akshara purusha*, through a process of self-contemplation (*svabhava*), recreates Itself as a multitude of beings (called *jivas* –

individual spirits) who then actualise (make concrete) the material universe by moving it from the wave to the particle state. This creative act (referring both to the act of the consciousness - *purusha* and that of the individual spirits - *jivas*) is called *karma* -work.

Karma generally means work (derived from the Sanskrit root *kr* – to do), but its use here forms a double entendre. *Karma* as work implies that what the *jivas* do in the world is work for the Divine, *Karma* Yoga. But it also refers to the fact that their actions are guided by the law of cause and effect (also called *karma* or the law of *karma*), and unless they awaken, they will perform less than ideal actions, subject to less-than-ideal outcomes, which, subject to the law of cause and effect, lead to poor results further down the track.

The *Bhagavata Purana* expresses a corresponding idea. Here, we learn that to create the material form of the Cosmic Being (the universe as the body of God), the Divine had to awaken the karmic tendencies of the *jivas* (this is another way of saying the Divine had to create beings and send them on their way)[85]. Through this process, the universe's constituents could come together into meaningful combinations, moving the universe from the wave and probability state to the actualised particle state. The karmic tendencies latent in the *jivas* are another expression of the result of the self-contemplation of the Divine. They denote what the Divine wants to become through each individual, which is at variance with what It wants to become through all other individuals. In the aggregate, however, they

---

[85] *Bhagavata Purana* III.6.3

CHAPTER 2

align with the Divine as divine law, infinite creativity and potential. Ultimately, this means that only through the Divine becoming the beings did the universe move from being a mere potential, a seed, to a concrete, manifested reality.

Before returning to the subject of the *jiva*, I will briefly outline the way to freedom for the *jiva*, *Karma* Yoga, described in more detail in chapter 5 of this book. The *jiva* has to use the same process by which the Supreme Being has brought it into existence, i.e. self-contemplation (*svabhava*). Through this process, each *jiva* realises which aspect of the Divine it represents. Relative to this realisation, we become aware of our own duty (*svadharma*), that is, the work that God wants to do through us and the work we have to do to serve God. Shri Aurobindo confirms this when saying that the path to safety is to follow the law of ones being (*svadharma*) by developing the idea of ones being (*svabhava*), which together form the process of our becoming.[86]

I will summarise this philosophy again as it may take time to understand initially. The Divine thinks us into existence by contemplating Itself. We must then contemplate ourselves (*svabhava*) to discover our divine essence and then enact it (*svadharma*). Through that, we become real. Again, here is a very different idea of spirituality than simply meditating ourselves into *nirvana* and nothingness, and the last to leave the world turns the light off. An individual obtains freedom by becoming what the Divine wants to become through that individual, i.e., by yielding to and cooperating with the divine creative urge, Eros, to

---

86 Sri Aurobindo, *Essays on the Gita*, p. 520

express itself through us. Fulfilling one's *svadharma* (one's own duty) is the process of *Karma* Yoga. I have described this in detail in my earlier text *How to Find Your Life's Divine Purpose*.

Continuing on the subject of the *jiva* in the *Gita*, we find Krishna proclaiming that an immortal portion (*amsha*) of His has become the *jiva* in the world of living beings, attracts to itself a body, mind, senses, etc., with whom it acts.[87] This statement confirms that the core of each being is divine, a portion of God, but what we make of it is left to our choice. The key is to understand this divine inheritance inherent in each of us, to let this understanding radiate to the surface, and to inform the quality of our decisions, expressions and actions. Little of this process has been realised or turned into reality at the current stage of human history. We are still just a potential. That's why the history of our species is one of war, atrocities, conquest and extermination of ourselves and other species, who are our brothers and sisters, too. If we see this divine inheritance in each of us, our history will finally change for the better.

PURUSHA, THE EMBODIED CONSCIOUSNESS

Purusha is a term used in the *Vedas* and the *Yoga Sutra*. In the *Purusha Sukta* of the *Rig Veda*, each aspect of the world is associated with the body of a cosmic being; hence, it represents embodied consciousness. This fact becomes evident in the *Samkhya* philosophy and the *Yoga Sutra*, which is based on *Samkhya*. Both systems allocate a separate consciousness to each embodied being. At first,

---

[87] *Bhagavad Gita* XV.7

this seems awkward. The yogi discovers in meditation that there is a witnessing, aware entity deep within us that is deeper, closer to us, and more essential than the body, the sensory mind, ego, and intelligence. Yoga calls this entity the consciousness because it is what is conscious, rather than just the contents of the mind, which primarily consist of unconscious data. Let's employ the metaphor of the TV, computer or cinema screen to explain consciousness. We may see the news, a documentary, commercial ads and a feature film all projected on the same screen, but the screen takes on the characteristics of neither of them. The contents of the projections pearl off the screen like water pearls off the surface of a non-stick pan or a lotus leaf. Similarly, awareness/ consciousness is not affected, imprinted or sullied by whatever you project on it. The mind and the subconscious are affected, but the awareness always remains pristine and unsullied.

This inability to be imprinted upon by content, however, also means that one person's consciousness cannot be differentiated from the consciousness of another. For this reason, the *Upanishads* and the *Vedanta* system proposed a single self, called the *atman*, which all beings share. Yoga nevertheless stuck to the concept of the many *purusha*s because yoga is an applied *Vedic* psychology. It starts with analysing the individual psyche and then proposes methods by which individuals overcome various mental problems or disorders (called *kleshas*, forms of suffering). In this approach, it would not be helpful to start the therapy by suggesting to novice clients that they all share the same consciousness. On the other hand, *Vedanta* begins with a completely different design brief. An analysis of the *Brahma Sutra*, *Vedanta*'s defining text, reveals that it is a mystical philosophy, not a psychology.

The *Bhagavad Gita* then would have been quite radical when, instead of aligning itself with the multitude of *purushas* along the lines of *Samkhya* and Yoga, it taught a single but three-tiered consciousness (*purusha*). The first tier consists of the bound (*kshara*) *purusha*, the consciousness of all individual spirits (*jivas*) within the so-called transmigratory existence, i.e. travelling from body to body to exhaust their *karma*. These *jivas* identify with their body. The second tier of the *purusha* of the *Gita* is the unbound (*askhara*) *purusha*. Also, here, we have a collective of beings, but they are spiritually liberated.

Interestingly, the *Gita* insists that the beings remain a collective rather than one single, undifferentiated mass, i.e. self-consciousness is not erased through liberation. The third and final tier is the Supreme Being (Purushottama), whose body is the universe and all other beings. The liberated beings thus retain their self-consciousness because they are not the Supreme Being but admirers, lovers and servants of the It.

The *Bhagavata Purana* also holds that the individual embodied consciousness (*purusha*) is not identical to the Divine, and the universe is seen as the body of the Divine.[88] Both concepts are also held in the *Yoga Sutra*, which says that the Divine is a special *purusha*, distinct from all others[89],

---

88 *Bhagavata Purana* XI.4.3-4
89 *Yoga Sutra* I.24

and that the Divine projects forth the cosmos through the utterance of the *pranava* (the sound OM – the Big Bang).[90]

What is now the exact relationship between the *purusha* and the *jiva*? In the *Bhagavad Gita*, it is stated that a *purusha* (embodied consciousness) becomes the *jiva* (individual spirit) by being associated with an aspect of *prakriti* (nature, divine creative force).[91] We already learned of the higher *prakriti* of the Divine, the *para prakriti*.[92] This *para prakriti* is sometimes also referred to as the *jiva prakriti*. The aspect of the *prakriti* that the *purusha* identifies with consists of the subtle and causal bodies, which form the mind, *karma*, *prana* and ultimately, the gross body. This identification is confirmed, for example, in the *Bhagavata Purana*, which states that the *jiva* (individual spirit) is the *purusha* (embodied consciousness) associated with the subtle body.[93] A similar statement in the *Bhagavata Purana* calls the *jiva*, the individual spirit, an emanation of the *purusha* (embodied consciousness).[94] The term emanation refers to the issuing out or radiating outwards from a source, that is, the spirit, which includes aspects such as mind, *karma*, etc., issues outwards from the consciousness of the individual. More generally, each individual is an emanation, a radiation outwards from our common source, the Purushottama, the Supreme Being.

---

90 *Yoga Sutra* I.27
91 Swami Tapasyananda, *Srimad Bhagavad Gita*, p. 353
92 *Bhagavad Gita* VII.5
93 *Bhagavata Purana* III.31.43
94 *Bhagavata Purana* III.26.4-7

ATMAN, THE UNEMBODIED SELF AND PURE CONSCIOUSNESS

The *atman* represents a more abstract concept and realisation than the *purusha* (embodied consciousness). It is fully obtained only in moments when one is wholly dis-identified with the body. Many Indian texts insist that awareness of the *atman* appears only when awareness of the body disappears, and awareness of the body only appears when awareness of the *atman* disappears. Therefore, we could translate *atman* as "unembodied consciousness", but this label is tricky as it conjures up images of poltergeists. For this reason, the terms unembodied self or pure consciousness are helpful in clearly distinguishing it from *purusha* (embodied consciousness). The term *atman* features heavily in the *Upanishads*, and I have taken "unembodied self" for example from the *Chandogya Upanishad*, which states that the *atman*, the pure consciousness and unembodied self of all beings, is all-pervasive like space and must be realised as Brahman (infinite consciousness and deep reality).[95]

Thus, a trajectory of abstraction exists along the line of *jiva*—*purusha*—*atman*—Brahman. All four represent consciousness to some extent, but the *jiva*, wholly identified with the body, is most subject to suffering and delusion. The terms *purusha* and *atman* represent stations of decreasing identification with one's current individuality. At the level of Brahman, identity permanently ceases, and only Cosmic Consciousness remains.

---

95 *Chandogya Upanishad* 8.14.1

The term "*atman*" is frequently featured in the *Bhagavad Gita* and the *Bhagavata Purana*. In the *Gita*, for example, Krishna teaches that the greatest yogis are those who, due to seeing the *atman* in all others, feel their joy and suffering as they would their own.[96] We now understand how important it is to have a term that implies the unity of one collective consciousness in all of us. If the *Gita* had used the term *purusha* here instead of *atman*, it would not have conveyed the same punch as *purusha*, which contains the notions of many. Having established that there is only one *atman*, we can understand how its realisation would make us feel the pain of others like our own, and that is that we have one common and communal deep self. On a side note, according to the *Bhagavata Purana*, this includes trees since it declares trees have *atman*, too.[97] This is, albeit, a view that not all *shastras* share.

I also want to highlight how much Krishna's idea of the yogi differs from the sometimes sprouted and spruiked concept of "shutting out the world through an act of will", which would make the yogi an aloof, unfeeling, uncompassionate character who has risen above it all. The ideal of Krishna's yogi is quite the opposite. His yogi is not insulated on a mountaintop of pure consciousness while the ignorant suffer below in the mire of sensory experience. On the contrary, Krishna's yogis feel all joy and suffering as if they were their own. Being able to do so and feeling empathy and compassion are some of the key concepts of *bhakti*. Firstly, there is nothing wrong with experiencing,

---

96 *Bhagavad Gita* VI.32
97 *Bhagavata Purana* I.21.5

whether the experience is joy or suffering. Secondly, the passage also clarifies that intensity is on the agenda of the Divine. Krishna wants us to experience the joy and suffering of all beings. It is more correct to say that through our common and shared *atman* (deep self), we are bound to share everything, but through our robotic conditioning, we have made ourselves so numb that we don't feel the hurt and pain of others anymore. Through this numbness, we have impoverished ourselves and the Divine. The Supreme Being embodies as the material cosmos and all beings, whether bound or liberated. Because we don't experience the world and life as intensely as possible, we also impoverish the Divine who feels and experiences the world through us. Hence Krishna's intervention.

Although the *jiva* is an outer layer of the psyche compared to the *atman*, the connection between both is nevertheless frequently pointed out. The *Bhagavata Purana* says that the *jiva* is none but the *atman*, who identifies himself with the egoic body-mind complex.[98] In other words, the difference between both is identification. Identification binds the deep self or pure consciousness to the surface self, the egoic body-mind. This statement aligns with the *Yoga Sutra*, which states that complete disidentification (*paravairagya*) is required to isolate consciousness from the contents of the mind.[99]

---

98 *Bhagavata Purana* XI.28.16
99 *Yoga Sutra* I.12

Chapter 3

WHAT IS OUR RELATIONSHIP WITH THE DIVINE?

After having gained a working understanding of what the Divine is and who we are, we can now turn to our reciprocal relationship. Only when we know what our relationship with the Divine is to be and what it is based on can we turn to *bhakti*, the next chapter's subject. Some hold that belief, faith, love, and devotion are enough, but without understanding and knowledge, these will often lead to sectarian cultism. The importance of understanding and knowledge will be explored more deeply in chapter 6, which deals with the relationship of *bhakti* and *jnana*, which also features prominently in the *Gita*. For example, without knowing and understanding that the Divine is also in those we do not understand, we could quickly become holy warriors or at least be judgemental and uncompassionate towards others.

With the understanding that we matter to the Divine, *bhakti* can succeed. If we could understand our importance to the Divine and that we make a difference to the Divine, we would easily be moved to invest more into our practice of *bhakti*. What stands in the way is our ancient misunderstanding that the Divine is like an emperor, pharaoh or king. Because God was supposed to be omnipotent, we took the closest available image of omnipotence, the one of a human imperial ruler, the so-called unmoved mover. The power of an emperor consists of the fact that he can apply his power to anybody else and move them in any direction or way he wants, but he himself cannot be moved because nobody else has the power to do so. Unfortunately, we have transferred this image to the Divine and imagined It as somebody who is omnipotent and immovable. According to this view, whatever we do or not do will not make a difference to the Divine. Why would we then bother to act in a better way unless somebody convinces us to do so to escape punishment or eternal damnation? Unfortunately, religion promoted this punitive relationship with the Divine instead of the ecstatic one that we should have been focussing on.

THE EGOLESSNESS OF THE DIVINE

The error in the above concept of the Divine is that a human ruler has an ego, whereas the Divine does not. The *Bhagavata Purana* confirms this fact when saying that the Supreme Being is without ego.[100] This statement implies that the Divine has no ego to judge us (the mechanical law of *karma* instead judges us, which, similar to the law of gravitation, does not require a humanlike enforcer to be effective) and has no ego from which to withhold grace. It is us who are withholding grace from us through our flawed choices and behaviour.

---

100 *Bhagavata Purana* III.12.37

The lack of ego becomes clear when we look at the *Bhagavata Purana*, where the Divine, here in the form of the Lord Vishnu, states that He is not free but rather subject to His devotees.[101] Through His fondness of His devotees, His heart is constantly under their sway, the passage says. Vishnu goes on to state that He does not even value Himself nor His consort Lakshmi, as he values *bhaktas* who worship the Divine as their supreme goal. Vishnu then states that accomplished *bhaktas* form the very centre of His being, and He is unaware of anything but them (and they of Him).[102] What more extraordinary declaration of love could there be than this, made by the Divine to us? Do not fall for the idea that we don't matter to the Divine and have nothing to contribute to God. We all matter, and it is through the beings, the *jivas*, that God is becoming Herself. The religions have almost exclusively described the being aspect of God, the transcendent, the Father. They have, however, elaborated little on the becoming aspect, the immanent, the Mother.

The *Bhagavad Gita* corroborates that God is not judgmental and accepts us however we come. In it, the Divine, in the form of Krishna, affirms that however flawed a person is and through whatever path they worship Him, He accepts and blesses them.[103] He adds that He is aware that people follow His path everywhere. This statement clarifies that true worship of the Divine is not limited to a particular religion, a particular deity or a cult, nor to a country, culture or ethnic group, which was also spelt out

---

101 *Bhagavata Purana* IX.5.63ff
102 *Bhagavata Purana* IX.5.68
103 *Bhagavad Gita* IV.11

by Shri Ramakrishna and Shri Aurobindo, who admitted to the same truth in all religions.

What does matter, though, is our understanding of what the Divine is. We need to recognise that the Supreme Being is not just an anthropomorphic representation of our favourite deity, but that worship of the Supreme Being changes us into persons supportive and respecting of all beings and forms of life. Our *bhakti* also needs to bring us to the point where we do not follow our own selfish designs but do God's work instead so that we are in service of Cosmic Intelligence.

That the Divine is open to all paths and forms of worship, as long as they ultimately lead to a complete understanding of all aspects of the Supreme Being, is made clear in an important passage in chapter seven of the *Gita*. Here, Krishna proclaims that through whichever path we desire to approach Him, He will strengthen and support us in that endeavour.[104] He welcomes us through whichever avenue, divine form, deity or religion we approach Him and meets us in a way and form we can understand Him.

In the next stanza, he confirms that whatever deity we worship, we will obtain the benefits that this deity can bestow. But such benefits, according to Him, are not granted by the deity, which is only a representation of the Divine, but by the Supreme Being Itself, infinite and eternal in all aspects.[105] Only complete realisation of the Supreme Being in all Its aspects, consisting of infinite consciousness, cosmic intelligence, the Divine as the material cosmos,

---

104 *Bhagavad Gita* VII.21
105 *Bhagavad Gita* VII.23

and as all beings and objects, leads to complete freedom. In other words, He says, "I am speaking to you here as Krishna, but I am not Krishna; I am all and everything, the universal form (*vishvarupa*)", which He reveals to Arjuna in the 11th chapter. That's important to understand. It is sectarians who are obsessed with the outer form that the Divine speaks through us. But the Purushottama is a nameless, infinite and eternal entity that speaks through us through a thousand voices and the voiceless, too. That's why Lao-tzu was right when saying that whatever can be said about the Dao is not the Dao. Only when we add up all voices of the Divine and then add the unspoken, too, can we gradually get an idea of what It is.

The *Bhagavata Purana* also confirms that the Divine responds to us in the way we can understand It and, therefore, adapts Its approach to meet our needs. It proclaims that whenever the mind is fixed on the Divine, whatever the motivation, It responds appropriately to that particular situation.[106] That's why we all see the Divine in so many different ways. We all get to see as much as we can handle and integrate, or slightly more so that we may gradually transcend our boundaries. It would be imprudent for the Divine to show Itself in a way that we cannot understand, as this quite possibly would shock us, and we could react with retardation. In other words, what we believe and know about the Divine says more about us and our limitations than the Divine Itself. This is almost verbatim what the Danish Nobel Prize laureate and nuclear physicist Niels Bohr said in 1908 about science. In what is

---

106 Swami Tapasyananda, Srimad Bhagavata, vol.3, p. 13

known as the Copenhagen Declaration, he stated that our scientific laws do not describe the world as such but only our knowledge of the world. The same must be said about religion. Hence, it is never a good idea to go to war because of one's religion or one's science.

Let's look closer into how the Divine adapts Its response to us. In the *Gita*, Krishna says that devotees come to Him for four main reasons: those who seek protection from hardship, those who seek boons and forms of gain, those who request spiritual knowledge and those who ask for nothing but come only to love. Krishna says that He responds to all of them according to their needs, but the last category comprises His dearest *bhaktas*, those who come only out of love, who come to give instead of receiving. That this is so makes clear that the Divine, although omnipotent, infinite, complete and eternal, is very open to receiving from us. That the Divine is receptive is again made clear in the *Bhagavata Purana*, where we read that complete intense *bhakti* (called *priti bhakti*) evokes a unique type of ecstasy in God.[107] This needs to be heard and understood. That we can evoke a unique type of ecstasy in God is a far cry from the concept of the unmoved mover. God is indeed moved by whatever we do, and all of our thoughts, actions, and words impact God.

How deeply we touch God becomes apparent in the following passage of the *Bhagavata Purana*. During Krishna's teenage years, the cowgirls (*gopis*) of Vrindavan became so enamoured with the *avatar* that they stole away from their husbands and family to engage in ecstatic

---

107 Swami Tapasyananda, Srimad Bhagavata, vol.3, p. 19

dilly-dallying with the *avatar* at night. This affection was, however, never carnally consummated since, according to *Bhagavata*'s teaching, whatever attitude or desire brings us to the Divine, the Divine will always convert into selfless devotion. After the local community of Vrindavan heavily censored the behaviour of the *gopis*, Krishna's final message to them was that even by serving them for an eternity, He could never adequately reward them for their glorious act of self-surrender and unselfish love, which led them to override any worldly concerns.[108] As He could never repay the debt He had incurred through receiving their devotion, Krishna proposed that the generous act of the *gopis* be its own reward.

Such is the love of the Divine for all Its children. The Divine is entirely aware of Its own powers and knows that for It to be perfect, loving, knowing, surrendered and beautiful is nothing special. It is to be expected. But if we humans, despite our frailty and limitedness, manage to be perfect, loving, knowing, surrendered and beautiful, then this is noted by the Divine as an act that It, relative to Its capacities, could never perform. Hence, we can create in God a unique type of ecstasy and intensity that God by Herself cannot bring about.

A very different picture of God is painted here than the one of the wrathful, irate, jealous, bearded man sitting on a cloud hurling lightings, floods and plagues at us. Here is a Divine conscious that it is not unique if God can love us totally and perfectly since God is perfection, love and totality. What is remarkable is when an imperfect, flawed

---

108 *Bhagavata Purana* X.32.22

and conflicted human can love God totally. Here is a Divine that understands that there is nothing more special in this vast world than such an act of love and surrender, and if we manage to do so, the Divine is in our debt.

That Krishna never deems Himself above the devotee becomes clear from the following episode in the *Bhagavata Purana*, taking place shortly before the great *Mahabharata* war, a setting where the conversation of the *Bhagavad Gita* takes place.[109] At the time, Krishna resides in the city of Dvaraka as King of the *Vrishni* clan. The sage Narada, the author of *Bhakti Sutras*, visits Him to show his respect. Lord Krishna immediately jumps up, bows down, touches Narada's feet and washes them. He then sits Narada on His own throne and asks him what service He can provide. Krishna acts this way because he knows it is much more difficult for a human being than for God to be sage-like.

Krishna consistently demonstrates that for Him, there is nothing higher in the world than the God-lover, not even He Himself. In the *Bhagavata Purana*, He states this explicitly, saying that not even He is as dear to Himself as His devotees are.[110] He also demonstrates how we should interact with each other. Our interactions should be determined by the fact that we can see God in each other. Therefore, our interactions should always be guided by love and respect for one another. This attitude is akin to what Jesus Christ taught, who said that we could recognise His disciples for their love for one another.[111]

---

109 *Bhagavata Purana* X.69.13-16
110 *Bhagavata Purana* XI.14.15
111 John 13:35

CHAPTER 3

If that is still not clear enough, we find in the *Bhagavata Purana* Krishna's proclamation that neither his brother Ananta (Krishna's brother Balarama was considered an embodiment of the serpent of infinity, named Ananta) nor His spouse Lakshmi (She is the consort of Vishnu, of which Krishna is an *avatar*), nor His son Brahma (Brahma, the creator, sprung from the navel of Vishnu), are as dear to Him as an accomplished devotee and *bhakta*.[112] Again, in the *Bhagavata Purana*, the Supreme Being declares Itself to be a devotee of Its own devotees[113] and a devotee of those devoted to Its service.[114] After many explicit declarations of love of the Divine for us, the uptake of *bhakti* should now present few, if any, obstacles for all of us.

WHY IS THIS RELATIONSHIP SO IMPORTANT FOR THE DIVINE?

The *Bhagavata Purana* declares God as the one desiring to be the many.[115] This revelation is essential for us to understand because, in many systems of spirituality, God is only described as the One with whom we are all desperate to become one. At the same time, we wonder how we are separate from God. All the while, we were unaware that God Herself desires to be the many, wishing to be us.

Further down, we hear that one who realises that the Divine has manifested as the many by Its mysterious power

---

112 *Bhagavata Purana* X.86.32

113 *Bhagavata Purana* X.87.59

114 *Bhagavata Purana* V.5.22-24

115 *Bhagavata Purana* II.10.13

(*yogamaya*) has understood the *Veda*.[116] Why this may be, is a justified question because without the One becoming the many, much of the suffering around us would not have occurred. But only through becoming us can the One become self-conscious in all its particulars and particles.[117] Without becoming the many, the One would only be conscious of Itself as the universe in a general sense. This would be a bit like me looking at Earth from space. Yes, I can understand that there is a planet, but only in a general way. My experience would be more complete and total if I could simultaneously experience Earth through all sense organs of all beings, i.e., if I could be in particular locations and times. That's what God is doing, which clarifies that one of God's objectives is intensity. Imagine the intensity of seeing, hearing, touching, tasting and smelling planet Earth through the sensory apparatus of trillions of beings (this includes animals, plants, fungi and microbes).

God's desire to become the many can also be understood from a quantum physical angle. As already stated, it is only through the presence of a conscious observer that a potentiality (in physics called a wave function) changes into the particle state and becomes what we experience as a concrete reality. Concrete reality (what is) crystallising out of simple potentiality (what could be) is the condition for the *lila*, the play of divine creativity, the process aspect of God, the Shakti. Without God becoming many, there is only the potential for the universe or, for example, our planet to become a concrete reality. What we call reality (*sat*) is, until

---

116 *Bhagavata Purana* XI.12.23

117 Debashish Banerji, *Seven Quartets of Becoming*, p. 297

then, only a probability or likelihood. Quantum physicists have pointed out that even complex objects like Earth are sustained in the particle state and, therefore, kept from returning to a wave function of probability only because, at any given time, some observers are always conscious of it rather than asleep. As a collective, which includes non-human lifeforms, we are an essential link in the process of the God immanent becoming Itself by crystallising as the material universe and multiplying Itself as a collective of conscious witnesses – us.

In his monumental text *Process and Reality*, Alfred North Whitehead introduced the term process to refer to God. Apart from the term cosmic intelligence or Shakti, I cannot think of any term more apt to describe the immanent aspect of the Divine. This aspect of the Divine has been chronically underexplored and under-described by all religions. Quite likely so because most religious authorities were males, and the male nature is more attracted to solid-state spirituality, including concepts such as consciousness, nirvana, emptiness and their human embodiment, the unmoved mover (who is always male). They all have in common that they are immutable and unchangeable, and they do not react to their surroundings in any way.

The term process, on the other hand, describes the dynamic aspect of God (Shakti), who is in constant flux, constantly evolves, and moves towards a dynamic equilibrium that continually recreates Itself without ever becoming static. For most male mystics, these ideas are hard to bear as they long for something that never changes, such as the transcendent aspect of the Divine, the pure consciousness. Both aspects of the Divine are real and vital to experience, integrate and understand. Our spirituality and religion during the last few thousand years have, however, suffered from the fact that process spirituality, Shaktism or Earth-based spirituality was always persecuted or at least pushed to the margins.

The initial aim is the label Alfred North Whitehead gives the part of us that God thinks into existence. It is called initial aim because while God aims to express an infinite number of permutations and computations of Herself by thinking all of them into existence, what we as individuals make of it may be far from God's initial aim. We all consist at the core of divine potential, but we are free to gloriously screw it up, to use a profanity. For this reason, it is correct to say that we co-create our destiny with the Divine. God sends us on our way through Her initial aim, Her idea of which aspect of Her each individual is to represent. But since we are made in the image and likeness of the Divine, we are made free, and freedom includes an extreme level of variation from the initial aim. We could go beyond the initial aim, fall short of it, or miss the mark entirely. The Hebrew term for missing the mark was later translated via Greek into the English term "sin". Sin originally meant that we missed the mark of what the Divine was trying to achieve through us. But instead of sinning, we alternatively are free to far exceed God's expectations.

All these avenues are open to us because the twin objectives of God's creativity, according to Whitehead, are intensity and novelty. I have already shown through various quotations that the Divine experiences the world through the collective of souls (*jivas*), and they make possible the intensity with which the Divine experiences the world. Let's now look at novelty. The study of astrophysics and the biological evolution of life shows that both processes are novelty generators. Each time, for example, when a metabolic by-product appears that none of the existing organisms on Earth can metabolise, a new organism evolves that can. Biological evolution, hence, constantly creates new varieties of organisms. The same occurs in astrophysics, where new stars, planets, galaxies, and, most likely, universes are always born. Even new chemical elements and compounds are added all the time.

A similar process takes place in individuation. Because the Divine is the Cosmic, i.e. the sum total of everything, including all individuals, it cannot Itself be an individual. To act on the level of the individual, the Divine has to individuate through us. The individuation process consists of the Divine thinking us into existence by out-projecting an aspect of Itself, an initial aim. Every time God thinks one of us into existence by out-projecting an initial aim, something or somebody new is created; that is, novelty is increased.

However, the initial aim is not a program we mindlessly follow because, in doing so, little intensity would be created. The individual produces the intensity, interprets the initial aim, makes it our own, puts it into action, and actualises it in our own individual way. Intensity comes about through the way each of us embodies our initial aim.

Of course, we could say that God is up to some precarious business. To paraphrase the *Bhagavata Purana*, every time we exceed God's expectations, a particular type of ecstasy and thrill is created in God. However, at the same time, the ample freedom we enjoy and our ability to co-create our destiny also give us ample opportunity to underwhelm God thoroughly.

Shri Whitehead's term "initial aim" is akin to the yogic term *karana sharira*, the causal body. According to yogic teaching, the causal body is the deepest of the three bodies: the causal, the subtle, and the gross. It is the only one that survives across the sum total of all embodiments. The causal body contains God's ideas of us as individuals; hence, we could call it an initial divine potential or initial aim.

There is another yogic term that the initial aim is related to, and that is the *Vijnanamaya Kosha*. The *Vijnanamaya Kosha* (deep knowledge sheath) is part of the five sheaths of the *panchakosha* doctrine of the *Taittiriya Upanishad*. The three superficial sheets, body, *pranic* sheet and mind, contain what we would call the surface self. The two inner sheaths connect us to the Divine. The fourth sheet, *Vijnanamaya Kosha*, includes the initial aim of the God Immanent. The fifth and innermost sheath (*Anandamaya Kosha*, i.e. ecstasy sheath) enables us to participate in the God Transcendent, i.e. pure consciousness. Like the causal body, the *Vijnanamaya Kosha* contains that aspect of the God Immanent, of cosmic intelligence, that we are to embody; i.e. what the God Immanent wants to become as and through us. The *Vijnanamaya Kosha* is not something given and then forgotten, but it is the divine aim we work towards when going from embodiment to embodiment.

CHAPTER 3

The scriptures often mention this complex relationship between the Divine and Her children, the beings. For example, the *Aitareya Upanishad* promulgates that the cosmos is exteriorised for the self-experience of the *saguna* Brahman, the Divine-with-form.[118] The Divine-with-form is often called the personal Divine, a term typically used to juxtapose the God Immanent with the God Transcendent, the formless Absolute. The term personal Divine does not imply anthropomorphism, but it means that this aspect of the Divine is personal to every single one of us. The *Aitareya Upanishad* goes on to declare that beings are made in the image of the Divine-with-form so that their instruments of external knowledge, i.e. the senses, mind, and intellect, may give evidence of the Divine's own reality. This means that God expresses Herself through Her beings, and the circle is completed when the beings experience God within everything, including themselves.

From the view of the Divine, we are, therefore, part of the Divine, and now it also becomes more apparent why the Divine does not need to exert any judgmental power or force to subdue us. On the contrary, the Divine does everything to foster our divinisation, that is, our ability to download divine capacities such as a complete understanding of the world and the ability to act for the Divine and all beings. For example, in the *Bhagavata Purana*, we find that the Divine subordinates Itself to Its *bhaktas*, although It is eternally free and is the master of all worlds.[119] This is taken further in a later passage of the *Bhagavata Purana*, where we find

---

118 *Aitareya Upanishad* I.I.1-4
119 *Bhagavata Purana* X.10.19

that from a certain point of development of the devotee, the Divine becomes the servant of the devotee.[120] This is so because, at this point, the devotees have committed themselves to be the servants of the Divine and have no more personal agenda. The Divine supports this attitude by serving and empowering the devotee.

Earlier in the *Bhagavata*, we learn that to serve the Divine, we need to serve all beings with the attitude that the Divine dwells in them.[121] There is no point in serving some divine image in private while at the same time treating God's beings with contempt and adversarialism. Whatever we do to all the children of the Divine, human and otherwise, through them, the Supreme Being will always be the direct recipient. By consciously understanding this fact and consecrating all our relating to other beings to the Divine, we ensure that what the Divine receives through our interactions with others is worthy of the Divine.

This is an important point! Every time we practice toxic relating and follow poisonous emotions, we would indeed poison the Divine, was it not for the fact that the Divine is immutable and unstainable. We do, however, poison the world by feeling and enacting toxic emotions. In this context, Shri Aurobindo points out that when we go beyond being governed by personal emotions and desires, and when our surface self no longer determines our actions, then the Divine can manifest through us Its purpose in the

---

120 *Bhagavata Purana* X.14.35
121 *Bhagavata Purana* VII.7.32

world, which is, according to Aurobindo the divinisation of all life and matter.[122]

HOW TO SEE AND WORSHIP THE DIVINE

We are now ready to establish guidelines regarding how the Divine should be seen and worshipped. We believe the Divine is remote and challenging to access, but it is we who are remote and challenging to access. So says the *Bhagavata Purana* that it is not difficult to please God.[123] For She is the innermost spirit in all beings and things and, therefore, can be communed with anywhere and in everybody.

The *Bhagavad Gita* announces that we will see all beings entirely in the self and also in the Divine, thus declaring the unity of the deep self and the Divine.[124] In the sixth chapter of the *Gita*, Krishna teaches that realisation must precede action when saying that those yogis serve Him present in all beings who have realised the unity of all existence.[125] In the all-important 12th chapter of the *Gita*, the chapter on *bhakti*, Krishna states that who is friendly and compassionate to all, free of adversarialism, jealousy and arrogance, established in meditation and content, equal in glory and shame, with mind and intellect established in Him, is dear to Him.[126] Also here, it is clear that the Divine is not interested in somebody who worships images in temples but is haughty and proud to other beings. No,

---

122 Sri Aurobindo, *Essays on the Gita*, p. 250
123 *Bhagavata Purana* VII.6.19
124 *Bhagavad Gita* IV.35
125 *Bhagavad Gita* VI.31
126 *Bhagavad Gita* XII.13

Krishna says, the way you treat others, you treat me. That's why Jesus Christ said, "Verily I tell you, whatever you do for the least of these brothers and sisters of mine, you also do for me"[127], and "Verily, whatever you did not do for one of the least of these, you refused to do for me".[128]

This close relationship with the Divine exists regardless of our mode of life, i.e., it is not limited to the powerful or exulted, but it applies even in the most humble position of life. And it is not limited to this lifetime either. In chapter seven of the *Gita*, Krishna promises that all who are established in the fact that the Supreme Being is the power sustaining all matter, spiritual capabilities and wilful actions will remain centered in the Divine even through the process of death.[129]

Understanding and knowing rather than belief is at the core of the *bhaktas'* quest for closeness and intimacy with the Divine. Shri Aurobindo understood this when he called for us to put ourselves passively into God's hands.[130] Putting ourselves passively into God's hands is not achieved by doing something; it is achieved by realising that the Supreme Being is not separate from us but is our innermost self and that of all beings. At the same time, It is the consciousness of the world and the sentient intelligence that has crystallised Itself as the material cosmos.

Deeply contemplating, understanding, and seeing this enables us to ultimately let this realisation radiate out into

---

127 Matthew 25:40

128 Matthew 25:45

129 *Bhagavad Gita* VII.30

130 Sri Aurobindo, *Essays on the Gita*, p. 559

our actions. Unless we achieve this, there is no value in the realisation. The value of a mystical insight lies not in itself but in the extent to which it makes us a changed person. A changed person is kinder, humbler, more supportive, and compassionate towards others.

Let's look now at how this would shape up to be. In the *Bhagavata Purana*, the Divine teaches that when we get outraged, we should remember the Divine in the heart of those who outrage us.[131] Instead of retaliating with vitriol, we should utter words of love to them. Doing so, the Divine will be drawn to us, says the *Purana*. The *Bhagavata's* injunction here is almost verbatim to Jesus Christ's approach to conflict resolution. Although it is the sensible thing to do, we nevertheless find it hard because we are submerged in a millennia-old campaign of adversarialism. This adversarialism has stained and sullied our minds, which can barely function without being jazzed up by competition, ambition and advantage-seeking over others. That's why we hear the *Bhagavata Purana* say that if, due to a purified mind, we see the Divine in our heart, we will attain spiritual freedom.[132]

Mental slavery is the outcrop of the Darwinian mind that sees a competitor in each being we meet and, therefore, devises endless schemes to outcompete them. The only long-term result of this attitude is that we will all die together. Better than the Darwinians, the *Bhagavata* understood evolution when it said it is a divine law that all

---

[131] *Bhagavata Purana* III.16.11
[132] *Bhagavata Purana* III.25.39

life forms flourish by mutual cooperation and meet their downfall by mutual antagonism.

Rather than antagonism, seeing kinship in everything around us, whether moving or unmoving, constitutes realising and worshipping the Divine. So says that *Bhagavata Purana* that authentic worship of the Divine consists of seeing everything, including trees, mountains, forests, rivers, the ocean and atmosphere, as ensouled by the Supreme Being.[133] Therefore, the true *bhakta* is experiencing reverence for all nature and beings at all times with sincerity. Imagine for a moment how our peace negotiations and attempts to prevent mass extinction of species, environmental holocaust and ecocide would progress if we would put this call into action. As a global civilisation, we are still on the destructive path because we refuse to follow this call, although spiritual visionaries of many cultures have, down the ages, advised us to do so, but to no avail.

Respect and love for God are not abstract concepts that one declares in a church, mosque, synagogue, or temple and then does not apply them outside. No, we must practise them in daily life. So says the Supreme Being in the *Bhagavata Purana* that if you want to win Me over as a loyal wife does a committed husband [or vice versa], then show your authentic love for Me by respecting my presence in all beings and nature alike.[134] We tend to show such love for close friends and family members but not for the rest of humanity. We may show it to our cat or dog but not to the

---

133 *Bhagavata Purana* III.12.41
134 *Bhagavata Purana* IX.5.66

rest of the animal kingdom. We may also show it to our front lawn or a few ornamental trees and shrubs in our garden but not to the rest of nature. This is because we have drawn an imaginary line between "us" and "other". *Bhakti* Yoga involves erasing those imaginary lines and serving God in everything, especially in the most unexpected places, such as our imagined enemies. We believe in enmity, adversarialism and antagonism because our past conflicts and grudges are deeply embedded in our subconscious. With training, it is possible to clear these programs from our conscious mind, but the subconscious mind requires much deeper attention. That's why the *Bhagavata Purana* says that we need to always remember the Divine, have both our conscious and subconscious minds surrendered to It, and perform all our actions consciously as offerings unto the Supreme Being.[135] Performing our actions as offerings can take place only if we recognise the Divine as the spirit that pervades within all beings and objects while simultaneously containing them like a vessel.

HOW NOT TO WORSHIP THE DIVINE

The discussion in the previous chapter on how to recognise and worship the Divine would only be complete with delving into potential pitfalls, i.e., how not to worship It. To this extent, Shri Aurobindo said that those who refuse to acknowledge the personal Divine pass over something profound and essential.[136] When Aurobindo speaks about the personal Divine, he does not invoke anthropomorphism,

---

135 *Bhagavata Purana* XI.29.9
136 Sri Aurobindo, *The Integral Yoga*, p.159

i.e. creating a Divine in the likeness of the human. He nevertheless acknowledges that the Divine is sentient, that It can feel and respond to us personally, in that It will respond to one devotee differently than to another (relative to the difference of the initial aim that gave rise to the person and also to what they make of it). In this sense, the term "personal Divine" is used rather than denoting the Divine as an individual. The other reason why many Indian mystics use the term "personal" is to juxtapose it with the impersonal Absolute, the God transcendent. The Divine is thus a being, not a human being, but a Cosmic Being. We may also call it Beingness, as there is nothing outside this infinite sentient being.

At the outset of the 12th chapter of the *Gita*, the chapter on *Bhakti* Yoga, Arjuna asks Krishna whether the Divine is better worshipped as personal or as the impersonal Absolute. Krishna's answer is straightforward: worshipping the personal Divine in a spirit of love and devotion is to be preferred[137] because the obstacles facing those who worship the formless Absolute are far more significant.[138] This is because, for embodied beings, it is difficult to follow an unclear ideal.

You can experience this clearly if you are in a complex conflict situation and now contemplate what advice the formless Absolute will give you for your actions. The answer will be little to none. At best, you get advice along the lines of being in the present moment. But being in the present moment will not get you far when dealing with warfare,

---

137 *Bhagavad Gita* XII.2
138 *Bhagavad Gita* XII.5

CHAPTER 3

genocide, victims of rape, etc. Being in the moment is too often the privilege of the well-resourced, well-connected, and well-educated bourgeois middle class of white industrial societies. The formless Absolute will not help us decide when to scale down the noble heights of our meditation pillow to use our mind in determining what is right or wrong and whether perpetrators need to be stopped and victims protected. It is the Divine-with-form, the personal Divine, the God immanent, who gives these instructions.

I will give you an example that illustrates the problem. I remember being baffled when one of my students told me they didn't see a point in rejecting Adolf Hitler since God was in Hitler, too. The statement that God is also in Hitler is, at face value, correct. The God Transcendent, the ocean of infinite consciousness, the formless Absolute, is in Hitler and Hitler in it, and to that extent, Hitler does not differ from any other being or object in the universe. But the statement that God is in Hitler is free of value when it comes to ethical consideration. The term free of value is another way of saying "worthless". The fact that God is in all beings does not exempt any such being from conducting themselves according to the rules of *dharma* (right actions, righteousness, duty). Nor does it exempt any bystanders from re-establishing *dharma* if they find it flouted. However, abstract metaphysical concepts (such as the formless Absolute) are sometimes used to excuse oneself from duty, a process called spiritual bypassing.

That's why Krishna says that for an embodied being, it is difficult to understand an unclear idea.[139] Pure, contentless

---

139 *Bhagavad Gita* XII.5

consciousness, *nirvana* and emptiness are unclear ideals. The advantage of the personal Divine is that it comes with evident ideals and ethical rules, such as protection of the victims, justice for all, correction of perpetrators and upholding public order. So says, for example, Arjuna to Krishna in the *Gita*, "I see that you are God and have all power. What I don't understand is that you are so concerned with abiding by a seemingly countless number of rules and upholding right conduct?" At the time, Krishna was the king of an ancillary dynasty, while Arjuna was the third in line to the imperial throne of India. Krishna reminds Arjuna that ordinary people look to outstanding personages, like both of them, for inspiration for proper conduct. Even though He, Krishna, and Arjuna could bend the rules and get away with it for some time, if they did, the general populace would take this as an invitation to do so, too. Therefore, the wise, so Krishna, will always give an impeccable example and conduct themselves to the highest specifications.

In a later chapter on ethics (Chapter 8), I will explain their importance to *bhakti* in detail. Here, I will only give a short introduction to the subject. In the *Bhagavata Purana*, the Divine says that sages and saints, cows, the poor and victims are dearer to God than anybody else and that those who persecute them will meet their Maker under unfortunate circumstances.[140] This statement is in spirit identical to Jesus's: "Blessed are the meek, for they shall inherit the earth".[141] The message here is clear: The Divine

---

140 *Bhagavata Purana* III.16. 10
141 Matthew 5:5

CHAPTER 3

has a particular spot for the weak, and if we want to impress the Divine, we are to treat them with the same respect and support as we would a king.

But why is there so much conflict among people in the first place, and why must we follow a complex set of rules and ethics? The *Bhagavata Purana* explains that there was a time (called the *Satya Yuga* or Golden Age) when people were cooperative and peaceful because they realised the Divine in the hearts of all beings and were capable of worshipping It there.[142] However, times changed, and people became mutually disrespectful and antagonistic toward each other because they only focused on each other's defects. Hmm, "mutually disrespectful and antagonistic of each other because they only focussed on each other's defects". Does this remind you of something? Have you watched the news lately or listened to a session of your country's parliament, assuming you are not living in a dictatorship where the case would be even worse?

This attitude of mutual disrespect and antagonism also made people incapable of seeing the Divine in each other's hearts. According to the *Bhagavata*, so that the Divine was not wholly lost, in the *Treta Yuga* (the world age following the Golden Age), worshipping the Divine in images, shrines, statues, etc., was introduced. We must understand that this form of worship was introduced because we could not anymore recognise the Divine everywhere, in everything and everybody. The *Bhagavata* is affirmative of image worship as it is a great shortcut, but it also says that image worship is of no benefit as long as one refuses

---

142 *Bhagavata Purana* VII.14.38-39

BHAKTI THE YOGA OF LOVE

to recognise the Divine in others and remains antagonistic and adversarial towards them.

In an earlier passage, the *Bhagavata Purana* has the Supreme Being complaining that people disregard Its presence as the innermost self in all and then make a great public show of worshipping It through images.[143] That sounds a lot like much religion practised today. The *Bhagavata* continues with the Divine warning us that ignoring Its presence in all as the self, and instead, foolishly offering worship to images, will make It very displeased. Therefore, any such person who victimises others is victimising the Divine residing in them. They and those who are proud and haughty are separating themselves from God and will never attain peace, so the *Bhagavata*. According to the Supreme Being, the right approach is worshipping images [as shortcuts] together with loving service to the Divine through all Its beings.

Combining both is not possible without authentically loving all beings. In fact, in this passage, the Supreme Being calls for an end to "othering", i.e. to stop self-centeredness and distinguish between self and other(s). By recognising the unity of all beings and everything in the Divine, we need to overcome the separation and estrangement of self-centeredness, and in this spirit, we can serve all beings through honour and love, a service that is then recognised and accepted by the Divine as service to It. Such service is the way to spiritual freedom.

Notice how this philosophy of divine love and service is the complete antithesis of the teaching of our modern

---

143 *Bhagavata Purana* III.29.21ff

society, which centres around receiving, taking and getting. In all the sources we are discussing here, the Divine states that the individual's freedom and an ideal and divinised society are created by focusing on giving to all and loving all via the avenue of seeing the Divine in them. Because our civilisation worships receiving, taking and getting, we are in a constant antagonistic and adversarial struggle with all "others", whether they are other individuals, interest groups, ideologies, religions, nations, or species. Deep down, it is our very philosophy of "othering" that is at the basis of environmental exploitation and destruction of cultures. Othering can have no place on the path of *bhakti*, for we need to sincerely try to see God in all those we have previously othered.

Chapter 4

BHAKTI, WHAT IT IS

Bhakti is not an emotion we can spontaneously conjure up, but it is a practice gradually refined over a long period. At the outset of this book, I invoked the great Sufi mystic Hafiz, who was destitute at the age of 20 because he could not get the beautiful woman he desired. At that point, Hafiz met a Sufi master who told him to turn his human love into divine love, love for Allah. It notably took Hafiz another 40 years to achieve this state, and his struggles are recorded in many of his beautiful poems.

The reason why Hafiz needed a solution for his unfulfilled love is because it made him miserable. Because he could not get his beloved, he lost weight, could not sleep and suffered until his mental health declined. This suffering illustrates that the way we ordinarily love is to get something. Ordinary human love is focused on receiving, whether this be a thrill, excitement, happiness, fulfilment, possession, stimulation, pleasure, security, escape from loneliness, status, affirmation, companionship, etc. Such love could indeed be called an emotion, as it is based on past lack, perceived need and neediness. We go out and love because something in us is missing, and we hope to obtain this through our beloved.

Whatever we hope to obtain through love, we then project this need onto the loved person, and as long as they supply for this need, the relationship works out. This process we call falling in love. When the beloved stops supplying this need, we fall out of love. Our partners often end the supply of our needs because they subconsciously realise that we relate to them from a projected need, a lack within us, rather than from who they truly are. This is ultimately only satisfying if our partner entered the relationship with similar motives. In many cases, the hormonal rush ultimately subsides, and they turn away from us or us from them.

Unlike this human type of love, *bhakti* is a mental/spiritual discipline focused on ourselves. We are gradually changing our love from wanting to receive to the attitude of giving. We do not constantly make supplications to the Divine to meet our needs, but we ask ourselves how we can love the Divine more and serve It more. This growth is available to us at all because love is itself a quality of the Divine. Because we share our innermost being with the Divine, such divine love is also possible for us. For this to become possible, though, we must undertake a process to convert our way of loving from the human to the divine. These ways are explored in this chapter.

Here, I will define *bhakti*, look at its prerequisites and qualities needed, list various types of *bhakti*, analyse their process, spell out the effects, and finish with its results and essence. But firstly, we need to establish that *bhakti* is not ideally practised in isolation but integrated into the larger complex of a complete yoga consisting of *Bhakti, Jnana,* and *Karma* Yoga. So says Krishna in the *Bhagavata Purana* that He has promulgated three paths of unification with

God, and there are no other ones: they are *jnana, bhakti* and *karma*.[144] Although Krishna limits the number of yogas here to three, He also says elsewhere that when we are incapable of absorbing the mind in Him, we should try to reach Him through the systematic practice of concentration, i.e. *Raja* Yoga.[145] A description of *Raja* Yoga takes up most of the sixth chapter of the *Gita*.

In Narada's *Bhakti Sutra*, we read that when reaching maturity, *Karma, Bhakti*, and *Jnana* Yoga will merge into a unified path.[146] In this triune path, *jnana* purifies the intellect, *bhakti* purifies the emotions, and *Karma* Yoga purifies the will. The term triune path, meaning three in one, was coined by Shri Aurobindo in his *Essays On The Gita* and later further embellished in one of his principal works, *The Synthesis of Yoga*. Both texts are dedicated to the importance of ultimately practising *Karma-, Jnana-,* and *Bhakti* Yoga side-by-side, even if, at first, we may choose whichever one of the three accommodates our still raw and unrefined nature most.

Aurobindo writes that the *Gita* teaches three steps, of which *Karma* Yoga can be taken as the first.[147] Here, we perform actions not for ourselves but in service to the Divine. We do not look at the outcome but at the process of working for the Divine, regardless of whether we succeed in our endeavours. Success and failure are met with perfect equanimity and offered to the Divine. I often have

---

144 *Bhagavata Purana* XI.20.6

145 *Bhagavad Gita* XII.9

146 Swami Tyagisananda, *Narada Bhakti Sutras*, p. 35

147 Sri Aurobindo, *Essays on the Gita*, p. 38

to elaborate on this attitude of equanimity and service when confronted with my students' despair in the face of mounting environmental, social and political problems. I get asked, "How do you stay hopeful? How do you motivate yourself to keep working for a better future, seeing that all seems so hopeless?" The point is that if we ask for hope and motivation, we are ultimately outcome-oriented. If there is a chance that we succeed, we will go and save the planet. But if the odds are stacked against us, we better avoid getting involved. The problem with this attitude is that it is again based on receiving and getting. We are in it because we get a kick from saving the environment. If it seems achievable, we are happy to chip in. In other words, a risk/ reward equation is going on here. How likely is it that we will succeed? How much effort do we have to put in? And how much reward in terms of self-satisfaction do we get? In the case of preventing environmental breakdown, success is very uncertain, and it seems like much effort is needed to save nature. Although we could get a lot of self-satisfaction out of it, the reward seems too far off; hence, the attitude of dejection seems more economical. We better refrain from investing our energies into a lost cause.

The attitude of the *Karma* Yogi is different. The *Karma* Yogi will not ask for a reward but simply do something because it is the right thing to do out of service to God. This is God's planet. We have no right to destroy it. Nature is breathtakingly beautiful. We can see God's beauty in it wherever we look. Hence, the point of whether we succeed or not does not occur. It's simply the right thing to do. Even if the *Karma* Yogi dies failing what they try to achieve, it would not matter. What matters is that they died doing the right thing.

With this attitude and process in place, we eventually practice *jnana*, the yoga of knowledge of the self, the consciousness. Its goal is not to become inactive but to realise that the doer is not us but the *prakriti*, the divine creative force, i.e., to recognise that the Divine moves us. This type of yoga aims at knowing, experiencing and seeing more and more aspects of the Divine. The more we truly see and appreciate the Divine in its totality, the more genuine love for It can grow. Without interrupting our *Karma* and *Jnana* Yoga, we finally see, love and adore the Supreme Being in everything we meet, see and do, in an act of complete surrender to the Divine, which is *Bhakti* Yoga.

In this volume, I have placed *bhakti* first, but I support Shri Narada's and Shri Aurobindo's view that *bhakti* is best not practised in isolation. For this reason, following the chapter on *bhakti*, I have included extensive chapters on *Karma*, *Jnana*, and *Raja* Yoga, explaining how their practice supports and augments *bhakti*.

DEFINITION OF BHAKTI

Bhakti means adoration, love, and surrender to the Divine. The term comes from the Sanskrit verb root *bhaj* – to divide. It is also used in the term *baksheesh*, which is used when asking for alms; in this context, it means "divide what you have and share it with me". In *bhakti*, our goal is not to unify ourselves with the Divine but to commune with It. We see we have a divine core, already one with God, the self or consciousness. But we also see that our surface self, i.e. our egoic body-mind, is vastly inferior in power to the surface self of God, the material universe as the crystallised body of God carrying within it an infinity of beings who are all computations and emanations of God.

For this reason, we are under no illusion that a true union with the Divine is impossible. What is possible is to devote our surface self and deep self to an eternal, loving service to and adoration of the Divine. Shri Ramakrishna expressed the difference by saying, "I do not want to be sugar, but I want to taste sugar". One hundred forty years have passed since this saying, and today, our enthusiasm for sugar has lessened due to health reasons. Nevertheless, he meant you could no longer taste sugar if you became sugar. The same applies to the Divine. If you could become the Divine, you could no longer behold and adore It. This beholding and adoring of the Divine constitutes the path of *bhakti*.

The 11th-century Hindu theologian Shri Ramanujacharya (Ramanuja for short) eloquently taught through his identify-in-difference doctrine (*beda-abeda*) that identity with the Divine (by way of our deep self being identical with the transcendental aspect of the Divine) and difference from the Divine (consisting of the difference between our surface self and the immanent aspect of the Divine) must be seen simultaneously side-by-side. The *Bhagavata Purana* also defines *bhakti* as the engagement in permanent service to the Divine rather than aiming for *moksha* (liberation), the release from the cycle of rebirth.[148] The *Bhagavata Purana*

---

148 Swami Tapasyananda, *Srimad Bhagavata*, vol. 1, xxxiv

calls *bhakti* the fifth *purushartha* (human objective). The orthodox four human objectives are:

- *Artha*, acquisition of wealth
- *Kama*, sexual pleasure and satisfaction
- *Dharma*, right action/ righteousness, which always applies, especially when it comes to the acquisition of *artha* and *kama*
- *Moksha*, spiritual liberation and freedom from the cycle of rebirth

The *Bhagavata Purana* adds *bhakti* as the fifth human objective, saying that loving and devoted service to the Supreme is the most important of the five and the highest destiny of the individual spirit (*jiva*).

The *Bhagavata Purana* explains further that *bhakti* implies the concentration of the entire psyche, usually engaged in knowing sensory objects, on the Supreme Being without asking for a reward.[149] The theme of not asking for rewards is discussed in more detail later. In the *Bhagavad Gita*, it is called surrendering the fruits (i.e. the reward) of one's actions to the Divine. The concentration of the entire psyche on the Supreme Being is something that only the most advanced *bhaktas* can do without further training. Aurobindo confirms the importance of this capacity when saying that *manana* and *darshana*, the constant thinking of the Divine in all things and seeing of It always and everywhere, is essential to the way of devotion.[150] Most of us will not have attained such an exulted state yet. Chapter

---
149 *Bhagavata Purana* III.25.32-33
150 Sri Aurobindo, *The Synthesis of Yoga*, p. 601

6 of the *Bhagavad Gita*, the chapter on *Raja* Yoga, will discuss using yoga methods to concentrate the mind. Narada's *Bhakti Sutra* defines *bhakti* as consecrating all activities to the Divine, utilising surrender.[151] Thus, it is consistent with the other two texts, the *Bhagavad Gita* and the *Bhagavata Purana*.

QUALITIES AND ATTITUDES SUPPORTIVE OF BHAKTI

Officially, there are no prerequisites for *bhakti*. The *Bhagavad Gita* states that even a hard-baked sinner attains *bhakti* if he comes to have unswerving love for the Divine.[152] In the next stanza, Krishna explains further that this steadfast love for Him (through divine contact) will transform any wretch into a righteous person.[153] That's the theory. Practically speaking, many qualities and attitudes move us forward in *bhakti*; without them, we are not going anywhere in a hurry, not least so on the path of *bhakti*. These qualities are listed in the 12th chapter of the *Gita*, the chapter on *Bhakti* Yoga. Let's have a look at them now.

Krishna states that those superior in yoga who, with their minds intensely concentrated on Him with a steady stream of love, worship Him with complete *shraddha*.[154] The term *shraddha* is complex and often truncated as the English term faith. But faith doesn't convey the sublimeness of the Sanskrit term. I would go as far as saying that as soon

---

151 Swami Tyagisananda, *Narada Bhakti Sutras*, p. 19
152 *Bhagavad Gita* IX.30
153 *Bhagavad Gita* IX.31
154 *Bhagavad Gita* XII.2

as one has accepted the translation of *shraddha* into faith, the transformative power of *shraddha* is not accessible to us anymore. I will treat *shraddha* here but have written an additional section on it in Chapter 10. Aurobindo has pointed out that *shraddha* has a past aspect, which he calls the memory of having emanated from the Divine, and a future component, the intuition that we will return to the Divine when our job here is done. The best translation for *shraddha* is, therefore, intuition-remembrance. I prefer using the original *shraddha*, but there is always the danger of overloading this text with Sanskrit, hence alienating you, valued reader.

A few stanzas later, Krishna exhorts us to concentrate our minds on Him alone and let our intellects penetrate Him, which combined will lead to permanent abidance in Him.[155] I have used the English term intellect here to translate the Sanskrit *buddhi*. Alternative options would be intelligence or reason. Krishna certainly encourages critical thinking here, as we should use our critical intelligence to understand the Supreme Being as much as possible. That this is not a misunderstanding becomes clear at the end of the *Gita*, in one of the last stanzas. Krishna concludes that He now has imparted to us this most secret of all secrets teachings (i.e. the teaching of the *Gita*). He suggests we reflect critically on it and then do as we deem fit.[156] Deem fit means take it or leave it, but act following your own understanding and not just because I say so.

---

155 *Bhagavad Gita* XII.8
156 *Bhagavad Gita* XVIII.63

Because of this emphasis of Krishna on our critical intelligence, the reading of *shraddha* as faith does not make sense. The term faith, for example, is used in the context of blind faith. Here, it means blind adherence to dogma, although we should know better. Another context is presented in the term good faith. We usually say we acted in good faith if our actions were flawed, but the reason for them being flawed was not known to us at the time. It thus means that we would have had to make an unreasonable effort to find out what happened; hence, acting in good faith is supposed to indemnify us from the demerit accrued of not having made this unreasonable effort.

But it is precisely this unreasonable effort that Krishna wants us to make when he says, "Let your intellect penetrate into Me" and "reflect on this entire secret teaching and then do what you deem fit". But why should we bother to make an unreasonable effort with our intelligence to understand Him? Swami Tapasyananda, a translator of both the *Bhagavad Gita* and the *Bhagavata Purana*, responds to his question by saying that unless we know what our connection to the Supreme Being is, love of It cannot become firm and constant.[157] This couldn't have been said any better. Our love for the Supreme Being wavers, and we struggle with *bhakti* precisely because we do not know and understand our connection with the Supreme Being. And if we do, then at least we tend to forget it frequently.

Let's continue our inquiry into the qualities and attitudes of the *bhakta* listed in chapter 12 of the *Gita*. Krishna says that those dear to Him cause fear to no one, and no one can

---

[157] Swami Tapasyananda, *Srimad Bhagavad Gita*, p. 256

frighten them. They are free from intense emotions such as euphoria, anger, and excitement.[158] Our need to dominate others and thus intimidate and frighten them comes from a deeply held fear of others. We pre-empt their attacks by attacking first. Hence, one who frightens others is the one who is scared himself. The second part of the stanza displays that Krishna has an understanding of what today we would call borderline personality disorder or emotional regulation disorder. Being in the throes of this disorder, we are addicted to producing intense emotions as otherwise we can't feel ourselves. We can't feel that we are important and think that not enough is happening in our lives to make us feel truly alive. Because Krishna understands this condition, He wants us to have distance from our surface self, which implies that we can watch our thoughts and emotions as if they were animals pacing up and down in an enclosure.

Krishna adds the following qualities:[159]

- desirelessness (to take things however they come and not worry about things that we currently do not have),
- purity (abstaining from toxic thoughts and emotions),
- resourcefulness (trust that whenever needed, He will send us the skills required),
- detachedness (the ability to let go of what we are about to lose),
- freedom from worry (the worst thing that can happen is that we die, but if we do, we return into His embrace)

---

158 *Bhagavad Gita* XII.15
159 *Bhagavad Gita* XII.16

- letting go of self-centeredness (although we think we are here because of ourselves, we are only one of the infinite permutations of Him, through which He experiences the cosmos. Hence, the best strategy is to place little importance on ourselves).

In stanza XII.17, Krishna asks us to let go of our tendency to chase the pleasant and avoid the unpleasant. This letting go is something we can easily do. Any mother will always clean away her baby's poop, feed the crying infant, do the dishes, go shopping, etc., although neither of these things are of themselves pleasant. In fact, in their accumulation, we could label them as mindless drudgery. Instead, we may prefer to sit in the Bermudas, watch the sunset, and slurp Martinis. But this is not what a mother thinks. Without a grudge, she will do whatever is required simply because the task is in front of her, she is present, and the task needs to be done. This is the attitude Krishna wants us to display. Interestingly, part of the attitudes of *bhakti* that Shri Narada lists in his *Bhakti Sutra* is that of a parent to the Divine. While this may be unachievable at first, the selflessness of a mother best reflects the attitude the *bhakta* should have toward the whole world.

Krishna then expands this attitude to the concept of *samah*, evenness, equality or equanimity.[160] He wants us to respond with equanimity towards friends and foes, evenness in honour and insult, alike in heat and cold, equal in praise and blame. Usually, we separate these pairs into two categories: one that we find pleasant and one we are

---

160 *Bhagavad Gita* XII.18-19

adverse to. Krishna says here that both categories are in constant flux, and the mix we get is outside our control. We can make the best effort, but after we have done that, we need to meet with equanimity the victories and defeats life dishes out to us and ultimately see and accept them as caused by our previous actions and the play of the Divine. In either case, after we have made our best effort, we need to accept them as ordained, stop emoting about them, and get on with our lives and duties.

Krishna asks us to perform our work as service to Him, to consider Him our destination and goal, and to surrender attachment and antagonism toward any of His creatures.[161] We may attach ourselves to other beings or antagonise them for various reasons. Krishna asks us to see them all only as permutations of Himself. If they come to us, we treat them friendly; if they avoid us, we accept that; if they seek conflict with us, we do not reciprocate. Instead, we try to defuse the confrontation by finding out why they feel threatened by us, and above all, we never initiate any conflict from our side.

An essential aspect of *bhakti* is our ability to surrender. So says Narada's *Bhakti Sutra*, true *bhaktas* are neither the doers of their own actions nor act for any gain.[162] They would instead abandon themselves like leaves being moved by the wind of the Divine. Shri Aurobindo confirms this by saying that the yogi must step aside and let the Divine take up the yoga through us.[163] While we call this

---

161 *Bhagavad Gita* XI.55
162 Swami Tyagisananda, *Narada Bhakti Sutras*, p. 81
163 Sri Aurobindo, *The Synthesis of Yoga*, p. 629

attitude surrender, Aurobindo teaches that it is not a passive letting go but takes place by bringing our being and will in alignment. When Aurobindo uses the term will, he talks not of something we use for our egoism, which we may call choice, but of a higher force naturally aligned with God. Aurobindo believes that there is only one will: God's will. Therefore, if we activate this will that aligns us with the Divine, we open ourselves to grace.

Narada's *Bhakti Sutra* confirms that God's grace is always present; only the ego prevents us from receiving it.[164] This is a fundamental realisation. Because our concepts of the Divine are still clouded by anthropomorphism, we imagine God as a giant human with an ego who may whimsically withhold grace from somebody whose face He doesn't like. But God is neither human nor has an ego from which to withhold grace. God is pure love, acceptance and life-affirmativeness; hence, grace is radiated out to all beings in all places at all times. It is our own individual ego which intercepts the receiving of grace. All *bhakti* is the practice of getting our ego out of the way so that we can receive the grace the Divine radiates out all the time. The objective here is that the Divine performs the yoga through us rather than our ego performing the yoga. Ego makes yoga more difficult because it tries to accrue benefits and advantages for us, thus sullying the spirit of yoga.

I will complete this section by listing the qualities needed for *bhakti*, spelt out by Shri Ramanujacharya, the 11th-century Hindu theologian. Ramanuja lists them as

---

[164] Swami Tyagisananda, *Narada Bhakti Sutras*, Sri Ramakrishna Math, Chennai, 2001, p. 124

- discrimination (ability to differentiate the real from the unreal and the essential from the non-essential)
- desirelessness (desires will stand in the way of surrender because having them implies that we continue to follow our own agenda)
- practice (*bhakti* has an active component and does not just consist of letting go and surrendering)
- service to others (being a servant of the Divine means to be a servant of all beings; it helps us to get over our self-centeredness)
- purity (the non-engaging in mental, emotional, spiritual and physical toxins)
- absence of the need for entertainment (when communing with the Divine, no entertainment is required; insisting on being entertained implies resistance to communing with the Divine)

Of course, Ramanuja places the bar here very high, and this list reflects the high standards of ancient *bhakti* authorities. Presenting such a list to modern readers may put them off because they may perceive such a standard as unachievable. I have nevertheless presented the list for two reasons. One may be called archaeological, which means I want to accurately present the historical roots of *bhakti* and show what it was like. The second reason may be called a graded approach. While one could feel inadequate at those demands and baulk, taken in a spirit of self-acceptance and self-analysis, the list is nevertheless helpful. I read through it from time to time and always find one area or another where I could do better without putting myself down. I take Ramanuja's list not as a prerequisite that needs to be fulfilled before commencing *bhakti* but as a dynamic list that I can use to assess my progress as I gradually mature.

TYPES AND FORMS OF BHAKTI

This section deals with traditional forms of *Bhakti* Yoga, that is, how *bhakti* was taught in the past. There is a significant variance in the approaches, and according to the *Bhagavata Purana*, this is because the attitudes and tendencies of individual *bhaktas* differ according to the dominance of particular *gunas* (qualities, i.e. the mix of intelligence, energy and mass in a person or object) within them.[165] To simplify this statement, different personalities need different types of *bhakti* practice. The defining list of forms of *bhakti* is the *Bhagavata Purana's* so-called nine limbs of *bhakti*.[166] They consist of:

- *Shravana* - Hearing of the exploits of the Divine, usually in the form of *avatars*. This limb is called hearing because the tales were handed down orally in the days of yore. In today's world, we would allocate the reading of sacred texts to this limb. Reading formed my initial exposure to *bhakti*. It is crucial when we want to choose our *ishtadevata*, which is the for us appropriate form of the Divine for the purpose of worship. Patanjali says in the *Yoga Sutra* that we find out which divine form is suitable for us by reading sacred texts (of various *ishtadevatas*).

---

165 *Bhagavata Purana* III.29.7
166 *Bhagavata Purana* III.25.25

- *Kirtana* – This involves the chanting and hymning of *mantras*, etc., associated with an appropriate form of the Divine. It is often done in groups and is then especially helpful for extroverts who find solitary meditation on the Divine difficult.
- *Smarana* – The remembrance of the Divine. This important aspect should be practised throughout the day and whenever possible. It is the ideal crisis intervention. Whenever you are in a critical situation, remind yourself that whatever you do, you do it for God and not for yourself. I have trained myself to remember the Divine before falling asleep, when I wake up, and whenever I should wake up at night. I found this practice extremely helpful. While remembering is usually done employing an icon, i.e. a simplified image, it is good practice to at least once per day to remember the Supreme Being in its entirety, i.e. the various aspects of the Divine, such as the God transcendent as infinite consciousness, the God immanent as cosmic intelligence, the universe as the crystallised body of the Divine, all beings and all objects as expressions of the boundless creative potential of the Divine. A traditional form of practice is to perform remembrance by uttering the names of the Divine through *mantra japa*.
- *Padasevana* – Service at the feet of the Divine, but also to see the whole world as a part (*pada*) of the Divine and to serve the Divine through all beings. Because we all play different roles worldwide, our *padasevana* may differ enormously. It involves experiencing our

- *svabhava* (law of our own being) and *svadharma* (law of our own becoming) in meditation and consecrating all of our actions to the Divine. The next chapter, the one on *Karma* Yoga, will fully explore these concepts. Our professional occupation ideally is done in the spirit of an offering to the Divine.
- *Archana* – Ritualistic worship. *Archana* involves a ritualistic offering to the Divine, usually in front of a visual image of the Divine. I practice this by performing my yoga practice, including *asana*, *pranayama*, meditation, etc., always in front of a visual representation of the Divine in the spirit of an offering. This creates the spirit of performing yoga not for yourself but as a gift to the Divine. A symbol may be appropriate for those who cannot visually represent the Divine. The key is to perform any version of *archana* with an authentic feeling of love for the Divine. If it becomes empty ritualism, then it is dead. The difference becomes evident when we can no longer see God in those we have complicated relationships with, particularly enemies or people we feel adversarial towards. It is in those that we need to see God most urgently.
- *Vandana* – Salutation. Whenever we greet another being with folded hands, we must consciously greet the Divine within them. That is the power of saying *namaste*; it means I greet God within you because I can see God within you. Additionally, if I cannot see God within you, I will keep reminding myself until I can. It also means that we should see God in the sun, the moon, the starry sky, the clouds, the ocean,

rivers and lakes, mountain ranges, forests, trees and animals. Ideally, we stand in awe and rapture daily before the whole of nature as the crystallised body of God, with all its beings inside of it. That's the best approach for *Vandana*.
- *Dasyam* – Servitude, slavery. Here, the more advanced layers of *bhakti* begin. We are cultivating the attitude of being a servant, or more radically, a slave, of the Divine. It is an essential practice for reducing the grip that the ego has on us. The *bhakta* gratefully accepts any form of humiliation or shaming. In these situations, it is healthy to see our ego cringe and wriggle like a worm in the mud and practice distance and disidentification from the ego. Krishna says he who is the same in glory and shame, a yogi he is. We are not here to rule and dominate but to serve.
- *Sakhyam*—Comradeship with the Divine, but also all other forms of relationships we could have with the Divine, including being the Divine's playmate, lover, or even parent. This requires advanced levels of exultation from the devotee and is better left to later.
- *Atmanivedana* – The total surrender to the Divine. The pinnacle of *bhakti*, described in the concluding stanzas of the 18th chapter of the *Bhagavad Gita*. I will cover it further down under the goal of *bhakti*.

The above list in the *Bhagavata Purana* is usually called the nine limbs of *bhakti*. It also goes by a second name, *saguna bhakti*, which is *bhakti* with form.[167] With form here because the nine limbs imply that we engage in a formal yoga practice. *Saguna bhakti* is then juxtaposed to *nirguna* (formless) *bhakti*, also known by a second name, *prema bhakti*, i.e. loving devotion. *Prema bhakti* is considered appropriate for more advanced souls. It is the practice of spontaneous, loving devotion to the Divine, which does not require the support of the above limbs. That this is so is also recognised by Narada's *Bhakti Sutra*, which states that *bhakti*, i.e. devotion, is only a means to be distinguished from supreme love (*prema*)[168]. This means that Narada considers *bhakti* the practice and *prema*, love, the goal.

The above list of the nine limbs of *bhakti* occurs several times in the *Bhagavata Purana*. It also gets mentioned when the demon emperor Hiranyakashipu asks his son what the best lessons he learned were during the education he was afforded.[169] However, the *Bhagavata Purana* also offers a truncated six-limbed devotional discipline, including salutation, praise, dedication of all action, service and hearing.[170] This introductory list mainly omits the nine-limbed list's last three more advanced aspects.

Narada's *Bhakti Sutra* chooses a different classification method and arrives at 11 types of *bhakti*.[171] They are:

- glorifying the Divine
- recognising the beauty of the Divine

---

167 *Bhagavata Purana* III.32.37
168 Swami Tyagisananda, *Narada Bhakti Sutras*, p. 132
169 *Bhagavata Purana* VII.5.23-24
170 *Bhagavata Purana* VII.9.50
171 *Narada's Bhakti Sutra*, stanza 82

- worship
- remembrance
- service
- being a friend of the Divine
- taking on the role of a child of the Divine
- taking the role of spouse or lover of the Divine
- total surrender
- complete absorption
- feeling the pain of separation from the Divine

Of these glorifying the Divine, worship, remembrance, service and total surrender are contained in the *Bhagavata Purana* list. Being a friend, child or lover of the Divine may be done by a particular devotee because it suits their nature. Arjuna in the *Mahabharata* was Krishna's friend. The *gopis* of Vrindavan pursued an erotic relationship with Krishna, which was, however, never carnally consummated. Shri Ramakrishna proclaimed that accepting the role of the child of the Divine was suitable for all, although he had phases where he took on other roles, too. There is no restriction to staying in any of the above attitudes. What is essential is that one achieves closeness with the Divine.

Some commentators limit the *Bhagavata Purana*'s phrase 'recognising the beauty of the Divine' to recognising the bewitching beauty of Krishna. At the same time, though, it is stated at every twist and turn that the whole universe is to be seen as the body of the Divine. In other words, we need to recognise the beauty of the Divine in all of nature. Many of us today have a sense of the beauty of nature, but often, we don't realise that this beauty in nature is an out-projection of the inner beauty of the divine Creator and Creative Force (Shakti). We, humans, would not be capable of recognising this beauty and perfection had the Divine not instilled us with Its sense of beauty. Hence, it is not enough to see something as beautiful; we must also see that this represents God's essential beauty.

Complete absorption in the Divine can be achieved by those who practice formal *samadhi* on the Divine. Ramanuja recommends this path, and Patanjali, too, says in the *Yoga Sutra* that the power of absorption (*samadhi*) comes from surrender to the Divine.[172] It is an advanced method for those who practice formal concentration yoga (*Raja* Yoga). Whereas Patanjali is more liberal with potential objects for meditation or concentration, Ramanuja accepts only the Divine as a meditation object.

Such absorption is a technique that suits those adept in formal concentration and meditation exercises, i.e., those inclined to *Raja* Yoga. Feeling the pain of separation from the Divine is for those of predominantly emotional temperament, i.e. *bhaktas*. Let's recall, however, that for swift success, all these techniques are combined and integrated with *Jnana* and *Karma* Yoga, too. We should not let such labels hold us back from practising a whole and integrated *Maha* Yoga (the great, universal yoga embracing all yogic disciplines).

In the *Bhagavata Purana*, we meet characters like Vidhura or Udhava, whose faces are awash in tears every time they meet or say goodbye to Krishna. Similarly, extreme ecstasy or extreme concentration can transport us to an

---

172 *Yoga Sutra* II.43

exulted state, as can extreme grief and pangs of separation. Another exponent of the emotional school of *bhakti* was the 15th-century Bengali mystic Chaitanya Mahaprabhu, who taught *prema priti bhakti*, self-abnegating love and joyful service.[173] He also taught that the highest form of *priti bhakti* has the character of illicit love because, like the *gopis*, you are risking everything, including the censorship of society, due to your divine madness. Also, *priti bhakti* comes in 8 stages.[174]

On the other side, Shri Aurobindo teaches that *bhakti* combined with *jnana*, i.e., knowledge of the Divine, is the highest *bhakti*.[175] This view is supported by many Indian theologians, including Madhusudana Sarasvati, who taught that *bhakti* must be supported by knowledge of the Divine and its attributes.[176] All schools of *bhakti*, though, have one thing in common: In its highest development, whether combined with *jnana* or extreme emotionality, the *bhakta* does not ask for reward, such as liberation, but only wants to render service to the Divine.

CONSECRATION

The initiation into the inner sanctum of *bhakti* begins when we consecrate our life to the Divine. Consecration here means that our actions are done with God in mind and as an offering to God. It does not necessarily mean that we do different things, but gradually, with everything we do,

---

173 Swami Tapasyananda, *Srimad Bhagavata*, vol.3, p. 16
174 Swami Tapasyananda, *Srimad Bhagavata*, vol.3, p. 20
175 Sri Aurobindo, *Essays on the Gita*, p. 284
176 Swami Tapasyananda, *Srimad Bhagavata*, vol.3, p. 16

we will ask ourselves more and more: is what I am doing here actually pleasing God? Krishna says He will gladly accept whatever we offer to Him with sincerity, even just water or a leaf. It is not that an act has to be fancy, extreme or outlandish; it is the sincerity and attitude with which we perform it that counts. So says Narada's *Bhakti Sutra* that renunciation of one's previous way of life means consecration of all activities, including secular (worldly) activities to God.[177]

The *Bhagavata Purana* agrees when stating that consecrating all actions to God means presenting them as an offering.[178] Important when making our actions an offering is that we see and recognise all beings as children of the Divine. About this, Jesus Christ says, "if you place an offering on the altar and have a grudge against your brother in your heart then your offering is not welcome as it would defile the altar. Go and make peace with your brother first then your offering is welcome".[179] Remember that Krishna said in the twelfth chapter of the *Bhagavad Gita* that those dear to Him treat friends and foes alike and fear none but frighten nobody either. What is required as the bedrock of consecration is that we see everything and everybody as God. Then, consecration is easy.

In the *Bhagavata Purana*, the Divine teaches that we should convert all of our mundane efforts to having God's satisfaction as our goal rather than pursuing our own

---

177 *Narada Bhakti Sutras,* stanza 8
178 *Bhagavata Purana* III.25.25
179 Matthew 5:23-25

agenda.[180] This is called surrendering the fruits of one's actions, *tyaga-karma-phalah*. The moment this becomes our focus, we are liberated from the fear of failure. The outcome of the action is surrendered to the Divine. We do our best and take failure, triumph, glory, or humiliation, however it comes.

But there is an even higher level of consecration. The *Bhagavata Purana* considers this next level when proclaiming that whatever we do with body, speech, and thought, we should offer to the Divine, both in terms of outcome (fruit) and agency.[181] This means to realise that it is, in truth, the divine creative force (Shakti or *prakriti*) that does everything through us and not us. Krishna states this in the *Bhagavad Gita* when saying, "All actions are done by my *prakriti*, only a fool believes to be the doer".[182] This stanza, and many others, declare that the agency is with the Divine and not with us. Think about it briefly: when you eat, are you metabolising the eaten food? No, the body does it even if you are asleep. Are you breathing your lungs? No, the body does it again, even when you are unconscious. Are you beating your heart? It seemingly beats by itself, most of the time without our awareness. Are you thinking your thoughts? Until recently, most of us would have said yes, but now neurologists tell us that when they ask us questions while our brains are wired up, they can see neurons fire seconds before we become aware of a thought or choice, that is, thoughts are generated

---

180 Swami Tapasyananda, *Srimad Bhagavad Gita*, Vol. IV, p. 66
181 *Bhagavata Purana* XI.2.36
182 *Bhagavad Gita* III.27

without our conscious awareness. In the aggregate, all of this means that we are not the doers, and giving up the sense of agency is a healthy attitude. Giving up the sense of agency is the final layer of consecration, the moment when we accept that we are enacted upon by God, who is the doer through us. When this is entirely and consciously accepted, we can become conscious vessels of and conduits for the Divine.

GOD-REALISATIONS AND THE INTELLECTUAL LOVE OF GOD

Shri Aurobindo says in *Essays On The Gita* that whoever loves God in all, lives and acts in God.[183] But how do we love God in all? We cannot unless we know and recognise the Divine in all and everything. Otherwise, to love God in all becomes some sectarian dogmatism that will not change our surface personality and behaviour. Krishna answers the question of how we can love God in all, an answer that forms the climax of the sixth chapter of the *Bhagavad Gita*. This is the chapter on *Raja* Yoga and meditation on the Divine, but it also forms the conclusion of the entire first six chapters of the *Gita*. Krishna states that those yogis are the most established in communion with Him, who, with their self, enter into His Being powered by love and *shraddha* (intuition-remembrance).[184] He exhorts us to bring our own *atman* (the self) in communion with the Divine Being through love and *shraddha*. To review the term *shraddha*, it is often poorly translated as faith, but

---

183 Sri Aurobindo, *Essays on the Gita*, p. 246
184 *Bhagavad Gita* VI.47

as Aurobindo has spelt out, it means to remember that before we embarked on our almost infinite sequence of embodiments, spanning several world ages, we were one with the Divine. On the other end of the timescale, we can have an intuition that after billions of embodiments are completed, we will return into the embrace of the Divine. Combining both remembrance and intuition is referred to as *shraddha* (intuition – remembrance). It serves as an inner compass to traverse the ocean of conditioned embodiment.

This *shraddha*, combined with love, brings our *atman*, our inner self, into communion (rather than union) with the Divine Being. It is crucial to differentiate union and communion here. Union with the Divine is our state before and after embarking on the world-age-spanning sequence of embodiments. In between, we may have more or less short glimpses of union, but only during mystical states, when the ego and mind are temporarily suspended. Because we need ego and mind to survive and fulfil the divine purpose of our embodiments, the highest we can aim for (while traversing our cycle of embodiments) is communion. Communion means that our deepest self is in a permanent state of blissful adoration of the Divine while our surface self keeps functioning and serves the Divine in the world.

This communion with the Divine Being is far from faith and belief. Because faith and belief are static states, not open to falsification (i.e. to know when we are wrong), they often lead to wrong concepts (such as that we believe that to please God, we should kill infidels). Through that, they may then be responsible for the many atrocities that have been committed in the name of religion down the corridors of history. If we rely on faith and belief, how do we learn when these are misguided? The prevalence of holy wars, crusades, witch burnings, holy inquisitions and murder and torture of heretics and infidels should show us that mere faith and belief are not enough. These historical errors also cannot be prevented by *bhakti* alone because our own emotions may signal to us that if we love God, we should show our love by killing infidels. But these aberrations can prevented by embedding *bhakti* in *jnana* (knowledge) and *buddhi* (intelligence).

The *Bhagavad Gita* lists three types of compound applications of *bhakti* and *jnana*. We could call them God-realisations or revelations of the Divine.[185] They are called *ekatva*—unity, *prthaktva*—difference, and *bahudha*—multiplicity. These must initially be realized sequentially but later applied simultaneously for our *bhakti* to remain free of egoic taint. Egoic taint here means that we use our supposed devotion to the Divine to gain power, fame, and wealth by manipulating people into conflict with others, citing religious and spiritual motives.

Ekatva means to see the unity of the deep, unembodied self, the *atman*, with the transcendental aspect of the Divine. *Prthaktva* means to know that we differ from the divine creative force, the Shakti or cosmic intelligence. The differential in firepower between the Shakti and our own intelligence, limited to the chip between our ears, is enormous. Similarly, the difference in size between our body and the cosmos as the crystallised body of God is

---

185 *Bhagavad Gita* IX.15

evident. There is a distinct separation between what our material and intelligent being can do and what God's material and intelligent being, the Shakti, are capable of doing. The third God-realization is *bahudha* – multiplicity. It means seeing how the God immanent has become the multiplicity of all beings and objects, resides in all of them, enlivens them and gives them their characteristics. Our *bhakti* cannot become complete unless we can see all these three realisations permanently or at least remind ourselves of their validity before making crucial decisions.

At the conclusion of the 18th chapter of the *Gita*, Krishna again presents the same facts in different words.[186] Here, Krishna tells us to surrender outcomes and agency of all actions mentally to Him, to practice intense devotion and communion of intellectual love to Him and to have our mind ever focussed on Him. I have gratefully accepted Swami Tapasyananda's translation of *buddhi yoga* as 'intellectual love of God'. This beautiful term the Swami adopted from 17th-century Dutch philosopher Spinoza. The term implies that we go beyond the emotional swoon of love to include the desire to know, understand and comprehend God as much as we can (independent of the outcome). This is why Krishna says elsewhere, "Let your mind rest on Me and let your intellect (*buddhi*) penetrate into Me".

The *Bhagavata Purana* supports this approach and exemplifies the earlier mentioned *bahudha* (multiplicity) version of *bhakti* by suggesting that we should recognise all nature, including sky, air, fire, water, earth, stars, living beings, trees, rivers, oceans, as the body of God and greet

---

186 *Bhagavad Gita* XVIII.57

them with prostrations of intense love and devotion as emanations of the Divine.[187] It is this attitude that indigenous people practised for a long time and for which modern industrial humanity ridiculed them as savages. Even when I studied Comparative Religion in the 1980's, animism was still considered the religion of primitives. Primitives because we deem our supra-cosmic and anthropomorphic image of a God, created in our own image, so superior to theirs. It is only now that we gradually begin to understand that it is precisely this awe and reverence with which the erstwhile primitives look at nature that prevents us from abusing, coercing and controlling it. And it is this abusing, coercing and controlling of nature which ultimately draws us closer to the yawning abyss of environmental holocaust and ecocide.

Of course, living in harmony with nature and all creation is possible, and it is fostered by loving devotion to the spirit that creates, supports, and exists in all and everything. This loving devotion, *bhakti*, is possible by surrendering to this spirit. So says Shri Aurobindo that because in our secret essence, we are one with the Divine, we can grow and evolve into Its likeness, i.e. emulate It.[188] In such a process of evolution, our surface self becomes informed by the various God-realisations we experience, radiating out to the surface and informing our surface self to become loving, supportive, forgiving, and compassionate towards all. In the beginning, when we practice *bhakti*, we may think mainly about getting and receiving experiences.

---

187 *Bhagavata Purana* XI.2.41

188 Sri Aurobindo, *Essays on the Gita*, p. 424

CHAPTER 4

For much of my life, I could have been profanely described as a mystical experience junky. Gradually, this morphs into an interest in changing our lower nature, focussed on survival, success, acquisition, ambition, competition, antagonism and adversarialism, to wanting to contribute to the Divine. To this, Aurobindo says that our salvation (from our robotic conditioned surface-self) cannot come without our evolution into the divine nature.[189] Love of the Divine is effective because it allows us to evolve into the likeness of the object of our adoration and call down divine love.

The calling down of divine love is usually referred to as grace. Let's recall the statement of Narada's *Bhakti Sutra*, which says that spiritual realisation is chiefly due to the grace of the Divine, made available to us by our own effort, our *sadhana* (practice).[190] Although this seems like a dichotomy at first, we realise that ultimately, spontaneous realisation and grace, and the work beforehand that enables it, always go hand in hand. I want to emphasise this statement as it is too easy to miss. Grace is essential for our evolution, but it is called down through our practice of spiritual techniques, our *sadhana*. It is *sadhana* that transforms us, not much else.

PURE LOVE AND ECSTASY

If we manage to see God in every creature we meet, this will profoundly affect our social interactions. It will turn our social interactions into offerings of pure love to God without expecting anything in return, as Narada's *Bhakti*

---

189 Sri Aurobindo, *Essays on the Gita*, p. 423
190 Swami Tyagisananda, *Narada Bhakti Sutras*, p. 170

BHAKTI THE YOGA OF LOVE

Sutra states.[191] Noteworthy is that this seeing of God everywhere is not motivated by reward but that we love because we cannot help loving God. This love so fills us that it overflows and must find an outlet. Such love cannot be conjured up by mere decision. It is produced by studying, understanding and accepting the philosophy of *bhakti* and by realisation produced by *sadhana* (the sum total of your yoga practices)—more on that in the following chapters.

Shri Aurobindo defines *prema*, divine love, as the holding or maintaining of the ecstasy of seeing the Divine. This holding implies an act of constant remembrance or repeated remembrance throughout the day. To do so, we must focus on the transcendental aspect of the Divine, the infinite consciousness, which manifests in an endless number of beings via the God immanent as process. This process is constantly developing without ever remaining the same. Although it appears fragmented into a multiplicity of forms, the God transcendent always remains unchanged. So says Krishna. We must maintain an attitude of love towards these myriads of forms, behind which we always recognise the one Divine. This recognition is the ecstasy of love.[192] Shri Aurobindo also gives a truncated rendering of this extensive formula. In *Records of Yoga*, he states that we must always remain conscious of universal love for the One, everywhere and in everything.[193] It is helpful to use the truncated formula throughout the day, but at least

---

191 Swami Tyagisananda, *Narada Bhakti Sutras*, p. 216
192 Debashish Banerji, *Seven Quartets of Becoming*, p. 334
193 Sri Aurobindo, *Record of Yoga*, Vol. 2, Sri Aurobindo Ashram, Pondicherry, 2001, p. 1470

once or twice per day, we must remember the Divine in Its entirety and all of Its aspects.

Aurobindo suggests that our focus on and remembrance of the Divine consists of an intricate relationship between love for the Divine, *prema*, and the ecstasy of realising the Divine, *ananda*. *Prema* is the active component of this relationship, and *ananda* is the passive one. To maintain *prema*, our love for the Divine, we must strive for an equal delight in all things. This equality or evenness is called *samata* in the *Gita*. Krishna, over and over again, asks us to be equal in the face of the duality of friend and foe, glory and shame, victory and defeat, heat and cold, by realising that these are all faces through which He speaks to us and which invite us to see Him, the unity behind all appearances. To maintain this is the state of ecstasy (*ananda*), and that is the source of love (*prema*).

EFFECTS OF BHAKTI

We shouldn't be afraid that *bhakti* could be austere and taxing. It can also be sumptuous and joyful. Narada's *Bhakti Sutra* states that *bhakti* is a supremely ecstatic experience, an un-corruptible and unalloyed state of absolute rapture, felicity and beatitude.[194] The *Bhagavata Purana* supports this by saying that we attain supreme bliss through an unbroken flow of love towards God.[195] Aurobindo states that absorption in the Divine does not bring only peace but also bliss and rapture.[196]

---

194 Swami Tyagisananda, *Narada Bhakti Sutras*, p. 56
195 *Bhagavata Purana* III.33.24
196 Sri Aurobindo, *The Integral Yoga*, p. 214

The intensity of ecstasy and rapture is caused by our *bhakti*'s attraction to the Divine. So says Krishna that nothing attracts Him as intense *bhakti* does.[197] He elaborates that since He is exceptionally fond of devotees of exulted mind, His heart is under their control.[198] This implies that He is attracted by the love and rapture of the devotee absorbed in Him. This, in turn, causes rapture in Him, which again increases the ecstasy of the devotee. We can understand now why the 14th-century Bengali mystic Chaitanya Mahaprabhu said that the highest *bhakti* has the character of illicit love, which may inspire the censorship of society. This is because loving the Divine with such intensity feels so good that one somehow expects it to be forbidden or illegal. Additionally, it can make one feel almost drunk with ecstasy, which, when pursued, can lead to erratic behaviour. Chaitanya Mahaprabhu tells us this is the right avenue to pursue and that we should not fear what the people say. In the mystical poetry of the earlier invoked Sufi seer Hafiz, the term "whine" refers to the elixir of divine love. The term "drunkenness", as used by Hafiz, applies to the state when this elixir is imbibed, and the "tavern" is code for the community of ecstatic devotees.

When approaching this type of absorption in the Divine, we mustn't be motivated by any form of gain, such as spiritual liberation, enlightenment, etc. We are to love the Divine for its own sake rather than the results, for motiveless love of the Supreme Being is superior to liberation, says the

---

197 *Bhagavata Purana* XI.14.20

198 *Bhagavata Purana* IX.4.63

Bhagavata Purana.[199] If anything, the focus should be on the rapture we cause in the Divine when beholding our love for It.

The ultimate goal and result of *bhakti* is the realisation of the Supreme Being. That this is indeed possible is stated in various passages. So says the *Bhagavad Gita* that the Supreme Being is attained by constant and exclusive *bhakti*.[200] An understanding of who and what the Supreme Being is in Its totality is required for such devotion. Otherwise, Krishna would not have used the term Supreme Being, Purushottama, here. He could have advised us to simply visualise Him, the *avatar* Krishna. But He did not say that. He used the term Supreme Being. This term includes the formless Absolute, a living and sentient Cosmic Being, embodied as cosmic intelligence and the entire material universe, giving characteristics to all beings and objects, aspects all simultaneously held and exceeded by the term Supreme Being.

At the outset of the seventh chapter of the *Bhagavad Gita*, Krishna announces that He will explain how employing yoga, a person surrendered to Him and absorbed in love for Him attains full knowledge of Him.[201] Following this announcement, He juxtaposes essential knowledge, i.e. *jnana* (self-realisation), which is insufficient for Krishna's purpose, and comprehensive knowledge, *vijnana* (God-realisation). This *vijnana*, so Krishna, consists in realising that he has a lower and higher creative force (*prakriti*), of

---

199 *Bhagavata Purana* III.25.33
200 *Bhagavad Gita* VIII.22
201 *Bhagavad Gita* VII.1

which the lower is the one that *Samkhya* and Patanjali's Yoga teach. The higher *prakriti* is the one through which the Supreme Being expresses Itself as an infinity of beings, which all are fractions, emanations and permutations of that very Supreme Being.

Krishna then continues that we need to experience and comprehend the Divine as taste in water[202], brilliance in fire, life in embodied beings[203], intelligence in the astute, heroism in the gallant.[204] Additionally, He says He is strength uncorrupted by desire and desire in alignment with the right action.[205] He then goes on to say that the Divine empowers and manifests all qualities in nature (as long as they align with divine ideals and law).[206] We can see and serve the Divine everywhere by studying and understanding these qualities. To do so, we need to comprehend that all the above qualities (and many more that the *Gita* lists in several passages) are in the Supreme Being. This means they are qualities that the Divine lends to objects and beings to make them what they are. But Krishna qualifies this by saying that while all objects and beings are in Him, He [in His entirety] is not in them[207]. This means that we need to recognise that everything that exists has its support and origin in the Supreme Being but

---

202 *Bhagavad Gita* VII.8
203 *Bhagavad Gita* VII.9
204 *Bhagavad Gita* VII.10
205 *Bhagavad Gita* VII.11
206 *Bhagavad Gita* VII.12
207 *Bhagavad Gita* VII.12

in itself represents only a tiny aspect of the Supreme Being. Hence, the Divine is not limited to these characteristics.

Let's recall that the chapter began with Krishna's announcement that He would show how one surrendered to Him and absorbed in love to Him attains full knowledge of Him. The key here is not just to take God as an *avatar*, a prophet, a supra-cosmic anthropomorphic ruler, who thrones on a cloud with his back turned to us, but to realise that we live inside of God. Everything we hear, see, smell, touch and feel is God (as long as it conforms to divine law and ethics) and must be recognised as such. To do so with an attitude of surrender and love to the Divine brings us into communion with It. This attitude of surrender and love is undoubtedly a challenging practice. Indeed, it is a very sophisticated and demanding yoga. But if we achieve it, Krishna promises He will see us as His very self.[208]

In the above passages, Krishna demands that all sensory experiences be converted to experiencing the entire cosmos and all objects as God. However, this conversion must occur without reducing the Divine to the cosmos because some aspects of the Divine, such as the God transcendent, are not contained in the cosmos. In a related passage, the *Bhagavata Purana* asks for the same to be done with deity worship. The *Bhagavata Purana* calls upon us to worship the Supreme Being alone through all deities rather than falling for the trap of mistaking any of the deities as the Supreme Being.[209] The Supreme Being must be recognised as the destination and goal of all spiritual endeavour and

---

208 *Bhagavad Gita* VII.18
209 *Bhagavata Purana* II.4.10

practice. Interestingly, the *Bhagavata Purana* does not discuss a particular deity or our particular *ishtadevata* (the form of the Divine suitable for worshipping a specific individual). Instead, it talks about all deities, i.e., multi-deity worship and polytheism. The *Bhagavata Purana* here calls upon us to go from deity to deity and recognise that the Supreme Being, the Divine, the One, hides behind all divine images.

Interestingly, this is precisely what Shri Ramakrishna practised and Shri Aurobindo advised. When we take this to heart, God will look at us through a thousand faces and images created by millennia of human cultures and civilisations on all continents. Similar to the earlier Gita passage, which asked to recognise the One in all objects and sensory perceptions, the *Bhagavata Purana* also exhorts us here to see God in the divine images of all cultures and religions. Aurobindo made this point by saying that the yogi must ultimately recognise God in all images and representations created. It would not be unfair to say that a yogi who cannot recognise God in a particular (*sattvic*) image has an unconscious block, and that unconscious block would prevent them from attaining *vijnana*, which is comprehensive God-realisation.

The *Bhagavad Gita* summarises many of the above points in a beautiful stanza, which says that by being established in communion (yoga) through practice (*abhyasa*), one attains to the Supreme Being if one does not lose one's focus and thinks of the Divine ceaselessly.[210] There are many important points made here. Firstly, the passage tells us not to fear using our minds. The mind is an important,

---

210 *Bhagavad Gita* VIII.8

powerful tool that can elevate us to incredible heights if appropriately used. Neo-spiritual movements often act like the mind is the enemy, something to be fought against and vanquished. On the contrary, the *Gita* believes that the mind can help us turn into a divine direction or its opposite (which the *Gita* usually calls demoniac).

For this reason, the mind must be made to think of the Divine as often as possible and ultimately see the Divine in everything. Seeing the Divine in everything is not entirely unachievable. It is just that there is not a lot of focus on it today.

The advice to think about the Divine ceaselessly may sound outlandish today. This is because we have created a civilisation that prides itself on spreading any mental focus between as many objects as possible. Think only about the fact that ringtones on handheld devices alert you to many messages received in various applications, none of which are probably critical. But you must attend to them, lest you lose social credit because your response time becomes too long. Hundreds of sensations (clickbait) are vying for our daily focus, and how can we not lose it?

Krishna answers this question by stating that we need to be established (*yuktena*) through practice (*abhyasa*) in communion (yoga). This establishment is not something that happens spontaneously. The term *abhyasa* practice, also occurs in the *Yoga Sutra* and is here juxtaposed with the term disidentification – letting go.[211] The *Yoga Sutra* thus creates a pair of opposites, in which practice (*abhyasa*) is a wilful, controlled, effortful process of applying ourselves

---

211 *Yoga Sutra* I.12

long-term. Also, in the practice of *bhakti*, we should not expect short-term spectacular results. At some point, Arjuna says, "It sounds great what you are promising but the mind to me appears too fickle to be able to control it." Krishna responds, "Yes, it is true that it is fickle, but through effort and practice, it can be controlled".

What Krishna means by controlling the mind is not to clamp down on the mind to stop it from thinking. Such an effort would be doomed to fail. He means to turn all thought God-wards, that is, to see the Divine in everything. That is by all means possible, and it will also ultimately make the mind silent because the mind now realises that it does not have to sort out the world. Somebody else, a greater power, has already sorted out the world; it, in fact, "is" the world. Through such practice, the turning of all thought God-wards, we ultimately realise that we live inside the Divine, like a fish in the ocean. We will then attain communion (yoga) with the Divine, which means to be established in service to the Divine.

THE ESSENCE OF BHAKTI

The essence of *bhakti* is described in some of the closing stanzas of the *Gita's* 18th chapter, the crowning chapter that summarises all the *Gita* teachings and offers its most advanced teachings. The passage begins by proclaiming that the Divine (here called *Ishvara*, the same term that the *Yoga Sutra* uses) resides in the heart of all beings while revolving them with Its mysterious power as if mounted on a wheel.[212] The Sanskrit term for mysterious power is

---

[212] *Bhagavad Gita* XVIII.61

maya. The meaning of this term was only later redefined by Shankara as illusion, and he did so to explain away the reality of the world. As many philosophers and scholars, including Shri Aurobindo, have pointed out, it is evident from a cursory glance at the *Gita* that this reading is not consistent with its teachings and an awkward, cumbersome re-interpretation of many of the critical terms of the *Gita* is needed to argue that it teaches the illusory character of the world.

In the context of the *Gita*, *maya* is divine power, power of creation and manifestation, similar to the terms *prakriti* or Shakti. The term *maya* is chosen over the others when its mysterious character is emphasised. It is difficult for the limited human intellect to completely comprehend why and how the Divine could do a particular thing. The term *maya* is also often compounded with yoga to form yoga *maya*. This compound illustrates that when the Divine expresses Itself as the world and all beings via Its creative force, Shakti, this is an act of yoga. Aurobindo often focused on this fact in his writings when stating that all life is yoga and that the entire two-billion-year evolution of life on earth was an act of yoga of the divine creative force to lift all matter to the state of divine consciousness. Aurobindo believed that the highest stage of yoga was achieved when we step aside and let the Divine practice Its yoga through us.

The mysteriousness of the divine creative force (*prakriti*, Shakti, *maya*) includes the fact that we assume ownership of our body and mind by utilising our ego. The *Gita* states that this is an erroneous assumption of our mind and ego but that instead the divine creative force moves us and takes us through our physical, mental and otherwise motions. We need to realise this fact and give up the false notion of the sense of agency and of owning the results of our actions. Such giving up of the sense of agency (i.e. the belief that we are performing our actions, that we own them) and the giving up of the results or fruits to the Divine constitutes the highest surrender and devotion to the Divine.

We are then told that the problem posed in stanza 61, viz., that we are moved by God as if mounted on a wheel, can be solved by seeking refuge in God by totally surrendering with our whole being.[213] By the grace of the Divine, we will then attain Its everlasting abode and supreme peace. According to Krishna, our problem is that, like an unconscious machine, we are moved by the divine creative force. Yet we believe that we are the agent, the doer, and we attempt to act to our own advantage and profit. This misalignment causes all of our problems because whether we are ultimately successful in all our small endeavours, which seem so important to us, is beyond the scope of our exertions. The problem is to be solved with a total surrender, i.e. realising that the Divine is enacting Itself through us and by consciously performing all acts for the Divine.

Such conscious performance includes the surrender of the body, i.e. following with our body divine command rather than the whims of our ego. Surrender of the heart means to love the Divine in all of Its expressions. Surrender of thought means to let the Divine think through us and

---

213 *Bhagavad Gita* XVIII.62

align ourselves with the agenda of the Divine, that is, to think life-affirmative and supportive of all beings rather than destructively. In Freudian terms, this would mean to be guided by Eros (desire to create, create beauty and foster more life) rather than by Thanatos. Thanatos represents the desire to destroy, to destroy life and to create ugliness. Many human cities and creations are exceedingly ugly. Leaving the destruction of natural habitats of other species in our wake, many of our designs are the work of Thanatos.

To think life-affirmative does not mean to not limit ourselves to protecting our own offspring but rather to look at all children of the Divine as our children, too. This includes all people, animals, plants, microbes, etc. To surrender to the Divine with one's speech is to speak the truth and what aligns with divine law. To surrender with one's intelligence means to know the Divine in all of Its aspects, i.e. the God transcendent, the God immanent as cosmic intelligence, the universe as the crystallised body of God, the Divine in the heart of all beings and the Divine as giving characteristics to all objects and phenomena.

The *Gita* asks us to let our minds be absorbed in the Divine, to worship the Divine, to be devoted to the Divine, and to offer obeisance to the Divine.[214] In return, the Supreme Being promises that we shall reach It. Letting our mind be absorbed in the Divine means recognising the Divine in all phenomena and not taking it for a deity or anthropomorphic god. To worship the Divine means to worship it through surrendering our sense of agency and the results of our actions. To be devoted to the Divine means

---

214 *Bhagavad Gita* XVIII.65

to feel intense sensations of love and longing towards God and to support God's agenda. To offer obeisance means formal worship, including bowing down before divine images, uttering divine names, and greeting the Divine with folded hands. Such acts cannot be mere routine; we must feel congruent with our actions.

The above actions can all be performed as they are things we can do. What we cannot do is feel intense sensations of love and longing towards the Divine. Some can already feel this way because they already have the right *karmic* tendencies in place. For others, this might be more difficult. How can we attain such an intense love if it is not naturally there already? To this, Narada's *Bhakti Sutra* says that supreme divine love, called *para-bhakti*, comes as the result of *Karma, Jnana* and *Raja* Yoga.[215] I cannot emphasize this enough. I never envisioned myself as a glowing *bhakta*, but extended practice periods in these three disciplines led me there without ever aiming for it. The following three chapters analyse how each of these three yogas contributes to supreme divine love.

---

215 Narada's *Bhakti Sutra*, stanza 25

Chapter 5
KARMA YOGA AND ITS IMPORTANCE FOR BHAKTI

In this chapter, I will analyse one of the three legs on which *bhakti* stands, *Karma* Yoga. I will first discuss the law of *karma*, the usage of the term *karma* as works to be performed, what *Karma* Yoga is and why it is done. Going into more detail, we will then look into self-contemplation (*svabhava*) and own duty (*svadharma*), which are the two terms to understand when figuring out our personal, divine duty. A discussion on sacrifice as offering and giving concludes the chapter.

THE LAW OF KARMA

Karma means action, doing or works and comes from the verb root *kr* – to do. It is used in the *Bhagavad Gita* and the *Bhagavata Purana* in the following vital contexts, essential to understand and differentiate:

- The term *karma* can be used in the law of *karma*, which means the law of cause and effect.
- It can be used in the context of actions performed in alignment with and service to the Divine and is then juxtaposed to egoic action or inaction.

- Finally, the term is combined with yoga to form *Karma* Yoga, and here, action becomes a spiritual discipline to develop and evolve our psyche.

The mechanics of the law of *karma* are so foundational to Indian philosophy that the *Bhagavad Gita* and the *Bhagavata Purana* take them for granted and have not explained them. I shall briefly quote and explain three stanzas from the *Yoga Sutra* to discuss the fundamentals. *Yoga Sutra* II.12 says that the root of suffering is the *karmic* storehouse, which bears seen and unseen results. Seen results are those we experience in this lifetime, whereas unseen ones are those reserved for future embodiments. In both cases, the main problem is that the cause is temporally so far removed from the effect/ result that we fail to note the connection. Most suffering we experience is caused by sub-optimal choices we made in the remote past. These sub-optimal choices have led to *karmic* seeds waiting their turn to sprout in the so-called *karmic* storehouse. The *karmic* storehouse is beneath our subconscious and is difficult to access. If only we could see and understand how our poor choices create more *karmic* seeds and how *karmic* seeds create what we now see as our fate or destiny, we would radically change our behaviour and not accumulate more negative *karma*.

Yoga Sutra II.13 states that as long as *karmic* seeds are in the storehouse, we are hurled out into the world in the form of embodiments that provide us with the right cocktail of pleasure and pain to awaken spiritually. This cocktail is tailored to our *karmic* needs and consists of types of embodiments, life span, and kinds of experiences. This

CHAPTER 5

means that our entire lifetime is a conveyor belt of lessons and tests where we are to learn and achieve assignments that we had not previously understood, such as compassion, support, appreciation of all life, harmlessness, fostering all beings, truthfulness, etc.

Yoga Sutra II.14 states that everything we consider good luck, privilege, pleasure, joy, etc., is caused by *karmic* merit, usually performed in past lives. The problem is that because we don't see the connection, we develop a sense of entitlement and do not use our current privileged position to do good for all beings. Our good *karma*, therefore, eventually exhausts, and we fall back into demerit. Respectively, all pain, suffering, bad luck, evil omens, etc., we experience now are not random, but we have placed ourselves into these situations through previously acquired demerits, usually in past lives. If we see and understand these connections, we would not be as concerned about whether we now experience pleasure or suffering. Instead, we would focus on performing only noble, ethical, and righteous actions, ignoring whether they are currently convenient or inconvenient. If they were convenient, we would know that they lay the foundations for good fortunes ahead. If they were inconvenient, we would see them as expiation and atonement for previous wrongdoing. Thus, we would act more in line with characters like Yudhishthira in the *Mahabharata* or Rama in the *Ramayana*, who were only concerned with doing the right thing.

A fourth stanza in the final chapter of the *Yoga Sutra* deals with *karma*. Stanza IV.7 states that in most people, *karma* is negative, positive or mixed (realistically, in most people, it is mixed because we don't focus enough on *karma*), but in accomplished yogis, it is neither. It is sometimes overlooked that this last stanza on *karma* describes an extreme level of achievement in which a highly accomplished yogi is surrendered to the Divine to such a degree that they are not acting from ego, but only the Divine is acting through them. Then, no *karma* at all is accrued. Until such sophistication is achieved, good *karma* is to be sought through righteous actions.

The above way of acting in the world without being touched by *karma* is also behind the Chinese term *wu-wei*, the doing without doing. No doer or ego gets in the way of an optimal action here. The elements move the practitioner to bring a state of imbalance back to an expression of the Dao. Similarly, Jesus Christ walking across the waters without wetting his feet is a metaphorical representation of the fact that there was no ego, no *karma*, no doer present that could make the water, here representing the unconscious, wet his feet and impinge on his travel by submerging him.

The *Gita* repeats the lesson of *Yoga Sutra* IV.7.[216] It states that as long as we act from the motive of personal gain and advantage, our *karmic* results will fall into three categories: the unpleasant state (often identified with those with damaging or sadistic intentions or those driven by extreme desires or pain), the pleasant state (for example those born into extreme wealth or power) and the mixed state (all of the rest). Also, the *Gita* proclaims that those who renounce

---

216 *Bhagavad Gita* XVIII.12

both fruit and agency of their actions to the Divine harvest none of these *karmas*.

The above line of thought is further developed in various stanzas in the *Gita*. In one instance, the *Gita* defines a person of refined intellect (*buddha*) as one who performs actions (*karma*) not motivated by egoic desires but rather purified by the fire of knowledge.[217] This means not to act from the narrow view of the personal ego but from the vantage point of the Divine. It is what Jesus Christ expressed when he said, "Not my will but yours be done".[218] The *Gita* here and in many other passages says that action itself is not the problem (it argues against an Indian tradition that espouses renunciation of action and life in society) but that egoic action is the problem. The next stanza makes this clear.[219] Without seeking personal benefit through our actions, being content rather than cunning and conniving, we are internally inactive, although outwardly engaged in action. Again, this beautifully expresses the Daoist principle of *wu-wei*, the doing-less doing, which the *Bhagavad Gita* achieves by making us act in service of a higher intelligence.

In the *Bhagavata Purana*, we learn that there is no God separate from the law of *karma*.[220] God can only award *karmic* results or benefits to a person relative to the degree of *karmic* merit they have achieved. God cannot bestow *karmic* benefits where there has been no action to achieve them. This means there is no point in seeking exemption from

---

217 *Bhagavad Gita* IV.19
218 Luke 22:42
219 *Bhagavad Gita* IV.20
220 *Bhagavata Purana* X.24.13-14

the law of *karma* by placating and petitioning God. Like regarding the laws of gravitation and all physical laws, so also regarding the law of karma, God is the exemplification and fulfilment of all laws, not their exception. God is the law of *karma* and the laws of physics, and they are valid because the power of the Divine is behind them.

Of course, the Divine is much more than just laws; all physical laws, including the law of cause and effect and *karma*, are an aspect of the Divine. Hence, there is no point in doing evil, damaging other beings and wishing them harm, and then attempting to placate God through petitionary prayers. The same teaching is expressed in the Old Testament of the Bible, the Torah, which says, "Vengeance is Mine, I will repay. In due time their foot will slip; for their day of disaster is near, and their downfall if arriving soon".[221] The New Testament repeats this almost verbatim, "Do not avenge yourselves, beloveds; instead, leave it to the wrath of God, for it is written: Revenge is mine, sayeth the Lord, I will repay".[222] The message of this initially opaque saying is that there is little point in trying to bestow demerit on others by thinking about them in a harmful way. They will earn their future according to their meritorious or de-meritorious actions, enforced by a mechanical law held in place by divine authorisation.

Do not think of the law of *karma* as being executed by an anthropomorphic enforcer or punisher. Such thinking would be as foolish as thinking that an angered God will pull you down when you lean too far out of the window.

---

221 Deuteronomy 32:35
222 Romans 12:19

CHAPTER 5

You will fall out of the window because you disregarded the law of gravitation. This law is mechanically enacted upon all beings and objects at all times, depending on their location on the surface of large gravitational objects (such as planet Earth) or distance to other larger gravitational objects (such as, for example, the sun or the supermassive black hole at the centre of our galaxy). Similarly, the law of karma does not require a humanlike enforcer but acts by itself without fail, like the law of gravitation.

Rather than trying to petition the Divine for release from consequences after we have made transgressions against others, the *Gita* states that whoever performs actions surrendered to the Divine and abandons egoic attachment to outcomes cannot be stained by sin, being in quality akin to a lotus leaf from which water pearls off.[223] The coming sections on self-contemplation (*svabhava*) and own duty (*svadharma*) will discuss in detail how we ensure that our actions are surrendered to the Divine and overcome egoic attachment.

A particular case of *karma* is discussed towards the end of the sixth chapter of the *Bhagavad Gita*, the chapter on *Raja* Yoga. Although an upcoming chapter deals with this path of yoga, this passage is explained here since it discusses the *karma* of the yogi. After Krishna discusses *Karma* and *Jnana* Yoga in the opening chapters, the sixth chapter deals with how to experience the Divine through formal meditation practice, i.e. *Raja* Yoga. Such meditation practice has to be combined with performing one's duty in the world and not as a drop-out. According to the *Gita*, one is not permitted to

---

223 *Bhagavad Gita* V.10

shirk from one's duty simply because one has yet to realise the Divine fully.

At this point, Arjuna becomes concerned about the fact that he has to split his attention between performing actions in society to his best but still limited knowledge on one hand, while at the same time engaging in formal meditation practice to reach God-realization on the other. In stanza IV.38, Arjuna states his concern that seeing he has to split his energy and efforts between two vastly different tasks, he may fail at reaching both objectives and hence fail in both this world and the next. To this, Krishna says that the doer of good never goes to ruin and shall not come to ruin either in this world or the next.[224] If such a yogi does not reach their aim in one embodiment, they will either be reborn in a noble and prosperous family, having the means to pursue their spiritual quest again, or they will be outright reborn into a family of yogis.[225] In both cases, the yogi will pursue their goal of attaining the Divine with renewed vigour.

It must be noted that the above stanzas should not be used for an attitude like "what I don't get done in this life, I will do in the next". Such an attitude would stand in the way of attaining the Divine in this life. The Divine asks for our totality and intensity. The path of *bhakti*, supported by *Karma*, *Jnana*, and *Raja* Yoga, is so effective because it summons all aspects of the human psyche to reach God. As Patanjali says in *Yoga Sutra*, the more intensely we pursue the goal, the closer we are to it.[226]

---

224 *Bhagavad Gita* IV.40
225 *Bhagavad Gita* IV.41
226 *Yoga Sutra* I.21

CHAPTER 5

KARMA AS WORK

This section deals with the use of the term *karma*, including the meaning of action, activity as works to be done, and passages that support this use. We do so in the lead-up to the next section, which looks at the meaning of the compound *Karma* Yoga as the yoga of action or active yoga. In an all-important passage of the *Gita*, Krishna states that all actions (*karmani*) are performed by His *prakriti* (nature, divine creative force), but deluded by egoism, we think we are performing them.[227] The view of the *Bhagavad Gita* regarding this particular matter is very much aligned with the findings of modern neuroscience, which finds that neurons related to certain decisions will fire a significant time before we think we have made a decision[228]. This means that the electrochemical apparatus of the brain makes a decision, and afterwards, we interpret that as having come to a conclusion based on volition. Similarly, Krishna teaches that it is the forces of nature, the *gunas* of *prakriti*, that make us do things, and after the fact, only the sense-of-I, ego, takes ownership. This delusion must be overcome, so Krishna, and of course, the repercussions here are entirely different to those of neuroscience. Nature (*prakriti*) in the philosophy of the *bhakti* texts is an aspect of the Divine; through it, the Divine moves us.

Shri Aurobindo writes in *Essays On The Gita* that performing actions is itself to be seen as a spiritual discipline that we undertake for self-finding and self-

---

227 *Bhagavad Gita* III.27
228 Robert, M. Sapolsky, *Behave: The Biology of Humans at Our Best and Worst*, Penguin Press, 2017.

realisation.[229] In his view, there is no discrepancy between mundane and spiritual actions, as all life and nature are an ongoing manifestation of the spirit. For this purpose, all actions must be turned God-wards, meaning they are to be performed for the Divine. Of course, not every action can be turned God-wards, and this means that certain types of actions, i.e. those that are merely self-pleasing and have no higher purpose, are increasingly retreating into the background. About this process, Aurobindo says that the knowledge of which work has to be done and which has to be avoided has to come entirely from within. It cannot be learned from books; it must be learned through self-contemplation.

The *Bhagavata Purana* has a more or less readymade recipe for achieving this.[230] Here, Krishna says that we will gain devotion to Him by converting all our mundane efforts with His satisfaction in mind. An important teaching! Orthodox theologies often portray God as being eternally complete, unmoved and having nothing to gain. But this is true only for the God transcendent, the infinite consciousness, the *nirguna* Brahman. The God immanent, the cosmic intelligence, the Divine as process, the Shakti, on the other hand, expresses Herself as the universe and all beings. Our actions can be either helpful towards the divine agenda (which, in Aurobindo's words, is the lifting of all life and matter via the billion-year-long process of evolution to the level of divine consciousness), or they can be impinging and decelerating. We can determine whether

---

229 Sri Aurobindo, *Essays on the Gita*, p. 572

230 *Bhagavata Purana* XI.11.23-24

our actions are accelerating God's efforts or slowing them down simply by inquiring whether they are satisfying to God. A disclaimer: if our mind is too tainted by subconscious desires, past trauma, etc., the answer we get can, of course, be wrong. That's where *Raja* Yoga and the process of deconditioning and purifying the subconscious is of extreme importance.

Like Aurobindo, Swami Tapasyananda teaches that self-improvement and spiritual advancement are the goals of desireless action.[231] That's why the *Bhagavad Gita* and the *Bhagavata Purana* at every turn teach to make service to and love for the Divine our motivation to act. While for those new to *bhakti* philosophy, this may all sound like a long shot, a cursory glance at our history over the last few thousand years shows that this change in attitude is precisely what is required. In the past, we were primarily motivated by competition, ambition, advantage, antagonism and adversarialism, all fuelled by looking at life through the lens of the individual ego and personal advantage. It is this attitude that led to endless wars, atrocities, extinction of species, destruction of cultures and nature, and us as a civilisation and species to the edge of the yawning abyss of environmental holocaust and ecocide. Considering the satisfaction of the Divine rather than ours, a course change might actually improve our situation.

Such a change can initially seem to lack immediate rewards and ask us to accept too many inconvenient actions. However, the *Gita* says that one who has given up performing acts motivated by reward but instead now

---

231 Swami Tapasyananda, *Srimad Bhagavad Gita*, p. 143

performs them from a sense of divine duty will continue doing them, whether pleasant or unpleasant.[232]

WHAT IS KARMA YOGA?

Having established the various meanings of *karma*, we can now look at *Karma* Yoga. Firstly, the lines between *Karma* and *Bhakti* Yoga are blurred. So labels, for example, the *Bhagavata Purana*, the surrendering of the fruits of all actions to the Divine, as *nish-karma bhakti,* although this phrase is the *Gita*'s principal definition of *Karma* Yoga. The term *nish-karma* means non-doing, and combined with *karma*, it would become the doing-less doing, which I have already discussed. When combined with the term *bhakti*, it becomes doing-less surrender or doing-less devotion. This means that we devote our actions to the Divine, are inspired by the Divine to act, and surrender our sense of agency to the Divine. *Bhakti-* and *Karma* Yoga are sister sciences (the term science here is loosely used as a system of knowledge) that support each other and benefit from being applied simultaneously or sequentially.

In *Essays On The Gita*, Aurobindo states that it is essential to give up the idea that individual choice determines which actions to take and what our duty is.[233] When the Supreme Being thought each of us into existence, what actions were to be performed by each individual formed the essential part of this very process. In other words, the Divine knows best what we need to do, but we usually don't. The Divine is thinking each of us into existence by using a fraction

---
232 *Bhagavad Gita* XVIII.10
233 Sri Aurobindo, *Essays on the Gita*, p. 36

of Itself, called an *amsha*, to form the *jiva*, the spirit of the individual. This *amsha* contains information on what works are to be performed by this individual. If we follow this information, we are performing *Karma* Yoga, which is the active part of the practice. The passive form of the practice is *bhakti*, by which we surrender to the Divine and make our service loving. This is the philosophy of the *Gita* in a nutshell.

Aurobindo further states that our spiritual and divine rebirth comes about by performing the very work we came into this life to do.[234] He uses the term rebirth here because, in our ordinary lives, we live and act from the ego and the delusion of personal advantage. To give up on this vantage point is like dying to the ego. This becomes the point of departure for being reborn into a more significant spiritual, divine birth. Here, the scope is to work for the agenda and program of the Divine (such as the divinisation of human society) and as an instrument of and for the Divine.

THE DEEP MEANING OF YAJNA

For this to become effective, our yoga must convert all actions into sacrifices to the Divine.[235] The term sacrifice has a negative connotation for many modern readers as it implies giving something for which the return is at least very uncertain or may not come at all. We could circumnavigate this by using the term "offering" for sacrifice, and I will frequently use it. But there is something deeper to be explored here. The term the *Gita* uses for sacrifice or

---

[234] Sri Aurobindo, *Essays on the Gita*, p. 251
[235] Sri Aurobindo, *Essays on the Gita*, p. 282

offering is *yajna*, which occurs often in this book. A *yajna* is a *Vedic* ritual in which an offering is made to the gods or spirits, usually with a particular outcome in mind. In *Vedic* society, *yajnas* were, for example, performed to have a good harvest or to obtain offspring. The underlying idea is to not just hope for a good outcome but be proactive and start the cycle by being in the position of the giver. This links the *Vedas* back to indigenous culture, which always observed a delicate balance between taking from nature and giving back.

The reason why our modern, hyper-individualistic civilisation is so toxic and destructive is because, at its core, is the concern for our own welfare and advantage and little else. Part of this culture is to look at the entire world as insentient, consisting of dumb and dead matter, populated by plants and animals that are little more than unconscious automatons, and other people who are competitors at best. Indigenous culture and the *Vedas*, on the other side, ascribe sentience to almost everything, leading to a philosophy called animism. Animism describes a world in which all objects are a crystallisation of spirit and have some form of intelligence. Notice how similar this is to the philosophy of the *Gita*, which constantly calls upon us to recognise God in all objects.

Because everything in the world is spirit and we derive so much benefit from the world, life in Indigenous culture and the *Vedas* consists of the art of giving back enough to the spirits. We attempted to give back at least as much as we derived from them, ideally more. You can still see this beautifully in Bali today, where a big part of the day-to-

CHAPTER 5

day life of the women is taken up with placing offerings for a multitude of spirits in many locations. These offerings do not imply the superstition of primitive people but a critical practice to keep in balance the tendency of humans to exclusively take from nature with their ability to give back.

In the *Vedas*, the god of *yajna* is Vishnu; in fact, *yajna* is another name for Vishnu, as stated in the *Gita*. Krishna, an *avatar* of Vishnu, calls for our entire life to be an act of giving, an offering or sacrifice to the Divine. Of course, this does not remain an abstract concept in the *Bhagavad Gita*, but it is to be expressed by loving and serving the Divine through all of Its children. This is the purpose of Krishna's exhortation: that our yoga must convert all actions into sacrifices to the Divine. In everything we do, we must ask ourselves whether what we do is good enough to offer to the Divine. If the answer is yes, we may go ahead. This answer can only be found through self-contemplation and not by perusing some list of actions that may find God's approval. The rationale for this is that the Divine expresses Itself through all beings differently.

Rather than following some external code of conduct that spells out how God would express Herself through the smallest common denominator of people or the median or average, we need to make our work a self-expression of our nature and turn it into a means of spiritual growth by moving closer to the divine ideal.[236] For this, we need to turn inside, connect to our divine core, and discover our role in serving the spirit manifested in the universe.

---

236 Sri Aurobindo, *Essays on the Gita*, p. 517

While some spiritual movements require us to enter a state of complete inactivity, the *Gita* suggests worshipping the Divine through our work.[237] This is significant because the *Gita* teaches that the world, the universe, all nature and all humanity are the meaningful work of the Divine expressing Itself. The world is not a purposeless accident; it is not a valley of sorrow and not an illusion. Everything has a purpose; it is only that humanity has created situations in which our lives may look meaningless. The *Gita* does not consider action senseless, hopeless or meaningless but quite the opposite. The question is, what sort of action and through what actions are we serving the Divine?

According to the *Gita*, Krishna considers *Karma* Yoga to include action, knowledge and devotion; that is, *Karma*, *Jnana*, and *Bhakti* Yoga are to be applied in unison.[238] This is important because *Bhakti* Yoga alone can quickly degrade into sectarianism, aka my god is better than yours. *Karma* Yoga can side-track us into mere activism without knowing what, why and for whom we are doing it. *Jnana* Yoga, on its own, can easily lead to an aloof, disinterested sitting on a metaphorical mountaintop, looking down on the toiling masses. The *Gita* suggests combining work with meditation practice, which teaches us that work is to be done by (through giving up the sense of agency) and for (through surrendering the fruits of the actions) the Divine, and so becomes *Karma* Yoga.[239]

---

237 Sri Aurobindo, *Essays on the Gita*, p. 524

238 Swami Tapasyananda, *Srimad Bhagavad Gita*, p. 109

239 Swami Tapasyananda, *Srimad Bhagavad Gita*, p. 166

CHAPTER 5

Krishna says in the *Gita*, "Be thou an instrument."[240] This means listening to what the Divine wants to become and enact through and as us. We are to be moved by a sense of duty, whatever the reward. In some activities, such as protecting the abused, protecting animals and nature, and contributing to saving the atmosphere and biosphere, success may be hard to get by or may even look beyond our scope. But Krishna says, do it anyway because it is the right thing to do and not because success may be at hand. Doing it with an eye on success means operating from the ego's vantage point. The ego will gloat as much about conquering the world as it would over saving the environment, a noble pursuit it may otherwise be. The point is to do the work for God and not for ourselves, not for our ego's aggrandisement.

In many ways, we can look at it as if we were to function as a cell in the body of God. If an individual cell in our body stops serving the agenda of the host organism, it becomes cancerous. If it can convince or reprogram enough other cells to rebel against the host organism, it will result in the death of the host body. Similarly, the historical decision of humanity to leave the indigenous state of society, described in the *Vedas* and the Old Testament of the Bible (in the latter as the Garden of Eden), to follow its own agenda by enslaving, coercing and manipulating nature can be likened to a cancerous growth on the biosphere. At that time, we decided to suit only our own human interests and discontinued serving the host organism, the biosphere. If all of humanity follows this course, the result will likely be

---

240 *Bhagavad Gita* XI.33

the death of the biosphere. But if we recognise ourselves not as something separate, not as the crown of creation, but as an organism within nature that should give back to other organisms and the biosphere at least as much as it takes, if we can see ourselves again as small cells in the body of God, then this course can be reversed, and we can find our way back to serving the Divine, all life and nature rather than trying to be its god and king.

The *Bhagavad Gita* calls upon us to perform all kinds of actions at all times in a spirit of devotion and surrender to the Divine.[241] By the grace of the Divine, we shall then attain the coveted state of *moksha*, spiritual liberation. Let's remind ourselves briefly what the spirit of devotion and surrender here means. It means knowing what the Divine is (i.e., not just the visual image of a deity or a historical avatar), having an intense love for the Divine, listening to It, and doing what It wants us to do. It means to realise that the Divine is the only doer in the world and that we are moved by It as if mounted on a wheel. It means to do what is the right thing to do and not because we fancy its rewards. All of these points in the aggregate constitute *Karma* Yoga, which is the active aspect of *Bhakti* Yoga.

WHY KARMA YOGA IS IMPORTANT?

The *Bhagavata Purana* states that the Supreme Being has taught three avenues to practice communion with It, and there are no others.[242] These are communion through knowledge (*jnana*), love (*bhakti*) and through action

---

241 *Bhagavad Gita* XVIII.56
242 *Bhagavata Purana* XI.20.6

(*karma*). This does not mean we should limit ourselves to one of them and shun the others, although we may do that initially depending on personal limitations. All should be practised eventually for efficacy, and the sooner we can do so, the earlier we achieve communion. Combining all three is the road to success in yoga, and Aurobindo's life was dedicated to showing this point.

Raja Yoga, the yoga of the *Yoga Sutra*, did not make the above list because it is not primarily a yoga leading to communion with the Divine, i.e., God-realisation. It is instead a yoga designed for self-realisation, which must ultimately be supplemented with *Jnana*, *Bhakti*, and *Karma* Yoga to lead to God-realization.

In the twelfth chapter of the *Bhagavad Gita*, the chapter on *bhakti*, Krishna states that if we are not capable of practising systemic practice of concentration (i.e. *Raja* Yoga), then we are to devote ourselves wholeheartedly to performing acts of service to Him.[243] Working for the Divine opens us to spiritual evolution. Unlike the previous passage in the *Bhagavata Purana*, where *Karma* Yoga is integrated into *Jnana* and *Bhakti* Yoga, in the present *Gita* passage, *Karma* Yoga is juxtaposed to *Raja* Yoga. For some, *Raja* Yoga, with its emphasis on technique, practice and *sadhana* (spiritual discipline), can be a hard ask. For those, performing acts of service to the Divine may be more accessible. For others, however, the situation may be the other way around. How do we really know which acts are pleasing to the Divine? Through the practice of yogic techniques, *Raja* Yoga will gradually decrease our conditioning and mental torpidity,

---

243 *Bhagavad Gita* XII.10

making answering all of these questions much more straightforward. Once these questions are answered, *Karma* Yoga's discipline, acting in service to the Divine, should be commenced immediately. This means that *Karma* Yoga may or may not be preceded by the practice of *Raja* Yoga (described in the sixth chapter of the *Gita*, in the *Yoga Sutra*, and 7th chapter of this book), depending on the needs of the individual.

Two stanzas down the track, in the twelfth chapter of the *Gita*, we learn that explicit intellectual knowledge of the teaching (*jnana*) is better than a formal practice of techniques (*abhyasa*)[244]. This requires explanation. Formal practice here stands for just going through the motions without clearly understanding why and how things are done. Just doing things is then juxtaposed with intellectual knowledge. In modern parlance, the term intellectual knowledge often implies that such knowledge is empty of experience, i.e. mere theory. This is not the view of Indian philosophy. Here, the intellect is something very high, higher than the mind. Hence, the term *Buddhi* Yoga is sometimes translated as intellectual love of God. Because the *buddhi* (intellect) is in alignment with the Divine, when such knowledge is achieved, it must have consequences rather than being sequestrated away in the mind, which could then support hypocritical actions. Explicit intellectual knowledge of the teaching (*jnana*) is thus usually the result of the formal practice of techniques (*abhyasa*) combined with a study of the scriptures (*shastras*) and must, therefore, constitute a more advanced state than the mere performance of

---

244 *Bhagavad Gita* XII.12

techniques (empty of understanding) themselves, that yet have to fructify into knowledge.

Stanza 12 then continues to say that meditation (*dhyana*) is even better than both practice (*abhyasa*) and intellectual knowledge (*jnana*). This again needs to be clarified. Practice in this stanza means the mere execution of techniques, having yet to achieve their culmination. In the context of this stanza, *jnana*, knowledge, means isolating the self and working towards self-realisation. *Dhyana*, meditation, here means meditation on the Divine with having achieved a certain degree of communion with the Divine. We could identify this state with *bhakti* or evolving towards God-realization. But stanza 12 goes further to introduce one of the most essential concepts of the *Gita*. Even better than that, it says, is *karma* (action)-*phala* (fruit)-*tyagah* (abandonment), i.e. surrendering the outcomes of one's actions to the Divine. In this stanza, then, the yoga is turned on its head. What is described in stanza ten as an introductory technique, i.e., the *Karma* Yoga, is now stated to be yoga's crown.

The reader should be clear of this because, of course, *Karma* Yoga is both. *Karma* Yoga may be the beginning of our path, but it will also certainly be there at its end, and what exactly it is for us depends entirely on our degree of surrender and devotion to the Divine. If such surrender and devotion are complete, we can become an instrument in the divine orchestra's play, as the *Bhagavata Purana* suggests.[245]

That *Karma* Yoga is not just the introductory discipline that it is sometimes made out to be is confirmed by Shri

---

245 Swami Tapasyananda, *Srimad Bhagavata*, p. xxxv

Aurobindo. He taught that our soul evolves through actions performed with an attitude of service.[246] This makes *Karma* Yoga not an end in itself but a means to self-realisation.

This is confirmed in a later stanza of the sixth chapter of the *Bhagavad Gita*, the chapter on *Raja* Yoga. Here, Krishna affirms that one who is established in the unity of all that exists (i.e. has achieved the results of *Raja* Yoga) and therefore serves Him as present in all beings (viz, practices authentic *Karma* Yoga), in truth abides in Him whatever be the situation (has achieved the goals of *jnana* and *bhakti*, too).[247] It is fair then to say that while Krishna puts *bhakti* into the centre of his devotee's relationship with Him, and while He lectures extensively on knowledge (*jnana*) and the path of concentration (*raja*), it is *Karma* Yoga that forms the very core of His message in the *Gita*. Krishna teaches that knowledge, concentration, and love must ultimately converge in an active life in the world that serves Him. This beautifully intersects and interdigitates with Krishna's message that the world is His body and the beings His children, His creative play, and His sense organs.

Think about it for a moment: If there was a Supreme Being, which for reasons that for our limited intellect at times are still somewhat nebulous, would embody Itself as the world and all beings, wouldn't the crown of Its teaching not be the enlightened and loving action that we see Krishna teach at every twist and turn? An action intended to further the world? It is, therefore, internally entirely consistent that the Krishna of the *Gita* always

---

246 Sri Aurobindo, *Essays on the Gita*, p. 251
247 *Bhagavad Gita* VI.31

CHAPTER 5

returns to *Karma* Yoga. *Karma* Yoga is the *Gita*'s mighty river to which all other yogas are tributaries. What we do in Krishna's world matters to Him because the world is His body.

SELF-CONTEMPLATION (SVABHAVA), OR LAW OF BEING

Let's turn to the frequently announced in-depth study of how we can know what God wants us to do, how this information is encoded into the very core of each of us, and how we decode that information. There are two key concepts we need to analyse in this context. They are self-contemplation (*svabhava*), the law of being, and self-duty (*svadharma*), the law of becoming.

The term self-contemplation (*svabhava*) comes with two different meanings and functions.[248] Firstly, the immanent aspect of the Supreme Being contemplates Itself and, via this means, thinks into existence a sheer infinite number of beings. The beings are all aspects, emanations and computations of It. In *How To Find Your Life's Divine Purpose*, I likened the God immanent's self-contemplation to a so-called Monte Carlo generator. The Monte Carlo generator is a software program initially created to determine how many combinations can occur if we spin a roulette wheel several times. As the software was further developed, it was applied to randomness models of financial markets. This is significant because each being is a potential course the Divine could take. The Divine is infinite creative potential and play (*lila*).

---

248 Sri Aurobindo, *Essays on the Gita*, p. 524

We may ask, "Why am I here cast in this particular situation"? Because the Divine does not have an ego from which to withhold Its own creative process. What can be, will be! Because the Divine computes infinite varieties or emanations of Itself (paths of what It could be), each individual is unique and never occurs twice. Whatever this individual has to express or contribute to the Divine concert should be expressed and contributed. This is the first meaning of the term *svabhava* – self-contemplation. It is the process by which the Divine brings forth infinite permutations of Itself, the *jivas* (individual spirits).

The second meaning of the term is that the individual has to practice self-contemplation to find out what the Supreme Being wants to express through this particular individual. The contemplation of the Divine gave rise to us, and now we need to contemplate our individual spirit to find out the result of that divine contemplation. In this context, we need to understand that because the Divine is the Cosmic, it can only enact Itself on the individual level by becoming us. The Supreme Being cannot squash Itself into an individual. But by individuating through an infinite number of us, It can act on an individual level. This is very important to understand because, by such understanding, we can lose the reluctance to become conduits for the Divine. The Divine cannot act on this level without doing it through us. Therefore, our cooperation with the Divine, called conscious co-creation, is extremely important to the Divine.

Additionally, because the Divine does not have an ego (ego means limiter in space and time), it cannot by Itself become an individual. It can only run Itself as a cosmic

Monte Carlo generator-like software and split Itself into a sheer infinite number of daughter programs, the *jivas*. Because the individual spirits are free to the extent to which they can liberate themselves from their own robotic programming, what they do with the information by which the Divine formed them depends primarily on them. That is, *jivas* can play along in the play of the Divine, and they may or may not do so to a certain extent. I don't want to keep repeating this point ad nauseam, but it has to be said that for the last few thousand years, give or take, humanity hasn't played along with the Divine. There is a long list of exceptions, but Shri Aurobindo stated that, by and large, humanity has not spiritually evolved in the last few thousand years.

For example, the reluctance to shift the world economy to renewable energies (to ward off climate catastrophe) has been linked to the estimated costs of US$2 Trillion (due to complexity, it is very difficult to give any form of accurate estimate). As I write this, the Stockholm International Peace Research Institute (SIPRI) has just released a report that the global military budget has just jumped to a mind-boggling US$2.44 Trillion per annum after the most significant rise in annual government spending in over a decade. In other words, we do have the money to fix climate breakdown, but we prefer to spend it on killing each other. This is due to humanity's lack of spiritual evolution. If we had spiritually evolved, we would realise with the *Bhagavata Purana* that beings flourish due to mutual cooperation (spending 2 Trillion on fixing climate change), and they meet their downfall by antagonising each other (blowing that money on military spending).

For a *jiva*, individual spirit, to realise its fullest potential, it needs to find out what the Divine wants to become through and as this *jiva*. Every *jiva* has a role in this cosmic drama, an aspect of the Divine to express. I have described this practice in *How To Find Your Life's Divine Purpose,* and a detailed description is beyond the scope of this present text. We prepare ourselves through a brief spiritual practice, preferably early in the morning and ideally somewhere in nature or at least alone. We then ask a sequence of questions about how I can serve You, the Divine. How do You want to embody as me and my life? What do You want to become as Me? What do You want to express through me?

After asking these questions, we listened intently. It is not because the Divine is silent if we can't hear. We must understand that the Divine has no ego from which to withhold the answer. Additionally, the Divine has already communicated this information when creating our individuality through self-contemplation (*svabhava*) out of the ocean of infinite consciousness. In other words, if we do not hear the answer, the problem is our inability to hear and our lack of receptiveness and openness. This inability to listen to and the various lacks are due to the thickness of our robotic conditioning, which we accepted during the aeon-long process of evolving from microbes to vertebrates and later humanoids. So says Swami Tapasyananda, self-contemplation, *svabhava,* is the potential we bring down from all our past lives.[249] Shri Aurobindo says that each individual is in self-expression a portion of the Supreme

---

249 Swami Tapasyananda, *Srimad Bhagavad Gita*, p. 425

Being; each being is a manifestation of an idea of the Divine.[250] This idea describes that beings evolve to spiritual maturity. What precisely this idea, this information is, is revealed to us through the process of *svabhava*, self-contemplation, which Aurobindo calls the law of self-becoming.[251]

In Alfred North Whitehead's philosophy, the self-contemplation of the Divine is called the initial aim. It is called initial aim because the Divine has an initial aim for us. This initial idea, or compound of ideas, appears via self-contemplation in our mind as the vision of what we could become. This vision will be modified, reduced or enhanced as we evolve through our *karmic* choices. When I say *karmic* choices here, I am referring to the fact that we determine who we will be in the future with each thought, spoken word, and act. The Divine then reacts to our attempts to embody the initial aim. God responds to our attempts to embody the initial aim by upgrading and specifying the initial aim, a process called co-creation.

We must understand that our lives are neither purposeless nor purposeless accidents, as our mainstream society, science, and economy will have us believe. Of course, if you succeed in making people believe this, it is much easier to mould them into the industrial production process afterwards. This process does not require empowered, self-realised individuals living their life's divine purpose, but they require industrial consumption automatons that have given up on their spiritual destiny. We are crushed souls, often propped up by antidepressants

---

250 Sri Aurobindo, *Essays on the Gita*, p. 519
251 Sri Aurobindo, *Essays on the Gita*, p. 372

and anti-anxiety medications, and are happy to buy any nonsense in the hope it makes us feel a little bit better. I am not saying that you should cease your medication without the advice of your psychiatrist. What I am saying is that the biochemical model of mental health claiming that there is simply something wrong with your biochemical make-up of your brain (which can be fixed by taking pills) is conveniently ignoring the larger subject that our society and civilization is making us sick (and has been doing so since a long time) by letting us compete against each other like 8 billion little hamsters running in their little hamster wheels inside their little cages faster and faster. These little wheels are all attached to one giant GDP-increasing machine, which gradually turns all nature and human relationships into money. There is nothing wrong with us if that set-up makes us mentally unwell. On the other hand if that set-up wasn't making us unwell, then something would be wrong with us.

We are here not just to consume silly products we don't need. We are here because the Divine wants to express Itself through us. After all, we matter to God. Every individual matters to God. Once you contemplate what the Divine wants to do through you and let this divine destiny happen through you, you will experience the absence of internal dialogue, peace, silence, the heart's voice, and being in the zone. You will also experience an absence of ambition, competition, adversarialism and antagonism. You will see that the Divine is moving all beings. Therefore, there is no point in antagonising them (unless they act *adharmic* – unrighteous, i.e., contrary to divine law).

CHAPTER 5

Contemplating what the Divine wants to express through us is a journey of self-discovery, self-expression and self-finding.[252] Of course, this is partly done through meditation and introspection, but once we have found what the Divine wants to do through us, we must become active and express it. What we are then to do is our *svadharma* (own duty). Aurobindo describes the connection between self-contemplation (*svabhava*) and own duty (*svadharma*) as the relation of a person's outward life to their inward being, the evolution of their actions from their soul and inner nature.[253] In *Seven Quartets of Becoming, A Transformative Yoga Psychology Based on the Diaries of Shri Aurobindo*, Debashish Banerji calls a person's *svabhava* their personal law of being, which contains the qualities they possess.[254] Related to that, his term for *svadharma* is the personal law of becoming. We need to find out what qualities we possess in the eyes of God before we can evolve our activities in that direction. Professor Banerji adds the critical term "personal" because *svabhava* and *svadharma* differ for each person. More on that later.

Aurobindo says that the action of the individual needs to be directed by their *svabhava*, the essential law of their nature.[255] According to him, it is the pure quality of a person's spirit and the inherent power of their conscious will. Conscious will has nothing to do with the whims of the ego, but it is the purposeful will of the Divine in

---

252 Sri Aurobindo, *Essays on the Gita*, p. 521
253 Sri Aurobindo, *Essays on the Gita*, p. 515
254 Debashish Banerji, *Seven Quartets of Becoming*, p. 391
255 Sri Aurobindo, *Essays on the Gita*, p. 274

us searching for the divine delight, joy and ecstasy of the divine play and activity. While this passage of Aurobindo may sound far-fetched to those newly introduced to this subject, there is no greater joy and satisfaction than handing oneself entirely over to the Divine and feeling how every movement, thought, and action is not done by oneself but by the Divine.

For this to occur, each individual must discover and follow their innate *svadharma*.[256] Our *svabhava* (self-contemplation or inner law of being) determines our *svadharma*, our personal law of action, which is our self-shaping, functioning and working.[257] It is an erroneous teaching that *svadharma*, the inner law of being, is a collective attitude. Instead, each being has a personal *svadharma*, a law of their inner being, which they must observe.[258] It is not enough to think about what is good, ethical, or right. We must find out what the right thing for us to do is. Our own duty is a personal thing between us and God. Nobody else can step in and tell us what to do, no soothsayer, astrologer, therapist, or spiritual teacher. The information is only relayed from the Divine to the individual.

SELF-DUTY (SVADHARMA) OR LAW OF BECOMING

We must do our self-duty (*svadharma*) to become what we already internally are. It is not enough to be, but we must also become. In this, we reflect the make-up of the

---

256 Sri Aurobindo, *Essays on the Gita*, p. 513-14
257 Sri Aurobindo, *Essays on the Gita*, p. 519
258 Sri Aurobindo, *Essays on the Gita*, p. 592

CHAPTER 5

Divine, which has a being-aspect, the God transcendent, and a becoming-aspect, the dynamic process of the God immanent, involving the rolling out of the universe and the evolution of life. Our law of becoming (*svadharma*) must naturally grow out of our law of being (*svabhava*). This was, of course, recognised not only by the *Bhagavad Gita*, the *Bhagavata Purana*, and mystics like Aurobindo but also by modern psychologists. Carl Jung, for example, said that each person carries a tension within them that they must express by becoming what they ought to become. If this tension is not creatively expressed, it can become destructive. For example, a person may reach for drugs to relieve themselves of that tension, anaesthetise themselves and experience some temporary relief and quiet. The founder of humanistic psychology, Abraham Maslow, said that a musician must make music, a painter must paint, and a writer must write. To ultimately be at peace with themselves, what a person can be, they must be.

The *Gita*, written several millennia before Jung and Maslow, states that it leads to more spiritual growth to perform one's own duty (*svadharma*), even if it is inferior in the scale of material values than getting much material advantage from performing the duty of another (called *para-dharma*).[259] No error is made, so the *Gita*, when performing work in alignment with one's own nature (*svabhava*). The *Gita*'s wording in another passage is even more radical. Here, we learn that even though work in alignment with one's own duty (*svadharma*) may not be fashionable, it is still superior to action foreign to one's

---
259 *Bhagavad Gita* XVIII.47

growth (*para dharma*), however, well we may perform it.[260] For even death in performing according to one's own law of becoming (*svadharma*), so the *Gita*, will lead to one's evolution, while duty alien to one's growth will lead to retardation.

Some of us may already have experienced this phenomenon when, having been talked into a long and arduous academic course, which was supposed to give material freedom and independence, we only find out when finally working in the profession that we hate it and have to leave. Turning around at such a late point may be challenging, but it is still better than spending a lifetime working in a profession that we have no affinity and calling for. That is why it is essential to become clear about one's *svabhava*, the law of one's being, as early as possible. Utilising self-contemplation, we must find out what our purpose in life is.

The *Bhagavata Purana* agrees with the *Gita*'s position that the pursuit of one's *svadharma* is the best course of action because one's own law of becoming cannot lead to bondage as long as it follows one's natural disposition (*svabhava*).[261] What is meant here is that following someone else's *svadharma* may lead to bondage (i.e. mental slavery) if one does not follow one's own natural disposition but somebody else's. We must ask ourselves whether we live our own life or somebody else's.

Today, there is an enormous impetus to push us into certain glamorous, financially rewarding, or supposedly

---

260 *Bhagavad Gita* III.35
261 *Bhagavata Purana* VII.12.31-32

secure professions via social media, television, peer pressure, financial pressures, etc. These professions may be unsuitable for us. So, we should not approach our choice of profession by considering whether others may admire a profession, whether they be parents, spouses, friends, etc. If they admire a particular profession, let them take it up. If they want to get rich or be financially secure, let them do so. Crucial is whether God has given us the gifts and calling to do well in a particular profession. If so, then the profession will come naturally to us, and we never have to think if the profession is right. We will be free of internal dialogue and be in the zone while enacting the profession. This is the case because the Divine will act through us; the Divine will do the work. Hence, doing will not be a doing from effort, a doing from the ego, but from surrendering to divine will. We will be moved by divine will; therefore, it will be an effortless or doing-less doing.

In the *Gita*'s concluding statements, Krishna announces that he will explain how one attains spiritual competency by devotedly executing one's natural duty.[262] Krishna only announces that he will make a particular statement to draw attention to and emphasise the following statement. He does so only if He wishes to express the extreme import of the following stanza. In the following stanza, Krishna says that we will attain spiritual empowerment (*siddhi*) by performing our own duty as an act of worship to the Supreme Being, the One from whom all beings have emanated and by whom all this universe is pervaded.[263]

---

262 *Bhagavad Gita* XVIII.45
263 *Bhagavad Gita* XVIII.46

This is extremely important to understand. It is one thing to meditate on the Divine, chant the names of the Divine, read sacred texts, and pray to the Divine. But what is the use of all that if the Divine has given us gifts related to what It wants to become as us, what It wants to do through us, and we ignore this information and go on to do something that makes us rich, famous and glamorous? I'm not saying what the Divine wants us to do will get us neither. It may or may not. To do the work that the Divine wants to do through us is essential on the path of *bhakti*. It is a form of loving surrender and devotion to let the Divine move us as if we were mounted on a wheel. To do so is to adore the Divine through one's actions. To refuse to do so is to worship one's own ego instead.

What we usually consider free will and choice is the voice of the ego. It will never satisfy and fulfil us. The reason is that the ego has no true will; it has only true whim. There is only one true will, and that is the will of God. If we let ourselves fall in line with the will of God, we become free. Otherwise, we remain bound by our own ego.

To follow one's own duty means to perform work, actions, or a profession that contributes to our evolution and spiritual advancement.[264] How so? We spiritually evolve to the degree to which we let ourselves be moved upon and enacted by the Divine. We are already doing this to some extent subconsciously, but we need to make this act a conscious surrender. Instead, we often worship our own ego and think we know better. However, most or all of humanity's miseries are created by acting out of

---

264 Swami Tapasyananda, *Srimad Bhagavad Gita*, p. 472

alignment with the Divine. But the Krishna of the *Bhagavad Gita* and the *Bhagavata Purana* is not interested in pushing unconscious pawns over a chessboard. He wants our conscious participation and co-creation. The more we consciously become aware that it is not us performing actions but the Supreme Being who is moving us, the more divine bandwidth we can channel and the more we can call down the Divine and surrender to It.

Such surrender is easy for some of us, but others may need preparation. To open ourselves to this act of surrender and to call down the Divine into us, the many purifying disciplines of *Raja* Yoga are often necessary. To discover our innate own duty, we may first have to free ourselves from the conditioning of upbringing, culture, environment, and desires that drive our decisions. According to Aurobindo, inner desirelessness is the pretext for bringing us in contact with the psychic law of our becoming.[265] Only then can our *Karma* Yoga become authentic and loving worship of the Divine.

VARNA OR CASTE AND WHY IT MATTERS FOR BHAKTI

In some *Gita* commentaries, the terms *svadharma* and caste frequently occur together. Indian castes have a certain superficial similarity to social classes in the West, the boundaries of which have been blurred somewhat since the advent of capitalism. Nevertheless, social classes still exist everywhere, and allocation to them today is primarily determined by the fatness of one's wallet.

---

265 Debashish Banerji, *Seven Quartets of Becoming*, p. 310

You may come across orthodox *Bhagavad Gita* commentaries that interpret Krishna's call to follow one's *svadharma* merely as sticking to the rules of one's caste. I am, of course, familiar with that line of argument and reject it following the same reasoning along which Shri Aurobindo and Mahatma Gandhi rejected it. The *Gita* talks about so-called *varnas* (colours), which are groupings through which society is ordered. One's *varna* is determined by one's *gunic* make-up (i.e. the preponderance in one's mind of certain qualities of nature called *gunas*). Somebody whose mind is predominantly *sattvic* (according to the late Professor Surendhranath Dasgupta, *sattva* means intelligence particle) belongs to the spiritual *varna* or priest caste (*brahmana*). If your mind is predominantly *rajas* (energy particle) with some *sattva* thrown into the mix, then you are part of the nobility, administrative and defence caste (*kshatriya*). If your mind is *rajasic* with some *tamas* (mass particle), then you are part of the merchant caste (*vaishiya*). With *tamas* alone as a predominant *guna*, one is part of the worker caste (*shudra*). In ancient India, membership in those *varnas* was determined by a person's mental tendency and quality, and it was neither hereditary nor did one have to stay in a *varna*. Aurobindo and Gandhi argued that the *varna* system of the *Gita* had nothing to do with a hereditary caste system, but it was a way of identifying how a person could ideally serve the Divine and humanity.

The view that qualities determine *varnas* (classes) is spelt out by Krishna when He says that whether we are a *brahmana, kshatriya, vaishya,* or *shudra* depends on the *gunic* qualities derived from our individual law of being (*svabhava*).²⁶⁶ So are the duties of a *brahmana*, born of their law of being, even-mindedness, self-restraint, simplicity, purity of action, speech and thought, patience, uncomplicatedness, self-realisation, God-realization, and devotion to the Divine.²⁶⁷ In other words, not heredity, but whether you display those qualities determines your *varna*. In the following stanzas, Krishna lists the characteristics of the other castes, and it is clear that he is talking about psychological types here, and the attempt to ascribe these qualities to hereditary members of today's Indian castes (or for that matter to the castes of any other society) would be a difficult, neigh impossible case to argue.

Another mystic and theologian who argues along these lines is Swami Tapasyananda, author of an excellent translation of the *Bhagavata Purana* and a superior commentary on the *Gita*. In his *Gita* commentary, Tapasyananda states that *varnas* are character types and have nothing to do with hereditary castes.²⁶⁸ Tapasyananda further explains that medieval understandings of *svadharma* linked it to hereditary castes, but true *svadharma* is in accordance with our mental constitution and higher development.²⁶⁹ He also states that the modern Indian caste system is based on birth, but the *varna* system of the *Gita* is based on the *gunic* constitution (i.e. the psychological make-up of our mind).²⁷⁰ Tapasyananda also proposes this

---

266 *Bhagavad Gita* XVIIII.41ff
267 *Bhagavad Gita* XVIIII.42
268 Swami Tapasyananda, *Srimad Bhagavad Gita*, p. 10
269 Swami Tapasyananda, *Srimad Bhagavad Gita*, p. 112
270 Swami Tapasyananda, *Srimad Bhagavad Gita*, p. 139

interpretation in the *Bhagavata Purana*, where we read that the modern caste system of India should never be mistaken for the *varna* system, in which a person's *gunas* (qualities) determine the *varna* (colour).[271]

Some modern authors still identify the *varnas* (colours) of yore with the castes of today because all the medieval commentators have argued along that line, even the great Ramanujacharya, who is otherwise impeccable. To this, Swami Tapasyananda responds that the old commentators have done great injustice to Shri Krishna in watering down His message as relevant only to members of the rigid Indian case system.[272] The divine duty to which one is called is one's *svadharma* and not one's caste. I include this point in this book because the themes *svabhava*, the personal law of being, and *svadharma*, the personal law of becoming, are so central to Shri Krishna's teaching of *bhakti* that without understanding them properly, the whole teaching becomes truncated at best and crashing down at worst. This was also the view of Shri Aurobindo.

I want to make clear that I am not here arguing for a romantic revival of the caste system. What I am saying is that to read a justification of the modern caste system into the *Bhagavad Gita* means to miss the profound meaning that Krishna's concepts of *Karma* Yoga, *svabhava*, and *svadharma* have for the whole of humanity. I have lived in India long enough to understand that today's rigid caste system is no representation of Krishna's teaching—more on that in a dedicated section on castes in chapter ten.

---

271 Swami Tapasyananda, *Srimad Bhagavata*, vol.2, p. 268
272 Swami Tapasyananda, *Srimad Bhagavad Gita*, p. 468

CHAPTER 5

YAJNA – MORE ON OFFERING AND GIVING

As promised, I will finish this chapter by discussing giving, offering and the *Vedic yajna* ritual. While a cursory glance at the subject might make us think that this is an outlandish theme to write about, you will soon see that it contains the core message of the *Bhagavad Gita*. The religion of our modern capitalist society is to have a go-getter attitude. Those who go and get what they want prevail in this type of society. The new-age movement has softened and rebranded the go-getter attitude and hidden it behind improving one's ability to receive or to manifest. But the focus is still on old-fashioned getting and taking, although we go at it with a somewhat more affable attitude. The focus in both approaches, the go-getter on one hand and the receiver/manifester on the other, is still ultimately the same. It is on having.

With Shri Krishna's interpretation of the *Vedic yajna* ritual, the focus is shifted to giving, being and becoming rather than getting, receiving and having. This shift is the central crux when trying to create a more compassionate society that is in harmony with the whole of the biosphere. As Aurobindo has shown in *The Secret of the Vedas*, initially, *yajna* was designed to give to the spirit world in abundance, and in turn, this would create abundance for humanity. At the time of the *Bhagavad Gita*, the *yajna* ritual had presumably become an act of bargaining with the spirit world to get a good deal from the spirits. The *Gita*, therefore, re-interprets the *yajna* ritual to bring it back to alignment with the early *Vedic* idea, where it is an act of selfless giving rather than the performance of a ritual with a specific outcome in mind.

Swami Tapasyananda states that *yajna* is the means to prosperity and spiritual success and that, in the *Gita's* terminology, *yajna* means self-sacrifice, i.e., giving oneself.[273] *Yajna* is to offer oneself in service to the Divine and all beings, and *yajna* means to give more than you take. In the context of the *Gita*, *yajna* means, as previously discussed, to turn all one's actions into a selfless service to the Divine. Part of that is to find out what the Divine wants us to be and become. The fact that *yajna* has a higher spiritual meaning than usually assumed is confirmed by the fact that *yajna* is also a name of Lord Vishnu, of which Krishna is an *avatar*.[274] In the *Vedas*, Vishnu is the recipient of all offerings. We need to realise that all of our actions are offerings to the Divine; therefore, it is essential with which attitude we make them. That's why Jesus Christ said, "If you place an offering on the altar while yet holding a grudge against your brother, your offering is not welcome as it will defile the altar. Make peace with your brother first, and then your offering is welcome".[275] Any offering or any action performed in the spirit of wanting to get an advantage over another child of the Divine cannot please the Divine.

In the *Gita*, Krishna exhorts us that unless all actions are done as *yajna*, as service to the Divine, they will lead to further bondage.[276] The reasons for this are apparent. Typically, through our actions, we seek to gain an advantage over others, as our actions are powered by egoic motives,

---

273 Swami Tapasyananda, *Srimad Bhagavad Gita*, p. 84
274 Swami Tapasyananda, *Srimad Bhagavad Gita*, p. 107
275 Matthew 5:24
276 *Bhagavad Gita* III.9

leading to identification and attachment, and also are motivated by desires and aversions. Due to that, all of our actions are leading to further *karma* and delusion. Krishna teaches us to avoid this by performing our actions as *yajna*, which means we consecrate our actions to the Divine. We are performing them as service to the Divine, in that we are offering ourselves, our actions, our sense of agency, and the results of our actions in what in *Vedic* terminology is called self-sacrifice, *yajna*.

In the following stanza, Krishna promulgates that the creator god created humans together with *yajna* and told them that by consecrating their actions to the Divine and the common good, they shall multiply and prosper, with all their needs met.[277] According to this teaching, abundance is created by having the welfare of all beings, all nature, and service to the Divine in mind; in other words, through coming from an attitude of giving. This philosophy starkly contrasts the credo of modern society, which seems to believe that abundance is created by cunningly and connivingly outsmarting everybody else and getting away with the motherload. I admit that this can sometimes generate wealth for a few, but in the long term, it impoverishes society. Look only at the fact that every year, a greater amount of wealth is concentrated in the hands of fewer and fewer obscenely wealthy individuals, while at the same time, the poorer 50% of the global population owns a smaller percentage of global wealth every year. It's a toxic recipe for class warfare. That Krishna will have none of it becomes apparent when He exclaims in the *Bhagavad Gita*

---

277 *Bhagavad Gita* III.10

that those are thieves who take without giving in return.[278] Stanza IV.24 of the *Gita* then re-interprets the formal constituents of the *Vedic yajna* ritual as a metaphor for life with offering and giving the central theme. In it, the giver, given, giving, and the receiver all form the process aspect of the Divine, the God immanent. Through this metaphor, we realise that there cannot be an egoic snatching away of resources from others; instead, abundance is collectively created by all beings mutually cooperating. On the other hand, impoverishment is created by working against each other and acting adversarially and antagonistically.

An essential aspect of the *yajna* ritual is the remnants or leftovers. For example, in a *Vedic yajna*, food is consecrated to the Divine, and some of it is poured into a sacrificial fire. A large amount of food is left over, which the participants may then eat. It is crucial that we not do away with these stanzas as pertaining only to Hindus or Indians. They do contain a universal message that can be understood by paying close attention to what the *Gita* says.

Stanza IV.28 lists yogic practices and the study of sacred texts as a valid form of *yajna*, self-sacrifice. Stanza IV.29 states that *pranayama* practice with a deep understanding of its *pranic* underpinnings is also valid *yajna*. Stanza IV.33 states that *jnana yajna*, knowledge offering, is the highest form of sacrifice. Knowledge here, of course, means spiritual knowledge such as self-realisation. Krishna states that obtaining spiritual knowledge is the highest form of offering we can make to the Divine. Spiritual knowledge is the highest form of offering because there is nothing

---

278 *Bhagavad Gita* III.12

as pleasing to the Divine as our spiritual evolution. The reason why this is the case is stated in stanza IV.37. Here, Krishna says that the fire of knowledge (*jnana agni*) burns up all negative *karma*, similarly as a fire reduces its fuel to ashes. These stanzas highlight the importance of *jnana* – knowledge, in *Bhakti* Yoga. *Bhakti* Yoga cannot be complete without *Karma* Yoga, which is serving the Divine through one's actions, but both cannot be complete without *jnana*, obtaining spiritual knowledge such as knowledge of the self and the Divine. *Jnana* Yoga will, therefore, be the subject of the next chapter.

Krishna responds directly to a question from Arjuna and states that He is the *adhi-yajna*, i.e. what is addressed in all sacrificial action, which people perform with their bodies and minds.[279] A few explanations here: When Krishna says I, He does not mean that the body of the *avatar* Krishna is the recipient of all acts of offering and service. He means Him as the Supreme Being, an allusion to the point that Vishnu, in the *Vedas*, is the recipient of all offerings. When Krishna says with body and mind, He wishes to express that it is not enough to go with one's body through the motions of performing certain rituals, such as yoga practice, without surrendering them as an offering to the Divine. Thirdly, He reminds us that there are practices that take place exclusively in the mind, such as surrendering all thought to the Divine, thinking in alignment with the Divine and offering one's meditation practice to the Divine. Fourthly, He clarifies that while formal rituals exist, all actions performed with body and mind should

---

[279] *Bhagavad Gita* VIII.4

be understood as an offering to the Divine. Herein lies the defining contribution of the term *yajna* to the philosophy of *bhakti*. All actions need to be transformed into declarations of love for the Divine.

These are all crucial aspects of *yajna*. *Yajna* is a ritual that reminds us that the whole cosmos is the crystallised body of God, and therefore, all of our actions need to become *Karma* Yoga and *Bhakti* Yoga. That is why Shri Aurobindo said, "All life is yoga". The most essential stanza on *yajna* in the *Bhagavad Gita* is IX.15, which I have already commented on earlier. Here, Krishna states that those who offer *jnana yajna* (knowledge offering) to the Divine worship Him as the all-inclusive whole, as the One (*ekatva*), the distinct or separate (*prthaktva*), and the immanent in multiplicity (*bahudha*). *Ekatva* means to see the unity of the deep, unembodied self with the transcendental aspect of the Divine. *Prthaktva* means to see ourselves separate and different from the divine creative force, the Shakti or cosmic intelligence. We have limited intelligence and power, but that of the Divine is unlimited. We have a limited body, but that of the Divine, the cosmos, is unlimited. The third type of God-realization is *bahudha* – multiplicity. It means seeing how the God immanent has become the multiplicity of all beings and objects, resides in all of them, enlivens them and gives them their characteristics. Our *bhakti* is incomplete unless we can see and understand all these three realisations.

In this chapter, I have shown that the practice and understanding of the principles of *Karma* Yoga are essential for *bhakti*. I hope the reader does not become dejected by

CHAPTER 5

this precise presentation of the science of *bhakti*. This did not come to me overnight but resulted from decades of study, inquiry and practice. The practice of *bhakti* is often hampered by the belief that it consists simply of bowing down before an image. The sophisticated understanding presented in this text (for which the present author takes no credit but which is due to the influences he quoted) will set us on track for a much deeper and more rewarding *bhakti* experience. Please understand that this cannot be gained by reading this text once. It is instead a life-long practice.

Chapter 6
JNANA YOGA AND ITS IMPORTANCE FOR BHAKTI

WHAT IS JNANA YOGA?

As with all other yogas in this text, I will mainly describe *Jnana* Yoga in relation to *Bhakti* Yoga. I am hoping to write a future text that deals exclusively with *jnana*. *Jnana* Yoga was initially described, albeit not under this name, in the *Brhad Aranyaka Upanishad*, namely in the dialogues of the *Rishi* Yajnavalkya with the emperor Janaka and with Yajnavalkya's wife Maitreyi. In these dialogues, Yajnavalkya formulated the so-called Brahman doctrine, which entails that the underlying reality of the universe and the human mind is infinite consciousness, the Brahman. To attain the Brahman, Yajnavalkya teaches a three-staged approach: *shravana* is listening to the truth expounded by one who has attained it. After that comes *manana*, reflecting on the truth heard. After thoroughly understanding and accepting it comes *nididhyasana*, a permanent establishment in the truth.

Yajnavalkya's approach will only suit those with a very sophisticated intellect, free of what the *Samkhya Karika* (a text propounding *Samkhya* philosophy) calls *viparyaya*, wrong cognition or error. If any wrong cognition is present, one's intelligence is prone to misunderstanding Yajnavalkya's teaching. Wrong cognition is present in the minds of most if not all, people. The *Yoga Sutra* of Patanjali is an attempt to make the abstract teachings of the *Upanishads* accessible to people who have error-prone minds. According to Patanjali, error (*viparyaya*) is one of the five fluctuations of the mind (*vrttis*) listed in the *Yoga Sutra*.[280] Patanjali's yoga, also called *Raja* Yoga, describes a system in which we first purify the mind from error, only after which it can be applied to *Jnana* Yoga. This purifying of the mind involves an extensive toolbox of *sadhanas* (spiritual practices and disciplines), which I give an overview of in chapter 7, the chapter on *Raja* Yoga. The *Gita* teaches *Raja* Yoga in chapter 6, where it is described as a tributary to *Bhakti* Yoga.

The 8th-century Indian theologian Shri Shankaracharya (I will call him Shankara for short) stated in his *Brahma Sutra Commentary* that the Brahman (infinite consciousness) cannot be attained through performing actions (such as yoga techniques) as otherwise it would have been demonstrated that the Brahman is caused. This cannot be because, by definition, the Brahman is the uncaused cause of everything. I will now critique Shankara's argument from the viewpoint of Patanjali yoga: by performing a yoga technique, I merely purify my mind and restore it to its original alignment with the Brahman so that I can abide in It. Doing so does not imply causation of the Brahman. Instead, it only demonstrates that

- A. my mind needed purification and

---

280 *Yoga Sutra* I.6

- B. the efficacy of yoga methods to achieve such purification.

Indian mystics who had similar views were Shri Ramakrishna and Shri Aurobindo. Aurobindo attained *jnana* in Alipore jail after practising a yogic meditation technique, which I will describe below in the "How to attain *jnana*" section. Aurobindo did not thereby believe he had caused the Brahman through his meditation technique. Of course Aurobindo understood and always proclaimed that the Brahman was the uncaused cause of everything.

Aurobindo also did not believe that *jnana* was the end of the spiritual path but rather its beginning. This belief was caused by the fact that Aurobindo attained self realisation relatively quickly. It did, however, kickstart a lifelong inquiry into *Bhakti* and *Karma* Yoga. So says Aurobindo in his *Essays on the Gita*, that the *Gita* emphasises self-realisation throughout its 6th chapter.[281] While this may be considered an end in itself, it is only the beginning of *Bhakti* and *Karma* Yoga.

Swami Tapasyananda, in his commentary on the *Bhagavad Gita*, defines self-realisation as a split in consciousness by which the conscious centre ceases to identify with the body-mind and stands poised in the witnesshood of Divine Consciousness.[282] Although initially, we may baulk at the idea that a split in consciousness is something to aspire to, it roughly tallies with Patanjali's concept of self-realisation. Patanjali calls it *kaivalya*, which translates as independence

---

[281] Sri Aurobindo, *Essays on the Gita*, p. 235
[282] Swami Tapasyananda, *Srimad Bhagavad Gita*, p. 374

but also as insulation. It means that one has realised the true self, which Patanjali calls *purusha*, as independent and insulated from the egoic body-mind. More strictly speaking, we need to isolate the witnessing consciousness, the true self, from the intelligence or intellect (*buddhi*). The ancient *Samkhya* teacher Panchasikha said that due to the vicinity of intellect and consciousness, we believe the intellect to be sentient and the consciousness to modify sensory data. The truth, however, is that both functions are entirely separate. He means that the intellect modifies sensory data but is not conscious. On the other hand, the consciousness is conscious, aware and sentient, but it cannot alter sensory data. The two functions are entirely insulated from each other, and whoever has permanent cognition of this insulation is self-realised.

The state of self-realisation is frequently mentioned in the *Gita*, which talks about seeing all beings in their entirety in the *atman* (the self)[283], whereas a different passage says that one who sees sameness in all beings and is established in spiritual communion (with the Divine) sees the *atman* residing in all beings and all beings as established in the self.[284] Chapter XIII of the *Gita* deals mainly with self-realisation and *Jnana* Yoga. In this chapter, Krishna differentiates between the field (*kshetra*) that is to be known, i.e. the egoic body-mind, and the knower of the field (*kshetra-jna*), that is, the consciousness or self (*atman*). Krishna states that according to Him, the knowledge (*jnana*) that distinguishes between the knower (*kshetra-jna*), i.e. the self, and its field

---

283 *Bhagavad Gita* IV.35
284 *Bhagavad Gita* VI.29

of operation, the egoic body-mind (*kshetra*), alone is actual knowledge (*jnana*).[285]

VIJNANA (GOD-REALIZATION)

Discussing *jnana* in relation to the *Gita* and *bhakti* would not be complete without delving into *vijnana*. In one of the pivotal stanzas of the *Gita*, Krishna posits the difference between essential knowledge (*jnana*, i.e. self-realisation) and complex knowledge (*vijnana*, i.e. God-realization).[286] The medieval commentators on the *Gita* missed the importance of this stand-out stanza, an omission that Shri Ramakrishna rectified. Shri Ramakrishna pointed out that the two terms here stand for the realisation of one's self and the realisation of the Cosmic Self, the Divine. He taught that *vijnana* (God-realization) is obtained through the realisation of the Divine as both personal (*saguna*, directly translated the term means with-form) and impersonal (*nirguna*).[287] *Nirguna* means formless or without attributes and refers to the formless Absolute (*nirguna* Brahman), the subject of Shankara's teaching. The term *saguna* means with form or attributes and points to all forms the Divine can take, i.e. a deity, an *avatar*, the collective of spirits (*jivas*), the entire cosmos, and the creative intelligence and force that permutates it (*prakriti*, *maya*, Shakti).

Swami Tapasyananda says that *vijnana* is to see the divine play in which the Divine becomes the *jivas* (individual

---

285 *Bhagavad Gita* XIII.2
286 *Bhagavad Gita* VII.2
287 Swami Tapasyananda, *Srimad Bhagavata*, vol.3, p. 9

spirits), the cosmos, and its master, the Godhead.[288] Tapasyananda's statement is significant, as in Shankara's philosophy, the world is static, i.e. it never changes its essence of illusion. Also, the only real entity, the Brahman, is static as it never changes its status of infinity, eternity, emptiness, qualitylessness and formlessness. Tapasyananda here uses the term *lila*, which implies the dynamic play of the Divine. While the Divine, the player, may be unchanged, the play undertaken is real and dynamic. Shri Aurobindo picked up Ramakrishna's teaching and developed it further. He says that *vijnana* is the direct spiritual awareness of the Supreme Being; through it, all is known, not only the self but also the world, its action and nature.[289] Also, here, Aurobindo admits more than just the static self but also the action of the Divine in a real and meaningful world.

Whether our actions in the world matter or are entirely illusory is based on our realisation and, ultimately, our knowledge of the world. If we realise the Divine is an active player in the real world, a much larger emphasis is placed on our actions and whether we contribute to the divine plan.

JNANA AND BHAKTI

Shri Aurobindo writes that the seventh to the twelfth chapter of the *Bhagavad Gita* lays the foundation for the close relationship of knowledge (*jnana*) and devotion (*bhakti*).[290] The *Gita* states that devotion (*bhaktya*) brings

---

288 Swami Tapasyananda, *Srimad Bhagavad Gita*, p. 208
289 Sri Aurobindo, *Essays on the Gita*, p. 266
290 Sri Aurobindo, *Essays on the Gita*, p. 263

one to the Supreme Being, and by knowing It (*jnatva*), we enter into It.[291] The mention of both demonstrates a close interweaving of both paths. Shri Krishna states that the knower (*jnaninah*) is single-minded in devotion (*eka-bhaktih*) and ever communing with the Divine.[292] It becomes clear from these quotations that the dichotomy that some create between *Jnana* and *Bhakti* Yoga is fictional. Because how could we have devotion to something we do not know? It would be an imagined devotion, a blind faith, a dogmatism. On the other hand, once God is known, nothing could be more straightforward and natural than *bhakti*. Hence, if both *jnana* and *bhakti* are real, they must always go hand-in-hand. We may, for example, start a simple *bhakti* practice by worshipping a divine image to the exclusion of others. Still, as the great *advaitic bhakti* philosopher Madhusudana Saraswati stated, the higher modes of *bhakti* can dawn only after unitary consciousness is attained. The term unitary consciousness here represents the realisation that there is one infinite consciousness behind all divine forms and deities.

In the *Bhagavad Gita*, Krishna states that great souls (*mahatmas*) know Him (*jnatva*) to be the immutable origin of all beings and, therefore, adore (*bhajanti*) Him with an undistracted mind.[293] Again, here is the seamless fusion of *bhakti* and *jnana*, the yogas of devotion and knowledge. Sometimes, *bhakti* grows out of *jnana*; at other times the other way around, but ultimately, they always go together.

---

291 *Bhagavad Gita* XVIII.55
292 *Bhagavad Gita* VII.17
293 *Bhagavad Gita* IX.13

For example, in the *Gita* Krishna states that He will bestow the intellectual love of God (*buddhi yoga*) on those who adore Him with delight and are firmly established in spiritual communion.[294] Later, the *Gita* says that by unswerving devotion (*bhaktya*), the universal form of the Divine may be known (*jnatum*).[295] Many other passages could be quoted, but these may suffice to show that *jnana* and *bhakti* are not two but one, and those who practice one to the exclusion of the other may well end up stultified.

HOW TO PRACTICE JNANA YOGA

What is today called *Jnana* Yoga in the ancient *Upanishads* is called Brahman knowledge. According to the *Rishi* Yajnavalkya, founder of the Brahman doctrine in the *Brhad Aranyaka*, the oldest of the *Upanishads*, it is attained through a process of reflection called *shravana, manana, nididhysana*. *Shravana* means listening to the teaching. *Manana* means reflecting on the teaching, while *nididhysana* means a permanent establishment in the truth. We can all listen to and reflect on teachings, but few will become spiritually liberated by such reflection without additional help.

By the time Shankara came around, who lived a few thousand years after Yajnavalkya, the Brahman doctrine was codified to such an extent that Shankara said the Brahman could not be known through any act or effort, but It could only be known through scripture. The particular scriptures that Shankara had in mind are the so-called *prashtana trayi* (triple cannon) of *Upanishads, Bhagavad Gita*

---

294 *Bhagavad Gita* X.10
295 *Bhagavad Gita* XI.54

and *Brahma Sutras*. This means that studying these texts comprises *Jnana* Yoga. The view that studying the *Gita* constitutes *Jnana* Yoga is also supported within the *Gita* itself. So says Krishna that studying the *Bhagavad Gita* means to adore Him with the offering of knowledge (*jnana yajna*).[296]

If we rely exclusively on scriptural study, there is a realistic chance that we will stay at the surface and that such research does not profoundly transform our actions. We may learn by heart a series of linguistic statements, which we may frequently utter to convince others and ourselves that we have indeed attained *jnana*, but this fails to transform our psyche. Although we may outwardly profess to be *jnani*, our actions may continue to betray our words.

Shri Krishna had precisely this in mind when stating in stanza II.6 of the *Gita* that he who is externally inactive [i.e. pretends to be a great meditator or *jnani*] but in one's mind continues to entertain desires, is a hypocrite. That is why the native Americans have a saying, "Don't tell us about your spiritual experiences. We will observe you and judge what you have seen and understood from your behaviour." The *Bhagavata Purana* agrees that merely talking about consciousness will not lead to liberation, whereas *sadhana* (spiritual practices) will.[297] Please note that the pendulum had now swung back, and practising yoga was again seen as more promising than mere listening, reflecting, and abiding. By the time the medieval period came around,

---

296 *Bhagavad Gita* XVIII.70

297 Swami Tapasyananda, *Srimad Bhagavata*, vol. IV, p. 3

there was an aversion to talking of *jnana* in yogic circles. This aversion becomes apparent in the concluding stanza of the 15th-century *Hatha Yoga Pradipika*, which states that unless the *prana* (life force) is made to enter the central nadi (*sushumna*), all talk of *jnana* is the nonsensical jabber of madmen.[298] Although such criticism is not new, a similar statement was made almost two thousand years earlier in the *Gita*, which states that sitting quietly and thinking that one has attained an unperturbed mind is hypocrisy.[299]

That's why more recent *jnanis* often practised yogic or tantric methods to obtain knowledge. I will give three examples: Shri Ramakrishna, Ramana Maharishi and Shri Aurobindo. Let's first have a look at Ramakrishna's case. Ramakrishna was the officiating temple priest at the Kali temple of Dakshineshwar. His case is interesting for a variety of reasons. He first attained realisation of the Divine with form through *bhakti* before practising *jnana*. According to his own statements, Ramakrishna performed devotional service to Kali for an extended period without achieving realisation. Frustrated, one day, he scaled the giant Kali statue in the main temple hall and threatened to impale himself on the sizeable sacrificial sword that the statue carried. It was then that he saw the divine form of Kali. While most devotees would have been satisfied with staying with their favourite deity, Ramakrishna was curious about what would happen if he went further afield. He then practised consecutive periods of meditation on

---

298 *Hatha Yoga Pradipika* IV.113

299 Swami Tapasyananda, *Srimad Bhagavad Gita*, p. 83

CHAPTER 6

Vishnu, Shiva, Jesus and Muhammad, respectively. Later, he stated that all these paths would lead to the same goal.

At that point in his life, the *jnani* Totapuri sought out Ramakrishna to teach him a lesson. According to Totapuri's philosophy, *Advaita Vedanta*, the formless Absolute, *nirguna* Brahman, was the only actual underlying reality. Divine forms and deities were stand-ins and crutches worshipped only by those who did not have the intellectual capacity to recognise their unreality. Totapuri instructed Ramakrishna on *Jnana* Yoga, but to his great surprise, Ramakrishna mastered it in a single sitting of 24 hours.

When Totapuri returned to check on his student's progress, he found that Ramakrishna was sitting upright in a rigour mortis-like state, with his whole body cold but only the top of his head hot. Ramakrishna had mastered what the *Vedantins* call *nirvikalpa samadhi* by absorbing his *prana* (life force) in the *Sahasrara Chakra* (crown *chakra*). This technique is listed in the *Vijnana Bhairava Tantra* as suitable for attaining *jnana*. It is, however, a technique safe only for advanced practitioners like Ramakrishna. Another widely published person who practised this method was the Indian civil servant, mystic and social reformer Gopi Krishna. He authored twelve books, including his 1967 personal report *Kundalini – Evolutionary Energy in Man*. In Gopi Krishna's case, because he was not adequately prepared, the technique backfired, and he had to go through a long period of suffering, which he described as being between death and madness, before his condition ultimately stabilised in realisation. It is not worth taking such a risk for the average practitioner.

223

Totapuri managed to get Ramakrishna out of his 24-hour *nirvikalpa samadhi* by repeatedly slapping and shaking him. He hoped that Ramakrishna had now experienced the supremacy of *jnana* over *bhakti*. To Totapuri's surprise, Ramakrishna stated that *jnana* is the state one eventually attains when leaving one's body for the last time, but while still in the body, *bhakti* is the adequate approach. Ramakrishna stated further that, while in the body, rather than attempting unification with the formless Absolute, we should aim to be a servant of the Divine and all beings.

This ties in with Shri Krishna's teaching in the *Bhagavad Gita*, where he explains that following an unclear ideal is difficult for an embodied being; it is much more problematic to follow the formless Absolute [than the Divine with form].[300] This is because we cannot learn what is right and what is wrong from the formless Absolute. We can, however, learn this from the Divine with form, such as Krishna, Jesus, or Buddha. Ramakrishna did affirm, though, that complete *vijnana* (God realisation) is only obtained by realising both the Divine with form (*saguna* Brahman) and the formless Absolute (*nirguna* Brahman).

The second case study is that of the Tamil 20th-century mystic Ramana Maharishi. Ramana did not himself write books. There is a considerable discrepancy in accounts of his teachings between books about him published by Westerners and Western publishers on the one hand and Indian publications on the other. I believe that the Western books and accounts give truncated and sanitised versions and that the Indian accounts show us a more complete

---

300 *Bhagavad Gita* XII.5

CHAPTER 6

picture of Ramana's orthodox spirituality. Ramana came from a very orthodox *Smarta brahmin* background. He tended to *jnana* right from the outset, but his *bhakti* was very strong, too. Ramana reported that the Lord Shiva spoke to him and told him to devote himself to an ascetic life. Ramana was to spend the rest of his life on or around Mt. Arunachala, seen by Hindu's as the southern embodiment of Shiva. Later in Ramana's life, there was a court case about whether a real estate development should go ahead on Arunachala. Ramana signed a court document declaring that the mountain was Lord Shiva's body and that no development could go ahead. A pure *jnani* could not have done that, as to a pure *jnani*, all matter is an illusion.

In Western books about Ramana, his story is told as if it merely consisted of a set of linguistic tenets, such as, "the body is an illusion, only the self exists". What here is not sufficiently explained is that Ramana was one of the fiercest Hindu ascetics of the 20th century. His *sadhana* (spiritual discipline), as Shiva ordered him, was complete disidentification with the body. Ramana practised this for his entire life, but the most intense period was the first 15 years after arriving at Mt. Arunachala at age 10. During this period, he disowned his body to such an extent that local boys started to pelt him with stones because they realised that he wouldn't defend himself. They went on to urinate and defecate on him as, due to his *sadhana*, he would not respond. Other *sadhus* (ascetics) eventually moved Ramana into an underground dungeon to protect him. They also started to clean up his wounds and feed him; otherwise, he would not have survived, such was his disidentification with his body.

To this extent, Ramana's *sadhana* is consistent with Shankara's teaching. Shankara stated that to reach *jnana*, one must disown the body, have no home and property, own no money and have no sexual and family relations. Western accounts, while sometimes mentioning these "excesses" of Ramana's earlier life, fail to appreciate that his teaching is emasculated if one continues to lead a life ruled by desires while claiming that the body is an illusion and only consciousness is real. Such discrepancy is precisely what Lord Krishna calls hypocrisy.

Ramana's life also does not make sense without understanding his *bhakti* relationship with the personal God Shiva, who commanded Ramana to perform these austerities to attain Him. I am not expounding on this to make a case here pro or contra asceticism. I aim to research, appreciate, and hopefully understand a person's spirituality, in this case, Ramana's, entirely, rather than cherry-pick individual aspects that one may find palpable, as is the case with Ramana and the modern Western neo-*Vedanta* movement. The Western neo-*Vedanta* movement cherry-picked Ramana's linguistic formulae (such as only consciousness exists) and ignored Ramana's actions (his asceticism, i.e. his total rejection of the body, property, money, home, sex and family). What the Western neo-*Vedanta* movement ignores is that the latter powers the former. So teaches Shankara, the leading proponent of *Advaita Vedanta*, who established the ascetic code that Ramana followed. Without total rejection of any form of bodily attachment, the former is, as the Hatha Yoga Pradipika says, "the jabber of fools", or in the words of the *Bhagavad Gita*, "hypocrisy".

CHAPTER 6

Our third case study for the *bhakti–jnana* relationship is the already profusely quoted Bengali mystic Shri Aurobindo. Shri Aurobindo was the scion of a wealthy Bengali shipping merchant family. He was sent to England for education in the late 1900s and studied at Cambridge, with the prospect of working for the British Raj in India. During that time, he encountered racism and gradually warmed for the cause of home rule, i.e. ejecting the colonial rulers from India. After initially publishing a journal calling for non-violent resistance, he eventually came to believe that this approach would not yield fruits. He then entered the armed resistance and eventually became one of its leaders. After a failed bomb attack on the high commissioner of Kolkata (then Calcutta), he was arrested and spent a year in Alipore jail awaiting trial. It was a foregone conclusion that he would be convicted and executed. After the sudden and somewhat unexpected death of the main witness of the prosecution, Aurobindo had to be let off. He went to French Pondicherry, where he dedicated the remainder of his life to spiritual experimentation, writing over 30 books, and teaching, which led to an *Ashram* forming around him.

What brought about the change from political activist to spiritual master was a series of spiritual awakenings Aurobindo had in jail. The two most significant are classical *jnana* (self-realisation) and *vijnana* (God-realisation) experiences. When faced with jail and unable to continue his political resistance, Aurobindo dedicated himself to meditation. Like Ramakrishna's crown-*chakra* technique and Ramana's body-disidentification technique, also Aurobindo's meditation technique is listed in the *Vijnana Bhairava Tantra*, although neither of the three mystics quoted this tantra as their resource. Aurobindo's technique is a so-called thought-negating technique, and he described it thus:

- First, sit and watch your mind, but do not think. Implied here is not producing thoughts actively but only watching them passively.
- Secondly, if and when a thought occurs, notice that it is not created inside the mind but enters it from the outside. The underlying model here is that the brain is not a generator of thoughts but instead functions like a radio receiver. According to this approach, thoughts are not seen as bio-electrical impulses generated in the brain but as atmospheric thought waves (*vrttis*).
- Thirdly, whenever you notice a thought trying to enter your mind, throw it back out.

I encourage you to put the book down and try out the technique after re-reading the instructions several times. Whatever the initial success, I suggest revisiting the method regularly to gauge progress. Of several dozen meditation techniques I practice and have practised, I do not regard this one as one of the easiest, but Aurobindo writes that after practising the method for three days, he was free, i.e. he attained *jnana*, self-realisation. Aurobindo stated that after throwing out thoughts for three days, his mind eventually became utterly silent. If he directed his now silent mind towards inquiry, he found it to have become more transparent, precise, and powerful.

CHAPTER 6

For most yogis, this experience would have been enough. They would have remained at the level of the silent self, the witnessing consciousness. But in Aurobindo's case, this self-realisation was only the precursor and opener for the subsequent God-realisation or *vijnana*. Aurobindo writes that a few months after his self-realisation, he experienced that his bed, his blanket, and his cell wall all turned in Krishna. His correctional officers and other detainees, many of them murderers, before his eyes turned into Krishna. These experiences, *jnana* and *vijnana*, led Aurobindo to his understanding of the *Bhagavad Gita*, which he eventually published as *Essays on the Gita*. Although a challenging 600-page read, and unfortunately not a stanza-by-stanza commentary, his is the most comprehensive, visionary and inherently consistent explanation of the philosophy of the *Bhagavad Gita*. Aurobindo explains *jnana* as a tributary to *bhakti*, and I follow this view in this text. Aurobindo nevertheless also taught that realisation of the Divine cannot be complete without self-realisation. Correspondingly, devotion to the Divine can only be complete by knowing the Divine. Therefore, *jnana* is not only a tributary of *bhakti* but also an essential structural element, without which *bhakti* can become calcified into dogmatism and sectarianism.

In my 2014 text *Through Mantra, Chakras and Kundalini to Spiritual Freedom*, I attributed Shri Aurobindo's swift success in his thought-negating meditation technique to two factors. The first is the fact that Aurobindo was during his time in jail, due to his insurgency activities, essentially on death row. If you are looking forward to a certain and soon death, there is little incentive to think about the future. Because there likely is no future, there is little point in worrying about unpaid taxes, having to call the plumber, or needing to carry the garbage out. The Armenian mystic Georg I. Gurdjieff, in his *Beelzebub's Tales To His Grandson*, stated that the only thing that could propel humanity's spirituality was a mechanism that would constantly remind us of our approaching death. Aurobindo had such a mechanism in place. While being on death row would be detrimental to any other human endeavour, it is the ideal setting for meditation.

The second factor is that Aurobindo was an ancient soul, i.e., he was ready to have these experiences and just needed to be nudged over the line. Ramana Maharishi was one day asked by some visitors why he recommended methods such as *Vedic* chanting, *mantra*, or *pranayama*, yet people had yet to see him practising any of those. Ramana replied that all those who attain spiritual states in this life, seemingly without having done extended periods of *sadhana* (spiritual practices), have done so in previous lifetimes. This truth is confirmed in the *Yoga Sutra*, which lists five avenues leading to spiritual empowerment (*siddhi*).[301] Of these, birth (*janma*) is the first on the list. Birth here means that you have attained spiritual empowerment by birth, i.e. you are born with it. It is, therefore, caused by *karmic* acts performed in previous embodiments.

Aurobindo's attainment by birth becomes very obvious in his choice of words regarding the above thought-negating technique. Aurobindo suggests "throwing thoughts back out once we have noticed them entering and before they can take hold in the mind". I don't know how

---

301 *Yoga Sutra* IV.1

that works for you, but if I "throw thoughts back out", it activates the doer in me and, with it, the sense of agency of which Krishna warns. This was no obstacle for Aurobindo, attesting to his maturity and exultation. For the rest of us mere mortals, I suggest replacing the active throwing out with passive letting go and releasing of thoughts.

An alternative approach would be the surrendering of thoughts to the Divine. As Krishna states, all actions are done by His *prakriti* (divine creative force), but in our delusion, we believe to be the doers. The term "all actions" here includes the action of thinking. We can step back from the thinking process by realising that the Divine is thinking all thoughts through us. Some may think that the offering or surrendering of a thought is too insignificant an offering. To this, Krishna says, whatever you offer Me with sincerity and love, even if just a leaf, a flower or fruit, that I will verily accept.[302]

A final word from Shri Aurobindo on the subject of *jnana* and *vijnana*: In *Essays on the Gita*, he calls upon us to realise the unity of all beings in Nature herself.[303] When spelling nature here with a capital N, Aurobindo wishes to invoke the Shakti, the becoming aspect of the Divine, behind which is still the un-manifest, the being-aspect of the Divine, the pure self.

EFFECTS OF JNANA

In the *Gita*, Krishna states that verily in this world, nothing exists as purifying as knowledge (of the *atman*, i.e. self-knowledge), as one perfected in yoga will find out in due

---

302 *Bhagavad Gita* IX.26
303 Sri Aurobindo, *Essays on the Gita*, p. 229

time.[304] This stanza is very significant. If we approach *bhakti* without knowledge (i.e., through belief and faith only), it can become an exercise of narcissism, where we extrapolate our ego on our preferred deity and make them the only object worthy of worship. We might then blight our soul with haughtiness and look down on all other children of God who worship the Divine through different avenues than the one we prefer. To develop such haughtiness is the real-life danger of *bhakti* without knowledge. With *jnana*, we see the *atman* within us and the same *atman* within others. Such knowledge will stop any sectarian zealotry in its tracks as we can only witness with humility God expressing Herself through other beings in entirely different ways.

The *Gita* makes this clear without a doubt, saying that a wise or educated person (*pandita*) sees the same self (*atman*) in a *brahmin* (a member of the priest caste), a cow, an elephant, a dog, and even a dog-eater.[305] In ancient India, dogmeat eaters were seen as having the lowest social status; they were outcasts. The idea is that a wise person will see the same *atman* even in the most socially despised. Imagine how our society would change if it could be built on that premise. All adversarialism, antagonism, ambition and competition would be gone in one stroke. Also, notice how much adversarialism, antagonism, ambition and competition have entered religions and spiritual practices and how much they would be purified if those practising them could see that we all share the same self and that

---

304 *Bhagavad Gita* IV.38
305 *Bhagavad Gita* V.18

this self is God. Most modern religions (except for the far-eastern religions) are *bhakti* religions. Yet because they often ignore the *jnana* element, they have become contaminated with the belief that only they represent the right path and members other faiths are infidels or pagans at best, worshippers of Satan at worst.

In the *Gita*, Krishna states that once we gain independence from sensory experience, we gain the joy of the *atman*.[306] Through that comes the infinite ecstasy from becoming absorbed in communion with the Brahman. This statement requires an explanation. As in the story of Ramana Maharishi, *Jnana* Yoga involves some form of *sadhana* that makes us independent from sensory gratification. That does not mean we must choose asceticism (for Ramakrishna and Aurobindo did not). It also does not mean that we may never choose sensory gratification, but it does mean that we need to become independent of it. For most modern humans, whenever there is stress, frustration, boredom, etc., the first response is to cover it up by employing sensory gratification, and that's why we have become addicted to it.

But the joy we experience through sensory gratification does not come from it but radiates out from the *atman* deep within us. The nature of the *atman* is ecstasy, which is why in the so-called *panchakosha* doctrine of the *Taittiriya Upanishad* (the teaching of the five layers on which yoga is built), the *atman* is called *ananda-maya kosha*, meaning the layer that empowers ecstasy.[307] The first step to discovering

---

306 *Bhagavad Gita* V.21
307 *Taittiriya Upanishad* II.2-5

the *atman* often requires some form of retreat, aloneness or isolation. Alone in nature, we can find the time, space and muse to realise that our innermost, intrinsic nature is ecstasy, which does not require external stimulus.

But in the above stanza, Krishna goes further. He says that if we stay in the joy of the *atman* long enough, we find beneath it and through it the infinite ecstasy of the Brahman, the infinite consciousness or world soul. Also here, Krishna points again to the fact that first comes *jnana* – self-realisation, and through it and after it comes *vijnana* – God realisation, an order that Shri Aurobindo so pointedly emphasised. Of course, the Brahman, the Cosmic Consciousness, takes longer to access, but once we become absorbed in communion with It, It delivers infinite ecstasy, so the *Bhagavad Gita* states.

Further extolling the virtues of *jnana*, Krishna states that *jnana* reduces the effects of *karma*, like a fire, which reduces a heap of wood to ashes.[308] Finally, Krishna says that He looks at the knower (*jnanin*) as His very self [i.e. extremely beloved].[309] This injunction should not be brushed aside as insignificant or as mere words. Krishna here states that self-realisation creates an intimate bond between Him and the devotee—a bond which will, of course, be infinitely increased once God-realization is obtained. We should not think that what we do does not matter to God. On the contrary, spiritual evolution and progress create a special kind of ecstasy in the mind of God. There is no greater

---

308 *Bhagavad Gita* IV.37
309 *Bhagavad Gita* VII.18

ecstasy for God than to witness the spiritual awakening of Her children, us.

We have now established what *bhakti* is and how it is practised. Additionally, we have learned how important *Kurma* Yoga is for *bhakti* and how, without it, *bhakti* can amount to little more than indulging in spiritual emotionality. Finally, we learned that *bhakti* without *jnana* can quickly descend into religious dogmatism and fundamentalism. But what if the heights of *Jnana* Yoga are too difficult for us to scale? What if our mind is confused, distracted and unfocussed, our breath unsteady, and our body too fidgety to sit upright for extended periods? The answer is that we must prepare ourselves with *Raja* Yoga, described in the next chapter, chapter 7.

Chapter 7
RAJA YOGA AND ITS IMPORTANCE FOR BHAKTI

WHAT IS RAJA YOGA

In this chapter, I will explain why and how *Raja* Yoga is essential for *bhakti* and all other avenues of yoga so far mentioned. *Raja* Yoga is a general term for the yoga of the *Yoga Sutra*, and its keyword is concentration. In his commentary on Patanjali's *Yoga Sutra*, *Rishi* Vyasa explains that the term yoga can be derived from the Sanskrit root *yujir yoge*, in which case the term yoga means to yoke or to commune.[310] With this meaning, the term is most often used in the *Bhagavad Gita*. There is a second Sanskrit verb root from which the term can be derived: *yujir samadhau*, in which yoga means to concentrate. With this meaning, the term yoga is used in the *Yoga Sutra*, and here all yogic methods (including *asana*, *pranayama* and meditation) are used to concentrate the mind to such an extent that it can ultimately be of laser-like, *samadhic* quality and see and cut through ignorance, conditioning, erroneous cognition and delusion.

---

310 Vyasa's *Yoga Bhashya* I.1

Although the *Bhagavad Gita* generally uses the term yoga to mean yoking the individual self to the Cosmic Self and communing with It, it also accepts the path of *Raja* Yoga, the path of concentrating the mind. So says the *Gita* that if somebody cannot fix their mind steadily on the Divine, they should approach the Divine through the systematic practice of concentration.[311] Apart from the preparatory limbs such as ethics, *asana* and *pranayama*, this systematic practice consists of the limbs *pratyahara* (independence from external stimuli), *dharana* (concentration), *dhyana* (meditation) and *samadhi* (absorption). Notably, these last four limbs do not differ regarding the meditation object chosen, but in how far the object meditated upon is duplicated in the mind. In other words, the degree to which an external meditation object and its duplicate in the mind have achieved identity. I have described all this in great detail in my explanation of the *Yoga Sutra* contained in Ashtanga Yoga Practice and Philosophy, and it is beyond the scope of this book to go into too much detail. However, in a general sense, the *Yoga Sutra* talks of the fact that our mind has been made scattered, dispersed and diffuse through negative imprints (such as trauma), which now surface as mental obstacles such as anxiety and depression, an unsteady breathing pattern and a fidgety body incapable of sitting still for extensive periods.[312]

Where the *Yoga Sutra* and the *Bhagavad Gita* differ is that the *Yoga Sutra* is very liberal when it comes to choosing a meditation object. The only limitation is that any chosen

---

311 *Bhagavad Gita* XII.9
312 *Yoga Sutra* I.31

object should be of *sattvic* (sacred) quality. Although the *Yoga Sutra* does include the Divine in its possible choices of objects, in the *Gita*, we find this to be the only recommended object. We would expect this in a text dealing with *bhakti*.

The *Gita* gives *Raja* Yoga a place because Krishna accepts that not everybody can go straight to *bhakti*, the yoga of devotion or *jnana*, the yoga of knowledge. This inability to go straight to the heart of the matter is because most practitioners have a mind oscillating between frantic activity (*rajas*) and torpid dullness (*tamas*), with very little time spent in the *sattvic* state. Such an oscillating mind must be purified, cultivated, and made sharp and luminous so that, in the end, it can know the Divine and be devoted to It in loving service.

The *Bhagavad Gita* begins its description of classical *Raja* Yoga with the advice that we should seek a solitary location, prepare a meditation seat, and assume a stable *asana*.[313] We now endeavour to make the mind single-pointed (*ekagra*) by absorbing it and the senses in the self to achieve spiritual communion. Additionally, the *Gita* advises us to keep the head, neck, and spine in an erect position, gaze towards the tip of the nose (*nasikagra*) without looking around, and, in a fearless, serene, and content state, meditate on spiritual communion with the Divine.

After Arjuna complains to Krishna that the human mind is too fickle and too liable to aggravation ever to attain communion with the Divine, the latter replies that although Arjuna is correct in his assessment of the human mind, it can nevertheless be domesticated through the

---

313 *Bhagavad Gita* VI.10-14

combined application of spiritual practice (*abhyasa*) and disidentification (*vairagya*).[314] Those studying the *Yoga Sutra* will notice that Krishna advises the same dual strategy to suspend the mind that Patanjali prescribes, too.[315] In other words, in this section of the *Gita*, Shri Krishna teaches straightforward Patanjali yoga. He agrees that if a person's mind is not yet capable of communion with the Divine, i.e. for *bhakti*, then the whole system of *Raja* Yoga may need to be applied to change the quality of that person's mind.

Notably, the choice of words for spiritual practice (*abhyasa*) and disidentification (*vairagya*) hints at *pranayama*. Spiritual practice (*abhyasa*) involves doing, conquering, and techniqueing, all activities yogis call solar. They are so-called because they are powered by the right solar nostril and the so-called *Pingala nadi*, which also supplies *prana* to the left analytical brain hemisphere and the sympathetic nervous system. Disidentification (*vairagya*) involves non-doing, surrendering and letting go, attitudes that yogis refer to as lunar. These are powered by the left lunar nostril and the *Ida nadi*, which also supplies the right, intuitive-holistic brain hemisphere and the parasympathetic nervous system with *prana*. The most straightforward means to balance both *nadis* is through the *pranayama* method *Nadi Shodhana*, i.e. alternate nostril breathing, which I have described in great detail in my book *Pranayama The Breath of Yoga*. There are other direct references to *pranayama* in the *Bhagavad Gita* and the *Bhagavata Purana*, which I will quote further down.

---

314 *Bhagavad Gita* VI.33-34

315 *Yoga Sutra* I.12

CHAPTER 7

WHY RAJA YOGA

As explained in the chapter on *Jnana* Yoga, the primary technique of attaining self-realisation in the days of yore was reflecting on scriptural passages. The problem with relying mainly or only on scripture to attain knowledge is that this approach has worked for an ancient society but is fraught with difficulties today. In several of my earlier books, I have written how the general mindset of humanity was degraded through entropy while history went through the so-called four *yugas* or world ages. This entropic process can easily be deducted from analysing the scriptures relevant to each *yuga*. During the first age, *Satya Yuga* (age of truth), the age of the *Vedas*, it was sufficient to practice *samadhi* (absorptive ecstasy) because the average person's mind gravitated in this direction. During the second age, *Treta Yuga*, the age of the *Upanishads*, a complex process of yogic meditation was added to raise Kundalini, which had dropped to around our ankles by then. The third age, *Dvapara Yuga*, the age of the *sutras* and philosophy, led to our brain hemispheres disconnecting from each other. This disconnect made humanity collectively oscillate between megalomania and depression, a disorder that brought with it the necessity to practice *pranayama*, particularly alternate nostril breathing to re-integrate both brain hemispheres and both branches of the nervous system. The fourth and current age, *Kali Yuga*, the age of the *tantras*, brought a profound disembodiment. This disembodiment led to an obsession with the body, particularly its external valuation, along with perceived ideas of beauty and an obsession with money and power. Yoga responded by emphasising the practice of *asana,* which can teach us to re-embody.

The theory of *Raja* Yoga is based on the already mentioned *panchakosha* doctrine of the *Taittiriya Upanishad*.[316] The *Upanishad* talks about the five layers or sheaths of which the human being is made up. The fifth and innermost layer, the ecstasy sheath (*Anandamaya kosha*), constitutes our relationship with the God transcendent, the *nirguna* Brahman. The fourth layer (*Vijnanamaya kosha*) entails the understanding of divine law, sacred knowledge of the order of the universe and the cognising of the master plan according to which all universes unfold, and divine creativity expresses itself as the world. This sheath coordinates our relationship with the God immanent, the *saguna* Brahman, and enables us to make a significant and lasting contribution to human society and life on Earth. This fourth layer is essential for *Karma* Yoga, and I have dealt with it in my text *How To Find Your Life's Divine Purpose*.

Bhakti and *Jnana* Yoga also deal with these two inner sheaths. The problem is that many yoga novices find it difficult to access these inner sheaths because of conditioning (*vasana*), subconscious imprints (*samskaras*), trauma, *karma* and suffering (*kleshas*) being stored and imprinted in the three outer sheaths. While the two innermost sheaths deal with aspects of the Divine and the self, impurities in the three outermost layers make seeing through to the two inner sheaths difficult or impossible. If somebody seems to have no spiritual tendencies, this is not because they will never be able to have spiritual experiences, but because

---

316 *Taittiriya Upanishad* 2.2 -2.5

currently, the three outer layers are too opaque to let the light from the centre radiate outwards to their surface self.

These three outer layers are *Anamaya kosha* (the body), *Pranamaya kosha* (breath and *pranic* sheath), and *Manomaya kosha* (the mind). Patanjali refers to them when he says in the *Yoga Sutra* that the obstacles to yoga are located in the body, breath, and mind.[317] These three layers are intricately linked, and it is here where the obstacles to spiritual freedom are located. Many contemporary systems of yoga address only one (or two) of the three layers in which obstacles are located. Some systems work mainly with the body by using *asana* or other forms of physical discipline. Other methods focus exclusively on the mind, such as meditation or mindfulness. Others again use breathing methods. Yoga is most efficient if it addresses all three levels – the physical, pranic and mental – by using techniques designed to purge conditioning from them, i.e. *asana* for the body, *pranayama* for the breath, and meditation for the mind.

To make our minds robust, our conditioning is stored in three separate locations, not just in the mind. It is also stored in the body and the respiratory pattern. This robust triple storage is why we encounter so much inertia when we want to change. If we want to let go of our past, we must purge conditioning from all three layers individually. It is precisely this that interlinked yogic *asana, pranayama,* and meditation do. They purify the body, breath, and mind.

The *Taittiriya Upanishad,* the *Yoga Sutra,* and the *Bhagavata Purana* agree that one may need to prepare through spiritual practices if one is incapable of communion with

---

317 *Yoga Sutra* 1.31

BHAKTI THE YOGA OF LOVE

the Divine.[318] Swami Tyagisananda, in his commentary on Narada's *Bhakti Sutra*, argues that success in *bhakti* arguably depends on divine grace, but such grace can never come unless we purify our minds through spiritual practices conducted through self-effort.[319]

Stanza 53 of Narada's *Bhakti Sutra* states that love for the Divine manifests itself in those who have made themselves fit to receive it through constant *sadhana*, spiritual practices and discipline. It is confused thinking to assume that love for the Divine is something that spontaneously drops out of heaven uncaused and uninvited. It must be deserved as it is the sweetest and most rewarding of all gifts. Narada here agrees with the *Bhagavad Gita*, which in the 18th chapter talks about different types of pleasure, being of *tamasic*, *rajasic*, and *sattvic* nature, respectively. *Tamasic* pleasure always results in delusion.[320] *Rajas*-driven pleasure is sweet in the beginning and poisonous in the end.[321] *Sattva*-derived pleasure (such as love for the Divine) is acquired by the long practice of spiritual disciplines. Therefore, it appears bitter (or at least laborious) initially but turns out to be sweet in the end.[322] *Raja* Yoga is the method for acquiring *sattvic* pleasure (such as divine love), which may seem arduous at first but yields outstanding rewards.

The *Gita* lists the paths of *Raja* Yoga (here called the path of *dhyana*), *Karma* Yoga (called by precisely this name) and

---

318 *Bhagavata Purana* III.28.27
319 Swami Tyagisananda, *Narada Bhakti Sutras*, p. 62
320 *Bhagavad Gita* XVIII.39
321 *Bhagavad Gita* XVIII.38
322 *Bhagavad Gita* XVIII.36-37

CHAPTER 7

Jnana Yoga (here called *Samkhya*, as it is often named in the *Gita*).[323] The path of *bhakti* (here called *upasana*—worship) is listed in the following stanza.[324] This is further evidence that Krishna accepts *Raja* Yoga as a fourth path, albeit seeing it mainly as a tributary and preparation for the other three. We will now look into the particular methods of *Raja* Yoga that attract the most scriptural attention.

METHODS OF RAJA YOGA

The two *Raja* Yoga practices most often mentioned in the *bhakti* texts are *pranayama* and *chakra* meditation. In the *Bhagavad Gita*, Krishna states that some yogis devoted to *pranayama* regulate the movements of *prana* and *apana* (the vital up and down currents) by offering the inhalation into the exhalation and the exhalation into the inhalation.[325] Krishna lists this as a *pranayama* technique because it is used to equalise the flow of *prana* and *apana*. Because it does not, however, involve manipulation of the breath itself (but rather just conscious observation), many *Raja* Yogis list this as a preparation for meditation or *kriya* technique. I have described the method in my 2014 text *Yoga Meditation - Through Mantra, Chakras and Kundalini to Spiritual Freedom*.

The *Bhagavata Purana*, too, testifies to the importance of the canon of *Raja* Yoga methods, including *pranayama*, *pratyahara*, and *dhyana*.[326] The importance of *pranayama*

---

323 *Bhagavad Gita* XIII.24

324 *Bhagavad Gita* XIII.25

325 *Bhagavad Gita* IV.28

326 *Bhagavata Purana* III.28.5-11

245

techniques is mentioned again.[327] The *Bhagavata* also states that mind, speech, and body need to be purified through *pranayama*, silence, and desirelessness, respectively, attesting to the importance of *pranayama* for the mind.[328] The *Bhagavata* additionally promulgates the practice of breath retentions (*kumbhakas*), both internal and external, embedded within alternate nostril breathing, referring to the complete *Nadi Shodhana pranayama* as Shri T. Krishnamacharya taught it.[329] The passage also talks about the importance of measuring the length of the breath by reciting *mantras* (rather than counting numbers in one's mind) and that *chakra* meditation must follow *pranayama*. This injunction does not necessarily mean *chakra* meditation must follow *pranayama* in each practice session. It instead means that once one has gotten hold of the *prana* and learned to cultivate the *pranic* sheath, one then moves forward to learn *chakra* meditation.

The *Bhagavad Gita* discusses fixing the life force between the eyebrows (*bhrumadhya*) to attain the Supreme Being.[330] It also gives importance to doing so at the time of death, but of course, this is a technique that yogis practice all life to attain the *darshana* (view) of the Divine with form (*saguna* Brahman). The *darshana* of the formless Absolute is gained by focusing the *prana* on the crown of the head (*Sahasrara Chakra*). Neither of these techniques is a beginner's technique. Beginners should introduce

---

327 *Bhagavata Purana* IV.9.80

328 *Bhagavata Purana* XI.3.26

329 *Bhagavata Purana* XI.14.32-33

330 *Bhagavad Gita* VIII.9-10

CHAPTER 7

this focus as an ancillary during *pranayama* and *chakra*-Kundalini meditation during prescribed times. It must also be mentioned that the eyebrow-middle is the eyes' focal point, whereas the mind must visualise the *Ajna Chakra* in the centre of the cranium.

Chakras also feature in the *Bhagavata Purana*, where we find advice on drawing *prana* up from the *Muladhara Chakra*[331] and on meditating on the heart *chakra*.[332] In another passage of the *Bhagavata*, we hear that the Supreme Spirit manifests Himself through the *chakras* in the spinal column.[333] I have given detailed instructions on how the Divine is doing that in chapter 13 of *Through Mantra, Chakras and Kundalini to Spiritual Freedom* and throughout *Chakras, Drugs and Evolution — A Map of Transformative States*. The subject is too extensive to cover here, even succinctly. The *Bhagavata Purana* states that the *chakras* initially point downwards, signifying their inactivate state.[334] They open and blossom upwards once activated through *sadhana* (spiritual practice and discipline). That they do so was also held by T. Krishnamacharya, and this is also why the *chakras* are referred to as lotuses in most yogic texts. Shri Aurobindo also performed *chakra* meditation, referred to in *The Synthesis of Yoga* and in his yoga practice diary, called *Record of Yoga*.[335]

---

331 *Bhagavata Purana* XI.14.32

332 *Bhagavata Purana* XI.14.36

333 *Bhagavata Purana* XI.12.17

334 *Bhagavata Purana* XII.14.36-37

335 Sri Aurobindo, *Record of Yoga*, Vol. 2, Sri Aurobindo Ashram, Pondicherry, 2001, p.1340, p.1462

In the *Bhagavad Gita*, Shri Krishna further elucidates the importance of the *chakras*.[336] Here, He advises attaining spiritual communion with Him at the time of death by closing all sensory gates of the body. This technique is variously called *Yoni* or *Shanmukhi Mudra* (described in my text *Mudras Seals of Yoga*). During it, one concentrates the mind in the heart *chakra*, draws all *prana* into the head, and utters the mystical syllable OM, denoting infinite consciousness.

PRACTICAL TIPS FOR INTEGRATING BHAKTI INTO RAJA YOGA PRACTICE

I recommend performing your *sadhana*, including *asana* and *pranayama* practice, before a suitable image of the Divine. How to choose such an image was covered in Chapter 4, *Bhakti* Yoga. Whenever performing yoga practices in front of your image, mentally proclaim that you are performing the practice for the Divine, dedicate the fruits (results) of the practices to the Divine, and surrender your sense of agency to the Divine. That means that you declare that you distribute whatever good is to come from your practice to the Divine and all beings and that you are aware of the fact that it is not you doing the practice but that the Divine is doing the practice through you, in the same way as Jesus Christ said it is not me doing the works but the Father through me is doing the works.[337]

Whenever you perform seated practice, such as during *pranayama* or *dhyana* (meditation), visualise the *ishtadevata*

---

336 *Bhagavad Gita* VIII.12-13
337 John 14:10

(the for you suitable form of the Divine) sitting atop your thousand-petalled lotus (*Sahasrara Chakra*). When completing your seated practice, fold the thousand-petalled lotus around your *ishtadevata* and draw it down into your heart lotus (*Anahata Chakra*). Keep it there throughout the day and remember it whenever possible by uttering the *ishtamantra* (the *mantra* associated with the for you appropriate form of the Divine). Upon commencing seated formal practice, take the lotus leaf enfolded *ishtadevata*, place it on the crown of your head and unfold the petals.

Initially, when practising *kumbhakas* (breath retentions) during formal *pranayama*, it is easy for the mind to get stuck in the practice's formalities. At such times, open your eyes during *kumbhaka* and practice *Trataka* (gazing) at the divine image before you. If you are using an anthropomorphic image, follow T. Krishnamacharya's advice to initially only look at the feet of the Divine. Raise your gaze only when prompted by the Divine to do so. *Pranayama* and *kumbhaka* constitute a sophisticated science that cannot be adequately covered in a short essay. Please follow the instructions in my text, *Pranayama: The Breath of Yoga*.

When studying yogic *chakra*-Kundalini meditation, learn first to pronounce the various seed-syllables (*bija aksharas*) into the six lower *chakras* during each inhalation and exhalation. Once you can perform this, pronounce several *bija aksharas* into each *chakra* during each in-and exhale. This extended practice gives you more time to visualise aspects of each *chakra*, such as the number of petals, the colour of each *chakra*, associated *yantra* (sacred geometry), the colour of the *yantra*, etc. Such increased complexity also calls for slowing down the breath, which in turn will support your *pranayama* practice. Once you have progressed to this step, start visualising your *ishtadevata* during each internal breath retention on top of your thousand-petalled lotus while pronouncing its *ishtamantra*. As stated by Shri Krishna in the *Gita*, this technique, visualising the Divine during breath retentions in *pranayama*, will ultimately lead to communion with the Divine.[338] For more information on the intricacies of yogic *chakra*-Kundalini meditation, please consult my text *Through Mantra, Chakras and Kundalini to Spiritual Freedom*.

In all daily *sadhana* situations, I suggest integrating *bhakti* into *Raja* Yoga practices as per above. There are, however, crisis situations when formal practices take too long. In these cases, place an image of the heart *chakra* in front of you and perform *Trataka* (gazing) on it until you can visualise it as your own heart *chakra*, i.e., project the image into your chest. Then, strike the root syllable (*bija akshara*) YAM into the *chakra* as if the root syllable were a mallet and the *chakra* a gong. Once you can feel the *chakra* or clearly see it, use the following affirmations:

- I am Divine love.
- I am an embodiment of divine love.
- I am pure love.
- I love and accept myself.
- I accept whatever thoughts and emotions come up.
- With every breath I take, the Divine is breathing love into every cell of my body.
- I live life as divine love.

---

338 *Bhagavad Gita* VIII.12-13

- I let the Divine speak, act through me, and communicate only from the divine love in my heart.
- I give unconditional love to all and genuinely love all beings as children of the Divine.
- My heart radiates divine love to all beings.

For more information on purifying the subconscious mind through affirmations, please consult my text, How To Find Your Life's Divine Purpose, which deals with the intricacies of *Karma* Yoga.

SUMMARY

This chapter aimed to show that *Raja* and *Bhakti* Yogas are not competing systems in conflict with one another but that *Raja* Yoga, for most aspirants today, constitutes a viable on-ramp for *bhakti*. Without having at least some vague experience of the Divine, *bhakti* is a steep ask for most people. *Raja* Yoga is the science that purifies the mind. With sufficient *Raja* practice under one's belt, direct experiences of the Divine gradually become inevitable, and the practice of *bhakti* is the next natural step. *Bhakti* itself also considerably improves the practice of *Raja* Yoga. The problem with *Raja* Yoga is that one can get bogged down with practising techniques. By placing one's yoga early on into the service of the Supreme Being, the typical pitfalls of *Raja* Yoga, wanting to progress and succeed, can be avoided. Practising out of devotion and service rather than wanting to get (such as achieving progress) is the so-called "good attitude" that Patanjali refers to in the *Yoga Sutra*.[339]

---

339 *Yoga Sutra* I.14

Chapter 8
ROLE OF ETHICS IN BHAKTI

This chapter aims to show that ethics are not a separate consideration or an after-thought when practising *bhakti* but are *bhakti*'s application and external aspects. Ethical considerations derive from the fact that those practising *bhakti* must understand that the entire universe and all beings are embodiments of the Divine and should be treated as such. Professing to love the Divine while mistreating others is an anathema and hypocrisy. For the true *bhakta*, it is impossible to let others suffer while remaining aloof, rising above it all, and gloating at one's spiritual realisation. So says Krishna in the *Bhagavad Gita* that in His view, those are the greatest yogis who, due to seeing the *atman* in others, develop such a sense of empathy with them that they experience their joy and suffering as their own.[340] We find here a profoundly different vision of yoga than spiritual boilerplate statements such as "everything is *maya*, suffering is an illusion, and everything is just perfect, as long as we can keep ignoring all problems". Krishna doesn't want us to become insentient and uncompassionate. The *bhakta* is right there in the midst of it all, compassionately sharing everybody's suffering.

---

340 *Bhagavad Gita* VI.32

Further down, the *Bhagavad Gita* states that those who surrender, having *sattvic* qualities and wisdom, never abandon their duties simply because they are unpleasant, nor do they perform actions merely because they are pleasant.[341] Such stanzas abound in the *Gita* because they are to be understood inversely. That is, we have to check ourselves whether we abandon duties simply because they are unpleasant. If so, this fact tells us that at this point, we do not surrender to the Divine and lack *sattvic* qualities and wisdom.

Both the *Gita* and Narada's *Bhakti Sutra* suggest that we do not make up our minds based on our whims but consult the *shastras* (sacred texts) as to what course of action to take. The *Gita* states that if we neglect the advice of the *shastras* and are guided by our desires, we will neither reach spiritual freedom nor worldly attainments.[342] Krishna then adds that the *shastras* must be understood before deciding which course of action to take. Krishna is not against desire per se, for He states that in all beings, He is desire not contrary to *dharma* (right action).[343] This means that He opposes desire when it is contrary to *dharma*. Shri Aurobindo spelt this out in *Essays on the Gita*, and it must be replied to by those who confuse themselves with statements such as that God is also in the wrongdoers.[344] The answer to that statement is yes, God is, but this fact is irrelevant when somebody's wrong actions are concerned.

---

341 *Bhagavad Gita* XVIII.10
342 *Bhagavad Gita* XVI.23-24
343 *Bhagavad Gita* VII.11
344 Sri Aurobindo, *Essays on the Gita*, p. 274

CHAPTER 8

Dharma (right action/ law) must be asserted based on the rightness of somebody's action and not on what they are essentially.

Narada's *Bhakti Sutra* states that even one who has attained realisation should always respect the scriptures because otherwise, there is the risk of downfall.[345] This means that even spiritual teachers can still fall for their own egos. Even after realisation, they are still subject to ethical rules and the *shastras*' guidelines concerning right and wrong. The history of spirituality over the last few hundred years offers ample examples of what happens if we begin to believe that we have become too big to follow the same rules as everybody else.

Swami Tyagisananda, in his commentary on Narada's *Bhakti Sutra*, explains that hating anyone is equal to hating God because there is only God. Any form of hatred must be let go of by the *bhakta*. Instead, our attitude toward everything needs to be love. By loving everything and everybody, we remind ourselves that God is in everything. We must pay particular attention to individuals we think we cannot love. If we seem unable to love them, it is usually a form of suppressed inner conflict that we externalise. Suppressed inner conflict in this context means that I believe I am incapable of loving person X because I see in them something that I cannot accept or struggle to accept in myself. Therefore, I project it onto another person, i.e. externalise the conflict, and now I can judge and persecute them for it. But deep inside, I am fighting against myself. The other person becomes a sacrificial animal that I

---

[345] Narada's *Bhakti Sutras*, stanzas 12-13

ritualistically offer (even if just through hating them rather than physically harming them) to appease and silence my inner conflict. This process occurs between individuals and groups within a society and in inter-societal conflicts such as disputes between nations.

Loving the Divine in everything does not mean we must put up with wrong and evil. Part of *dharma* is the duty to assert right actions, stop perpetrators, and protect victims. We mustn't attempt to stop perpetrators while ourselves coming from an attitude of hatred because otherwise, in the process, we become those we profess to hate. But how is it that God accepts all the evil done in the world, and is it not God's duty to stop it? In the *Mahabharata*, Krishna was assailed precisely with these arguments and was told He was responsible for the slaughter of Kurukshetra, as He could have changed the minds of the evildoers.[346] Krishna argued that every person is born free. Therefore, the Kauravas were free to choose the path of evil, and they did. They, thus, met their end because of their actions. It is not the job of the Divine to change the minds of individuals, but individuals must tune into the Divine, do the right thing, and fulfil divine law and *dharma*.

Let's now switch to the *Bhagavata Purana* and see what it says about ethics. We find that nobody who suppresses other beings attains to the Divine, while those who see everybody as equal and are peaceful, pure, and benevolent to all do.[347] Such qualifications make it very clear that realising and knowing the Divine is essential but useless unless it changes our attitude and behaviour

---

346 *Mahabharata* XII.53

347 *Bhagavata Purana* IV.12.36

towards others. We can go as far as saying that the value of a realisation or spiritual experience lies not in itself but in how far it changes our behaviour towards others. The *Bhagavata Purana* confirms this by stating that a person's life is meaningful and purposeful to the extent that their wealth, energies, intelligence, and utterances are utilized for the good of others.[348]

This attitude is precisely the crucial point in our ethics of *bhakti*. It leads us to conclude that the modern desperate hunt for spiritual experiences is overdone and their importance overemphasized. If we understand and accept the philosophy of *bhakti*, we might as well go straight to the point and treat all beings as if they were God. They indeed are, and it is this point that *karmically* drives spiritual liberation and not fancy psychedelic experiences that may give us an initial dopamine high. Such epiphanies will, after a short time, wear off. We may then require more spiritual experiences, but none of them may ever change our behaviour. We are thus again on a quest to receive and get. This time may not be about wealth and pleasure but spiritual experiences. The emphasis on obtaining and getting, however, is still the same. What truly changes us is to switch our focus to giving. This switch is what powers the *karma* that brings liberation about.

The *Bhagavata Purana* says that serving all beings begins with accepting that the Divine dwells in them and that It is, therefore, the recipient of all of our actions.[349] This acceptance is the key to ethical action. If we understand

---

348 *Bhagavata Purana* X.22.35
349 *Bhagavata Purana* VII.7.32

and accept this point and make it the departure of all our actions, we do not need a sophisticated, nigh complicated catalogue of commandments and rules. The *Bhagavata Purana* confirms this by stating that all beings should be considered embodiments of the Divine.[350] Beings here clearly do not just mean humans. It is imperative that we let go of our speciesistic outlook. The *Bhagavata* says that we should also consider animals our own children.[351]

Above all is the guideline that we should look at all beings as the same, an attitude that the *Bhagavad Gita* calls *samata* — evenness, equality, or sameness. So says the *Bhagavata Purana* that we need to honour all beings as manifestations of the Divine, whether they be holy, outcasts, tormentors of holy people, peaceful, ferocious, or cruel personalities.[352] A quick disclaimer here: if somebody is evil, we first have to recognize God within them and not treat them with the same evil they project against us. We must respond to them with love, which may change their behaviour. If it doesn't, and if they break the law, damage and victimize other people or even nations, then we need to bring the full force of the law against them. But not in a spirit of hatred or superiority and "other", for they are not other; they are us. We all partake of the same *atman*, the divine self. We need to correct perpetrators against divine law in a spirit of loving support, and this cannot change even if we have to wage war against them. In the long term, it is in nobody's interest to perpetrate against divine law,

---

350 *Bhagavata Purana* X.85.23
351 *Bhagavata Purana* VII.14.9
352 *Bhagavata Purana* XI.29.13-14

even if, in the short term, they hope to gain some short-sighted advantage through it.

The above *Bhagavata Purana* passage goes on to state that those who constantly seek the presence of God in all beings will give up any competitiveness because they see all as equals. They will give up jealousy towards those they deem superior and contempt for those they consider inferior [because they see all as equal children of the Divine]. Finally, seeing the Divine equally in all beings will make us cease placing too much importance on ourselves. In other words, seeing the Divine in all stops us from taking ourselves too seriously.

Placing too much import on ourselves provides a serious obstacle on the path of *bhakti*. We matter to the Divine in that regard that we are an expression, an emanation of the Divine, an avenue through which the Divine computes Itself. But obstacles are created if we live our life with a feeling as if we are the centre of our private little universe. In reality, one centre of the universe, the Divine, computes Itself simultaneously through a sheer infinite number of little selves, one of which is us. In that regard, the import is not on ourselves individually but on the Divine, which expresses Itself through all matter, nature, and all living things.

For this reason, the *Bhagavata Purana* continues, we should prostrate before all beings, seeing them all as manifestations of the one Supreme Being. Such seeing is also the meaning of the Indian greeting *namaste* (or *namaskar*, or *pranam*), in which one places one's hands in a prayer position (*Anjali Mudra*). It means I recognize the

Divine within you. We then practice this recognition of the presence of God in all beings, in thought, word and actions. If you study this text closely and accept its content after due consideration, then this amounts to practising the recognition of God in all beings in thought. It will require constant remembrance; whenever we face a challenging and conflicted relationship, we must frequently remind ourselves that God is in that seemingly conflicted person, too. We must also remind ourselves that our relationship with that person is complicated only because we have difficulties seeing God in them. To the extent we learn to do this, our relationships will improve.

But what about practising the recognition of the presence of God in all beings through word and action? It is here that ethics come into play. While it is possible and to some extent necessary to have a catalogue of ethical guidelines, the safest and most straightforward way is before we say or do something to ask ourselves whether we are aware of the fact that the being in front of us is at its core God. Recognizing this does not mean that they have to be perfect or don't make mistakes. If they are unaware of their divine core, they are bound to make mistakes and act hurtful. But whether or not somebody else is aware of their divine core and whether we are aware of it has little to do with each other. As a *bhakta*, we need to be able to see God in somebody else whether they do so or not. Because whether we can or can't primarily say something about our own relationship with the Divine.

If we can see the Divine in all other beings, we will notice that our relationships with others will gradually heal. Some individuals are so dependent on a toxic response that they will seek us out based on our propensity to give such a response. Upon becoming aware of our unwillingness to supply such a response, they will usually seek out somebody else.

If we all become aware of each other's divine core, we will all become inclined to cooperate mutually. And that is precisely what the Divine is trying to do through us. Such mutual cooperation based on reciprocal recognition of our divine core forms the bedrock of a divine or divinized society.[353] To the extent that we do not recognize each other's divinity, we will continue to interact in mutual conflict due to the erroneous view of life consisting of conflicting interests. The outcome is that we will harm and destroy each other, as we have done for the bulk of our history. For this reason, the *Bhagavata Purana* says that it is a divine law that living beings destroy each other and ultimately themselves by mutual feuds and that they prosper by mutual cooperation.[354] With this in place, we can now understand that a society's prosperity, peace, and civic cooperation derive from its spirituality and spiritual understanding. There is no other source for it.

---

[353] The term "divinized" implies that the society is not just divine per se but has undertaken a transformative effort to become divine.

[354] *Bhagavata Purana* I.15.24

Chapter 9
METAPHYSICAL ERRORS AND WHAT THE DIVINE IS NOT

In this chapter, I will discuss metaphysical errors and erroneous conceptions of the Divine. This is necessary because their acceptance forms critical obstacles on the path of *bhakti*. If we don't know who we are devoted to, who we love, and who we are to surrender to, how then can our *bhakti* be functional? Additionally, even if we think we know who we are devoted to, our concepts nevertheless may be erroneous. What is the value of such previously held-onto beliefs? And how do we know if we are wrong if we do not critically investigate our convictions employing reason? Considerations such as these are why many *shastras*, such as the *Brahma Sutras* or the *Mandukya Karika*, contain chapters in which false and erroneous beliefs are examined and rejected. Additionally, critiques of rival schools are often dissected and refuted.

We must remember that only about a thousand years ago, *bhakti* in India was a grass-roots movement perpetuated by people who felt what they were practising was right but couldn't articulate why this was the case. It was only with the advent of the 11th-century Indian theologian Shri Ramanujacharya (T. Krishnamacharya was a follower of Ramanuja) and his refutation of Shankara's teachings that *bhakti* received its philosophical underpinnings. I must admit that neither Ramanuja nor Shankara are particularly pleasant to read. Their style is argumentative, and the entertainment value of their writing is akin to that of lawyer's arguing a court case, i.e. it's not to everybody's liking. Nevertheless, many modern yoga practitioners do have a critical intellect, and often only once our intellect is completely satisfied that a particular course of action is the right one, we can take this course of action with conviction and dedication. On the other hand, many students don't follow through with their *bhakti* or practice it without focus because they still harbour insecurities in the recesses of their minds. Once these are removed, however, we can practice *bhakti* with the dedication and sincerity it requires.

THE UNMOVED MOVER

Teaching the subject of *bhakti*, I frequently come across arguments such as, "I cannot believe in God due to such and such recent atrocity". At the base of this statement is an anthropomorphic concept of God, which is the outcome of projecting the sheer limitless power of ancient pharaohs, kings, or emperors on the Divine. In ancient days, the most potent entities we could think of were rulers like the pharaoh. The pharaoh's power consisted of his ability to exert force on any other person to make them conform to the pharaoh's will, but no other person was powerful enough to change the course of action of the pharaoh. The pharaoh was, therefore, the unmoved mover. Because the pharaoh could move everything, but nothing could move the pharaoh, everything that took place in the empire was thus either caused or at least accepted and not intercepted by the pharaoh. This course of reasoning was then extrapolated onto God, in which case it becomes even more difficult to accept because it is easy for us to imagine an at least morally conflicted or aloof pharaoh, but it is unthinkable to imagine a God that allows or ignores evil.

In response to this problem, theologians had to dedicate an entire branch of their teaching, called theodicy, to explain how God can still be good and just even though the world is full of evil. Theodicy becomes entirely unnecessary if we realise that we have turned around the scriptural statement that defines the human as created in the image and likeness of the Divine and have instead created a God in our own image.[355] To do so, we projected the image of a human ruler into the sky. This image of God as an air-born man of giant proportions and capabilities has nothing to do with the Divine. Instead, it says something about our own spiritual limitations.

But the problem does not end here. I practised techniques taught by various spiritual movements for most of my life. It was common for members of these movements, sects or cults to describe their leaders or founders with statements akin to, "he is the father I never had". We have created a God in our own image and projected our needs for the perfect father onto the Divine. Again, this has nothing to do with the realistically existing Divine but is reflective of what in Freudian psychology is called the incomplete bonding or failed attachment to the father figure. Because most of us did not experience the bonding, closeness and

---

355 Gen I:26

acceptance with and from our fathers that we wished for, we are now saddling our relationship with the Divine with this psychological incompleteness. For this reason, theologians had to struggle with issues that should have better been addressed in counselling and therapy sessions.

God is not a giant human. The Divine does not even have an ego to concentrate Itself in a particular time and space to become a human. The Supreme Being is infinite consciousness and cosmic intelligence. God has crystallised as the entire material universe, giving all objects and beings their characteristics. But God, being the universal, can, on the individual level, i.e. within a limited spacetime continuum, act only by acting through us. This means that if we want evil stopped, we cannot wait for God to do it. But we must allow God to act through us, which is precisely what Shri Krishna is trying to convince Arjuna to do.

Because we have choices relative to our level of self-awareness, we also have the option to act in evil ways. Human society, the way it is today, reflects how much of the Divine we have drawn down (Aurobindo refers to this as the drawing down of the supermind) and how much of It we have ignored. When we see wars, atrocities, destruction, etc., we should first and foremost question humanity and its integrity and not try to offload responsibility to a non-existent, giant, white, bearded man in heaven.

Talking about him, look at the depiction of God in Michelangelo's *The Creation of Adam*, which is part of the Sistine Chapel ceiling. This is not the Yahweh of the Old Testament, for in Judaism, it is not even allowed to produce images of Yahweh. The elderly gentleman that we see in Michelangelo's painting is none other than

CHAPTER 9

Zeus, who found entry into Christianity via Hellenistic philosophy. Together with Zeus's image, part of his characteristics also entered Western concepts about God. While Zeus, at times, was a prudent ruler of heaven, he could also be selfish, philandering and conniving. No surprise then that the European Enlightenment gradually did away with God until Friedrich Nietzsche could finally proclaim, "God is dead, now man is free"! Over a hundred years later, gazing into the yawning abyss of environmental holocaust and ecocide, we are beginning to wonder where this supposed freedom will lead us. But maybe the additional $2.4 trillion in military expenditure will help us to get clearer.

In this chapter, I will then attempt to dispel the following erroneous concepts about God and the world:

- That God is a giant human in heaven
- That the world is an illusion
- That the formless Absolute is the highest attainment and that consciousness is all that exists
- That *Karma* Yoga is an inferior or introductory discipline of yoga
- That *Bhakti* Yoga is the only way of approaching the Divine
- That the individual self and the Divine Self are one and the same

GOD NOT A GIANT HUMAN IN HEAVEN

Swami Tapasyananda writes in his commentary on the *Bhagavata Purana* that the Abrahamic religions hold the peculiar unconscious belief that God is an individual entirely different from nature.[356] The problem with this belief is that God is seen as an individual with a particular personality. God cannot have a personality but is the sum total of all the highest potentials that all personalities combined could theoretically achieve. This is embedded in Alfred North Whitehead's term "the initial aim". God thinks all individuals into existence and pursues a different initial aim for each being. But because we are made in the image and likeness of God, we are free to reject the initial aim or cooperate as much as we deem proper. Krishna acknowledges this even at the end of the *Bhagavad Gita*, where he says, "Consider everything that I have said and then act as you deem fit".[357]

The second problematic connotation with Tapasyananda's statement about the Abrahamic religions is that it makes God not only anthropomorphic (i.e. a human-like individual) but also supra-cosmic. Supra-cosmic means that God is entirely different from nature and somehow thrones above it in heaven. Earth (and nature) is a valley of sorrows or at least fundamentally different from the Divine realms, whether heaven, emptiness or *nirvana*. But God is not supra-cosmic, but the cosmos is the crystallised body of God. We live inside of God as individual cells live inside our bodies. Like a single cell can refuse to cooperate with the host organism and become cancerous, human individuals and cultures can choose to do so and are doing so as we speak.

Swami Tapasyananda's criticism does not stop at Abrahamic religions but also extends to Hindu schools of

---

[356] Swami Tapasyananda, *Srimad Bhagavata*, vol.3, p. 27
[357] *Bhagavad Gita* XVIII.63

thought. In his commentary on the *Bhagavata Purana*, he states that the Chaitanya school of Vaishnavism (which led to the modern Hare-Krishna movement) claims that Vishnu is only an emanation of Krishna (Mainstream Hindus, on the contrary, believe that the human *avatar* Krishna is an emanation of the godhead Vishnu).[358] The followers of Chaitanya Mahaprabhu do so because the *Bhagavata Purana*, in a single stanza, says that Krishna is the Bhagavan (i.e. God) Himself.

The *Bhagavata Purana* is a vast text containing some 30.000 stanzas. Some stanzas are obscure, while many support the mainline argumentation of the text. Tapasyananda states that the above statement (of Vishnu being an aspect of Krishna) is not consistent with all other statements of the *Bhagavata*. To quickly restate the *Bhagavata Purana's* theology, the text argues that God is firstly the formless Absolute, the infinite consciousness, secondly a cosmic intelligence that works through and as the divine creative force, thirdly the entire material cosmos which it has become, fourthly an endless number of beings and objects through which It expresses Its infinite creative potential. Krishna is a so-called *avatar* (embodiment, emanation) of this Divine who is exceptionally expert at expressing this philosophy, already spelt out in the *Upanishads* and other texts.

Shri Aurobindo captures the problem of the *Bhagavata Purana* or the *Bhagavad Gita* particularly well. He says we hear Krishna say "I," and because we all tend to anthropomorphise, we believe Krishna just to have referred

---

358 Swami Tapasyananda, *Srimad Bhagavata*, vol.1, p. xxviii

to the human man Krishna. Thus, the classical blue-skinned image, dressed in yellow silk, with peacock feathers in his hair and possibly a flute at His lips, appears in our minds. Aurobindo, however, says that when Krishna speaks "I", He means not the embodied *avatar* but the Purushottama, the Supreme Being.[359] At this point, we need to always briefly stop and remind ourselves that the Supreme Being consists of at least the four main aspects described in the previous paragraph, but probably more because God can possibly never be entirely understood by the limited human intellect. Nevertheless, we must get as close as possible at any given time.

The problem does not, however, end when the term Purushottama is introduced. It is instead here where it really begins. Purushottama is a compound word consisting of *purusha* and *uttama* and, in this context, is rightly translated as Supreme Being. Arguably, Supreme Beingness would be even more to the point, but it's hard to pinpoint what this term refers to in English. Some modern commentators have used the phrase Supreme Personality of Godhead to translate *purusha-uttama*. They do so because the English term "person" has its roots in the Sanskrit *purusha*. But the term person has a different meaning in English. Here, it implies the idea of having a distinct personality from another. For example, we may have a vicious personality instead of a virtuous one. In the judiciary, the term person denotes a legal entity with certain rights; for example, corporations have been given the rights of legal persons identical to humans. This concept of personhood is entirely

---

359 Sri Aurobindo, *Essays on the Gita*, p. 433

different to the idea of *purusha*. The English term person can be traced back to the Sanskrit *purusha* because it is the pure consciousness, the awareness which bestows on an individual their personhood. We cannot become a person if we have no consciousness or awareness.

In Patanjali yoga, the *purusha* is the pure consciousness, the self or *atman* of the *Upanishads*. It is contentless, infinite, pure, formless and immutable. Like the *Bhagavad Gita*, the *Yoga Sutra* says that *purusha* cannot be cut by water, burned by fire, pierced by thorns, or cut by blades because it is the eternal self. While our personality is our surface, the *purusha* is the deepest divine self. In their depth, everybody is divine, and at the surface, none of us is.

To make it even more transparent, all personalities have their root in the Purushottama, the Supreme Being. Our personalities are our limited interpretation of the initial aim by which God has thought into existence every single one of us. Because the Purushottama is, therefore, the indirect source of all personalities (or more precisely, one of the aspects of the Purushottama is the sum total of all initial aims), It cannot be limited by a particular personality. The Purushottama is the Cosmic. It is all persons simultaneously and, importantly, more than that. The term personality also cannot be applied to an infinite and eternal entity, as the Purushottama is. One personality versus another always implies limitation.

Humans have always struggled with the complexity of the Supreme Being. It is okay to simplify, but we lose its essence if we simplify too much. We may use anthropomorphic images of God (or non-humans, too) as shortcuts for the sake of simplicity, but at least once per day, we need to remind ourselves of what God really is.

So says Shri Aurobindo that the Supreme Being is not the limited personal God of so many exoteric religions.[360] Rather than that, It is the one Supreme Soul of whom all deities are aspects, their individual personalities being only a limited development in cosmic nature. This Supreme Being, so Aurobindo, is not a particular name and form of Divinity, such as the one we may choose as our *ishtadevata*. All such names and forms are only faces of the one Divine who is the Universal Divine of all worshippers and all religions.

When choosing an *ishtadevata* (the for us suitable form of the Divine), we need to stay pluralistic and remind ourselves that this cannot be the right *ishtadevata* for everybody. If we choose Krishna, we cannot deny that others will choose Jesus and vice versa. Otherwise, we become orthodox, fundamentalist hardliners who are not interested in whether or not somebody else attains God-realization but only in the fact that we are right and others are wrong. This often plays itself out in following the right faith versus the followers of Satan. Here, however, religion is denigrated to becoming the vehicle of our old problems, adversarialism and antagonism. A truly spiritual person is concerned whether or not somebody else realises the Divine and not whether they do this through the same avenue they themselves have chosen. If it is important to me that other people follow my path, it is because I am unsure whether my path is correct, and therefore, I need other people's confirmation. If I have genuinely attained

---

360 Sri Aurobindo, *Essays on the Gita*, p. 343

realisation, I will only care if others do so, too, and not whether they do so through the same avenue that I used.

Aurobindo also emphasises the need to love the universal Purushottama (Supreme Being) rather than some sect or cult.[361] To get stuck in the outer trivia of spiritual movements and religions is what he calls exoteric. Aurobindo further states that the weakness of the emotional religions (we can assume that with this term, he meant the *bhakti*-based religions) is that they always get too absorbed into some or other divine personality.[362] It is essential to focus on the esoteric aspect of a religion, that is, realising and loving the Purushottama—the Supreme Being.

THE WORLD NOT AN ILLUSION

It is a spiritual boilerplate statement that the world is an illusion and everything is happening in the mind. These concepts have done much damage to spirituality by enabling spiritual bypassing and need to be revised. At the core of the illusionist theory lies the re-coining of the term *maya* as illusion. The term, however, originally implied divine power rather than illusion. So translates Swami Tapasyananda the term *yoga-maya* as the power of manifestation.[363] The *Bhagavata Purana* states that *maya* functions as ignorance in the individual spirits (*jivas*) but as creative power in the Divine.[364] In the same passage, the

---

361 Sri Aurobindo, *Essays on the Gita*, p. 287

362 Sri Aurobindo, *Essays on the Gita*, p. 329

363 Swami Tapasyananda, *Srimad Bhagavata*, vol. 2, p. 207

364 *Bhagavata Purana* X.87.14

universe is described as non-different from God. How can the universe be an illusion if it is non-different from God?

The *Bhagavata* calls *maya* the creative power of God[365] and the same text says that those who know the self recognise the entire world as *sat* (truth), i.e. as really existing.[366] This is because all form is an expression of the Divine. To explain this point further, the *Bhagavata Purana* gives the example of an object made from gold not being rejected as illusory just because it is made from another substance. Similar to gold being the substance from which ornaments are made, God is the substance from which the universe is created. God indwells the universe as its substance in the same way as gold abides in ornaments made of it. Additionally, the passage calls God the One without limbs and sense organs, who is nevertheless the power that supports grasping, locomotion and sensing in all creatures. This means that we are sensing a real world because the Divine powers our instruments of cognition. The concept of the world as an illusion has no place in this philosophy.

A similar boilerplate statement is that the multiplicity of objects and beings we see is false, and only the unity behind it is real. This needs to be corrected. Both unity and multiplicity are real and divine. So says the *Bhagavata Purana*, who understands that the Supreme has manifested Himself as the many by His *yoga-maya* (divine power), has understood the *Veda*.[367] There is nothing wrong here with

---

365 *Bhagavata Purana* X.87.38
366 *Bhagavata Purana* X.87.26
367 *Bhagavata Purana* XI.12.23

the many. In Tapasyananda's edition of the *Bhagavad Gita*, the term *maya* is translated as God's mysterious power, by which the Divine takes birth through Its material nature (*prakriti*).[368] It is a futile attempt to read illusion into the term *maya* here. Again, in a different passage of the same text, the term *atma-maya* is translated as inherent power or will.[369]

Also, Shri Aurobindo is very critical of calling the world an illusion. In *Essays on the Gita*, he states that the world is not an illusion but that the *Bhagavad Gita* throughout admits to the world's dynamic reality.[370] According to Aurobindo, the *Gita* does not adopt the severer view of the extreme [*Advaita*] *Vedantists*, according to whom the world is only an appearance. Such a view would strike at the very roots of all works and actions (*Karma* Yoga). What Aurobindo means is that if the world truly was an illusion, the *Bhagavad Gita* could not afford work, action, and duty to play the prominent role it does.

Again in *Essays on the Gita*, Aurobindo compares *maya* to *prakriti* (nature or divine creative force) and states that *maya* does not mean illusion.[371] Aurobindo states that *maya* consists of the power of process (using Alfred North Whitehead's terminology here), *prakriti*, which is the interplay of its three fundamental modes, the *gunas*.[372] Let's recall that Whitehead described the dynamic or immanent

---

[368] Swami Tapasyananda, *Srimad Bhagavad Gita*, p. 119
[369] Swami Tapasyananda, *Srimad Bhagavad Gita*, p. 135
[370] Sri Aurobindo, *Essays on the Gita*, p. 251
[371] Sri Aurobindo, *Essays on the Gita*, p. 154
[372] Sri Aurobindo, *Essays on the Gita*, p. 252

aspect of God as process, which in the language of the *shastras* is *maya* and *prakriti*.

In *The Integral Yoga*, Aurobindo states that the belief that the world is an illusion was caused by the failure to bring down the supermind.[373] By "bringing down the supermind", Aurobindo means becoming a vehicle for the intelligence of the Divine, which expresses Itself in the ecstatic play of the real world and real beings. In his main work, *The Life Divine*, Aurobindo explains that the *Vedic* seers used the term *maya* to denote divine power.[374] For the *rishis*, *maya* meant the power of infinite consciousness to comprehend itself as infinite existence. Through *maya*, the static truth of essential being becomes the dynamic truth of creation.

Further down in *The Life Divine*, Aurobindo even reckons with the source of the belief that the world is an illusion.[375] The source is simply the fact that if a mystic absorbs their *prana* in the crown *chakra* and thus enters the state of (what in Patanjali's language is called) objectless *samadhi*, (or in the language of Ramakrishna) *nirvikalpa samadhi*, (or in Aurobindo's own language), *nirvana*, the world seen from that state appears unreal. To this, Aurobindo says that the fact that world existence seems unreal to us when we pass into the spiritual silence of *nirvana* does not of itself prove that the cosmos was all the time an illusion. The world is still real to the consciousness dwelling in it. The only thing

---

373 Sri Aurobindo, *The Integral Yoga*, p. 40
374 Sri Aurobindo, *The Life Divine*, p. 115
375 Sri Aurobindo, *The Life Divine*, p. 436

established is that the world appears unreal to the one experiencing *nirvana*; that is all.

CONSCIOUSNESS NOT ALL THAT EXISTS

Closely related to the belief that the world is an illusion are those that the formless Absolute (*nirguna* Brahman) is the highest attainment one can have, and that consciousness is all that exists. In this section, I will show that while the experience of the formless Absolute is significant, serving and aiding the Divine lovingly and with devotion in its divine play is just as sacred and essential. Additionally, consciousness is real, and its direct experience will ultimately aid self-realisation, but divine consciousness has crystallised Itself into this world and the universe, and all beings have become Its body. They are, therefore, just as real and sacred, and to say that only consciousness exists denigrates the importance of God's becoming the world and all beings and that God is working on divinising society.

How did the view that the world is an illusion and only consciousness is real develop? I have written on that subject in both of my books on the chakras and will do so here only succinctly.[376] Authentic experiences of *purusha*, *atman*, *nirguna* Brahman, the formless Absolute or the infinite consciousness, are powered by absorption of one's *prana* in the crown *chakra* (*Sahasrara*), whether the one who makes the experience is aware of that fact or

---

376 *Yoga Meditation – Through Mantra, Chakras and Kundalini to Spiritual Freedom* and *Chakras, Drugs and Evolution – A Map of Transformative States*

not. When *prana* is absorbed in that *chakra*, consciousness appears, and the world disappears. If the experience is long and deep, such as the view of the formless Absolute, no cognition of the world can take place at that time. This is because the formless Absolute can only be seen when identification with the body for the time being is wholly given up. Together with the perception of the body, any sensory verification of the universe's existence disappears. At the same time, the formless Absolute appears. Let me give an example.

When Arjuna saw the *vishvarupa* (the universal form of the Divine), he described it as looking simultaneously into 1000 blazing suns.[377] If one gets to this point, the experience is so powerful that it drowns out all experiences one had until that point and possibly those in the future. One may then fall for the fallacy of reducing the experiences of all other *chakras* to those of the *Sahasrara Chakra*. Such reduction is understandable, as nothing is more potent than directly seeing the God transcendent. Although it is understandable, it is nevertheless incorrect. When coming back from this experience and declaring the world as unreal, one fails to understand that the very God transcendent one was just blessed to have seen, has embodied as this very world. The Divine also has embodied as us whom It has sent into this world to become Itself as us. This means that the process of the God immanent of expressing and becoming Itself as the world and all beings is as holy, sacred and authentic as the experience of the God transcendent. There is no discrepancy between the reality and sacredness

---

[377] *Bhagavad Gita* XI.12

CHAPTER 9

of the formless Absolute on the one hand and the world and all beings in it on the other. Let's also recall that Shri Aurobindo stated that the perceived unreality of the world during mystical states does not prove that the world is unreal, as it is still perceived as real at times of standard embodiment. It only proves that the world appears unreal during mystical states.[378]

In one of the *Gita*'s most significant passages, Krishna discusses essential knowledge (*jnana*, i.e., self-realisation) and complex knowledge (*vijnana*, i.e., God-realisation).[379] The first person to expound on the meaning of this stanza was Shri Ramakrishna. Shri Ramakrishna taught that *vijnana* (God-realization or comprehensive knowledge) is to see the divine play in which God becomes the *jivas* (individual spirits), the world, and the enactor of the divine play.[380] This *lila* is not an illusion but a real expression of divine creativity and ecstasy. The Divine supports the universe by becoming the collective of the *jivas* (i.e., all beings). This is revealed in the state of *vijnana*. Therefore, we must not stop at *jnana*, which is only essential knowledge, i.e., self-realisation, for otherwise, we do not recognise the sacredness and importance of the world and all beings.

Shri Aurobindo expanded the findings of Shri Ramakrishna and moulded them in 35 textbooks into a comprehensive and internally consistent system of mystical and evolutionary philosophy, which shows that it is not only consciousness that is real. In *Essays on the Gita*, Aurobindo

---

378 Shri Aurobindo, *The Life Divine*, p. 436

379 *Bhagavad Gita* VII.2

380 Swami Tapasyananda, *Srimad Bhagavad Gita*, p. 208

says that the Supreme Being (Purushottama) is higher even than the immutable Brahman (i.e. the *nirguna* Brahman) and that loss of ego in the impersonal, formless Absolute is only an initial step towards union with the Purushottama.[381] It serves to recall that the 15th chapter of the *Bhagavad Gita* describes the mystery of the Purushottama as containing in Itself the formless Absolute, the community of bound *jivas* (those who are identifying themselves with their bodies) and the community of free *jivas*, who have attained realisation. Aurobindo further clarifies that the real goal of yoga is a living union with the Purushottama and not just a self-extinguishing disappearing into the impersonal, formless Absolute, which would be the reasonable thing to do if one deemed only consciousness as real.[382]

Aurobindo advises against a self-annihilating spirituality at every turn. He makes clear that the *Bhagavad Gita* rejects the belief that all we have to do is to disconnect *purusha* (consciousness) from *prakriti* (nature, divine creative force, in this case, the world) and merge into the formless Absolute, as this remedy would abolish the patient together with the disease.[383] Aurobindo teaches that we are here for much greater things than simply dissolving ourselves into infinite consciousness. According to him, the world follows a divine plan, and each individual is a part of this plan. We are reminded of Jesus's words, "The things I did you will do and greater things you will also do".[384]

---

381 Sri Aurobindo, *Essays on the Gita*, p. 91
382 Sri Aurobindo, *Essays on the Gita*, p. 132
383 Sri Aurobindo, *Essays on the Gita*, p. 216
384 John 14:12

Further into that vein, Aurobindo states that in the earlier chapters of the *Gita*, we get insistence on self-realisation (i.e. *jnana*).[385] This early insistence on self-realisation can be confused with the end of our spiritual evolution, but this is only the beginning of *Bhakti* and *Karma* Yoga. Let's recall that Aurobindo first attained self-realisation while awaiting a show trial in Alipore Jail. This experience kickstarted his higher yoga, inquiry into the Divine, and life of service to the Divine. Aurobindo is concerned that we will limit our evolution when believing there is nothing to achieve beyond meditating ourselves into self-annulment. He says that if we continue our evolution to *vijnana*, instead of obsessing over self-annulment, we will glimpse an ampler solution, the principle of self-fulfilment in divine nature.[386] This self-fulfilment culminates in loving surrender to the Divine (*Bhakti* Yoga) and acting in service to the Divine (*Karma* Yoga).

KARMA YOGA NOT AN INFERIOR DISCIPLINE OF YOGA

Some commentators view *Karma* Yoga as an inferior path for those who have yet to evolve enough to practice complete inaction, i.e., *Jnana* Yoga. Alternatively, some see it as a path gradually leading to inaction and introspection. But this is not the view of the *Bhagavad Gita*. In Aurobindo's words, in the *Samkhya* philosophy, the realisation of the *purusha* (consciousness) leads to cessation of action.[387] In the *Gita*,

---

385 Sri Aurobindo, *Essays on the Gita*, p. 235
386 Sri Aurobindo, *Essays on the Gita*, p. 289
387 Sri Aurobindo, *Essays on the Gita*, p. 227

on the other hand, it leads to divine action. Krishna teaches that it is impossible to be wholly inactive and lead a life exclusively devoted to introspection. In Krishna's view, action itself is not the problem; it is the fact that we are attached to the false belief that it is our own consciousness (the *purusha* or *atman*) that causes our action rather than the Divine. Krishna says we must recognise that the Divine is enacting Itself through us. That's why in the 18th chapter, He says that the Divine revolves us as if mounted on a wheel.[388] Recognising this fact is called "giving up the sense of agency", i.e., letting go of the belief that we are performing the acts. Additionally, Krishna calls for surrendering the fruits of the actions to the Divine; that is, we are not attached to the outcome of our acts, whether we are successful or not, but in each situation, are simply doing the best, dedicated to the Divine, whatever the outcome is.

Like Krishna, Aurobindo also urges us not to yield to the spiritual tendency to rise above it and withdraw into non-engagement from the world. He says that the quietistic tendency in the human must recognise its own incompleteness.[389] According to Aurobindo, kinetic action, on the other hand, is the fulfilment of God in the human and the presence of the Divine in all human action. Further, Aurobindo points out that for the yoga of the *Bhagavad Gita*, action is not only a preparation but also a means for spiritual liberation.[390] While *jnana* (knowledge) is essential, by its union with works (*Karma* Yoga), we dwell

---

388 *Bhagavad Gita* XVIII.61

389 Sri Aurobindo, *Essays on the Gita*, p. 143

390 Sri Aurobindo, *Essays on the Gita*, p. 79, 86

in consciousness not only when inactively calm but also amid stress and intense action. Similarly, *bhakti* (devotion) is significant by itself, but combined with *Jnana*, and *Karma* Yoga, we come to dwell in the Purushottama (the Supreme Being), who is master at once of the eternal spiritual calm and the eternal cosmic activity.

Aurobindo points out that the later teachings of the *tantric Shaktas*, who even made *prakriti* or Shakti superior to *purusha*, are already evident as a remarkable feature of the *Bhagavad Gita* and perceptible here as the great cosmic action, activity, and power of cosmic energy (divine creative force, Shakti or *prakriti*).[391] Combined with the theistic and devotional elements, the *Gita* teaches that the human, embodied in the natural world, cannot cease from action. Our very existence here is an action; the whole universe is an act of God, and mere living means to be part of this Divine activity. Hence, *Karma* Yoga is not just an inferior path for those who can't sit still or an introductory path for those still learning, but it is an intricate aspect of complete yoga all the way up to its pinnacle.

BHAKTI YOGA NOT THE ONLY WAY OF APPROACHING THE DIVINE

Although I have written a textbook on *bhakti* here and see myself as a *bhakta*, I will argue against the fundamentalist notion that *bhakti* is the only suitable form of yoga for this world age and the most direct way to the Divine. *Bhakti* is a challenging practice. For it to succeed, we need to have a sophisticated conception of the Divine and, with it, get

---

391 Sri Aurobindo, *Essays on the Gita*, p. 107

as close to reality as possible. That's why Krishna exhorts Arjuna to let his mind rest on Him and let his intelligence penetrate Him. To allow our mind to rest on the Divine is relatively easy. We just need belief and blind faith. But what if our blind faith in its conception of the Divine is incorrect? What if we were led astray by teachers who were possibly well-meaning but did not know better? In this case, we would be like the proverbial blind led by the blind.

Bhakti can be an exceptional spiritual motor, potentially driving us on the spiritual path with more velocity than any other form of yoga. That is true, and considering the exultation one can reach, it could be rightly called the pinnacle of yoga (although other aspects of yoga can also mount a claim for this title). But in order to not become emotionally blind and fundamentalist, *bhakti* must be embedded into a framework of *Raja*, *Karma*, and *Jnana* Yoga. Embedded in such a framework is the way Krishna teaches it in the *Gita*. Without a reasonably good concept of the Divine, *bhakti* may otherwise lead us to look down on those who worship another god. Embedded in the other yogas, *bhakti* will make us understand that all gods are images of and avenues to the very same Purushottama, who is nameless and, at the same time, has a thousand names.

In *A Synthesis of Yoga*, Aurobindo describes several ways of making the mind receptive to the Divine.[392] One of them is to make the mind so still through meditation practices that one can literally hear the Divine and then become capable of following Its instructions regarding one's actions. This is a difficult path for most, but it is the path Aurobindo took. It is

---

392 Sri Aurobindo, *The Synthesis of Yoga*, p. 802-7

CHAPTER 9

an avenue taken in some schools of Buddhism but also plays a role in Patanjali Yoga[393] and in *Vedanta*.

A second approach forms the path of *bhakti*, whereby one focuses exclusively on the heart centre and trims one's emotions on the personal Divine. Although this approach, especially for those of an emotional bent, has some advantages over the first one, Aurobindo explains that this path is more prone to error since the emotional being is more likely to be tainted with the impurity of ego and self-centeredness. He states that it is too likely to be tainted by lower emotions, belief in miracles and reliance on divine intervention.[394] One is, therefore, more likely to be here led astray by one's faulty intuitions. This would then make itself known through haughtiness, spiritual pride that one's deity or *avatar* is better than others or even the only true one, and looking down on others who do not share one's religion or religious ideals and declaring them as infidels or inferior. Any such attitudes will void all spiritual advancement created through *bhakti* as they will boost the spiritual ego, a creation almost more dangerous than the materialistic ego. Aurobindo says that devotion without knowledge often leads to bigotry and is raw, crude, blind and dangerous, as the crimes and follies of the religious have frequently shown.

Aurobindo next describes the path of focussing on the *chakras*.[395] Focussing on the *chakras* is performed until a partition in the mind is established, in which one can focus

---

393 *Yoga Sutra* I.2
394 Sri Aurobindo, *The Synthesis of Yoga*, p. 804-5
395 Sri Aurobindo, *The Synthesis of Yoga*, p. 805-6

on the descent of the intelligence of the Divine through the higher *chakras*. Aurobindo says one needs to come to the point where the thinking process takes place above the head in the subtle body, which helps draw down the intelligence of the Divine. This is the path the present author took.

A fourth path is purifying the intellect (*buddhi*) until its reasoning power and capacity of deduction and inference are so great that they cut quickly through misapprehensions. J. Krishnamurti, for example, was an exponent of this path, and it is also featured in *Samkhya* and the *Yoga Sutra*. Here, *tamas* (mass) and *rajas* (frenzy) are gradually purged from the intellect until it is sharpened and represents pure *sattva* (intelligence). Aurobindo argues that each of the four paths has weaknesses when pursued independently and that the ideal scenario is that all four are combined. According to him, they should not be combined through wilful action but by surrendering to the Divine and letting the divine Shakti choose to which degree the paths must be mixed and at what time one is preferred over another. While this demands from the practitioner an extreme level of maturity, openness, and willingness to listen, what we can take away is that it is crucial to combine *bhakti* with other forms of *sadhana*, such as *Raja-*, *Karma-*, and *Jnana* Yoga, until one has gained complete *vijnana* (comprehensive knowledge) of the Divine.

THE INDIVIDUAL SELF AND DIVINE SELF NOT ONE AND THE SAME

As previously explained, in moments when our *prana* is absorbed in the *Sahasrara Chakra*, the world disappears, and the *darshan* (view) of the formless Absolute is obtained.

CHAPTER 9

Both cannot take place at the same time. Because of this, when returning from the experience, we may declare that only the *nirguna* (formless) Brahman exists and nothing else. Following this reasoning, some philosophers declare that the individual and the divine self are the same because only the Brahman exists during such time. They state that at the time of the experience, some form of conscious entity is present, of which the experiencer is aware. This is then seen as the individual self, which, upon merging with the Divine Self, is experienced as identical. This would be of extreme importance because if it can be shown that we have no individual self of any significance, the path of *bhakti* is inconsequential. After all, there would be no individual self from which we can love and worship the Divine. Identity between both selves leaves us only the dissolution and disappearance in the formless Absolute. It also means that enlightened work towards an enlightened humanity is useless because there is no worker, no work and nothing to work on, a nihilistic view held by *Advaita Vedanta* and some schools of Buddhism.

Bhakti proposes a different solution: during the mystical union, the individual self of the mystic is suspended, and only the Divine Self is experienced in Its infinity. There is, therefore, no union of two selves but only the Divine Self (Brahman). Upon leaving the mystical state, the individual self reappears and is again seen as different from the Divine Self. This view is supported by the 11th-century Indian theologian Shri Ramanujacharya (Ramanuja for short), Shankara's great adversary. In his *Shri Bhashya* commentary on the *Brahma Sutra* and his *Vedanta Sara*,

Ramanuja says that the divine and individual selves are different.[396] Ramanuja says that the identity of the individual selves with the Brahman appears so because the Brahman is the self of these individual selves, which are Its body. He wishes to express that the individual self wraps like a mantle around the Divine Self, which alone is experienced in a deep mystical state. Hence, one is duped into believing that both are identical. Remember that Krishna repeatedly says I am the self in the heart of all beings? In our core, then, is the Divine Self, but this is not the individual self. There is nothing individual about the Divine.

Ramanuja also brushes away the argument that the waking state is as unreal as the dream and the deep sleep state, a mainstay of *Advaitic* philosophy formulated in the *Mandukya Upanishad* and Gaudapada's *Karika* (commentary) on this *Upanishad*. Both texts hold that the waking state is annihilated when the dream state starts. The dream state is annihilated when the deep sleep state commences, which in turn is destroyed when the waking state recommences. Hence, all three are unreal, and only the fourth state, consciousness, occurring permanently in all three, is the true and real state. Refuting this philosophy, Ramanuja says that because of the difference in the nature of both, the waking state is not like a dream.[397] The knowledge found in the waking state is not unreal like that in the dream state because in the waking state, there are no defects in the sense-organs, and the knowledge is not sublated as false. Please note that this view is very similar to Patanjali's,

---

396 *Vedanta Sara of Ramanujacharya* III.5.44
397 *Vedanta Sara of Ramanujacharya* II.2.28

CHAPTER 9

who says that both states cannot be compared because the dream state primarily consists of conceptualisation and error, whereas the waking state is mainly one of right and wrong cognition. All of this matters because the *Mandukya Karika* philosophy is often quoted to assert the continual existence of a single divine self (called *Turiya*, the fourth state). In contrast, the separate existence of an individual self is declined by showing the discontinuity of the waking, dream, and dreamless sleep states. These arguments are shown here as invalid, a fact which supports the existence of an individual self, separate from the Divine Self.

The next important point to discuss is Ramanuja's clarifications on the *panchakosha* doctrine of the *Taittiriya Upanishad*. I have already described it in Chapter 3, under the subheading *Why is this relationship so meaningful for the Divine?* Succinctly, while the outer three layers represent body, breath and mind, the innermost layer, the *Anandamaya kosha*, is the consciousness, the divine self. In *Vedanta Sara*, Ramanuja argues that the 4th sheath, the somewhat elusive and misinterpreted *Vijnanamaya kosha*, is the individual self and seeing that it's different from the 5th and innermost sheath, the *Anandamaya*, the two obviously cannot be the self.

In *Vedanta Sara*, referencing *Taittiriya Upanishad* II.1.1 Ramanuja argues that the *Anandamaya kosha*, the Divine Self, differs from the *Vijnanamaya kosha*, the individual self. He says that that which is denoted by the term *Anandamaya* is the Brahman because only in the Brahman is the highest bliss, which is therefore called *Anandamaya kosha* (power of ecstasy sheath). He further grants that the individual self possesses intelligence and the power of seeing, yet it cannot be the cause of the universe, which is the Divine [the Brahman]. He again quotes the *Taittiriya Upanishad*, which states ' "From the same self, the spatial ether came into existence", declaring that the *Anandamaya* [the divine self] is the cause of the universe and, therefore, different to the individual self. Ramanuja further says that the *Vijnanamaya* is so-called because knowledge is the fundamental characteristic of the individual self, whereas the *Anandamaya* is the Brahman whose essential characteristic is supreme bliss.

Ramanuja also states that the affix *maya* in the names of all sheaths signifies abundance rather than illusion. It is already established that the innermost sheath, the *Anandamaya*, refers to the Brahman, and there cannot be illusion in the Brahman. The *Taittiriya Upanishad* states that the Brahman Itself is the cause of all bliss. Therefore, the innermost sheath cannot be called the illusion of bliss sheath.

I found Ramanuja's assertions that our innermost core is the divine self and wrapped around it is the individual self to be the missing links that comprehensively explained all remaining questions of yoga philosophy. When in deep meditation, we dive into our core and find an eternal, infinite, and changeless entity. We share this entity with all other beings, and this forms the cause of compassion. Because we share this divine or cosmic self with all others, it is easy to feel exactly what they feel.

However, calling this entity the individual self is incorrect because it has no individuality. The divine self in me seamlessly blends into the divine self in you because there is only one. All of us partake of this one divine self. We are all the same in the divine self, but in the individual self, we all differ. The individual self is only worthy of that name if it is where our individuality is encrypted. Otherwise, we are better off not to use the term individual self at all.

The true individual self is the *Vijnanamaya kosha*, that part of our psyche that represents the initial aim through which the God immanent thought us into existence. Because each individual represents a different initial aim of the Divine, it is called the knowledge sheath. Each of us has a particular knowledge through which we all differ from each other. This different knowledge is related to the various aspects of the God immanent we each are to represent here on earth. The *karana sharira* (causal body) is another term yogis use to describe this individual self. Again, the causal body is the carrier of God's vision of each of us, the initial aim.

One thing remains to be explained, and that is the similarity in terms of *vijnana*, i.e. the comprehensive knowledge (God-realisation) that Krishna called for in the Gita on the one hand and the term *Vijnanamaya kosha* (deep knowledge sheath).[398] Shri Ramakrishna stated that *vijnana* consists of the combined realisation of the *nirguna* and *suguna* Brahman, the formless Absolute and the Divine-with-form. The formless Absolute is revealed by diving into the *Anandamaya kosha*, the ecstasy sheath. This experience is ecstatic and removes all fear of death since it reveals to us

---

398 *Bhagavad Gita* XII.2

that after dying our last death, we will return to the infinite ecstasy of the Brahman. But what the *Anandamaya kosha* does not reveal to us is how we need to live our lives and what we need to do to serve the Divine and to let the Divine enact Itself through us. This information is only revealed by meditating on the *Vijnanamaya kosha*. It shows us how the Divine becomes Itself by enacting Itself through us.

Jnana means realising that the transcendental aspect of the Divine, the *nirguna* Brahman, is the self in the heart of all beings. In the God transcendent, the many become the One. *Vijnana* means realising the One becoming many, but also how the God immanent expresses Itself through the initial aims, *Vijnanamaya koshas,* or individual selves of an infinity of beings.

Chapter 10
CLARIFICATION OF TERMS

In this final chapter, I will present scriptural snippets that will enhance a clearer understanding of specific terms, which, if misunderstood, would impede progress in our science. It will also allow me to elaborate on certain concepts further and express some ideas I have yet to have the opportunity to embark on. The terms discussed here are

- Mind
- *Avatar*hood
- *Shraddha* (formerly translated as faith)
- *Shastra* (scripture)
- *Yugas* (world ages)
- Castes - additional notes and references

MIND

During the Middle Ages, the body was considered weak and corrupted. In both the Orient and Occident, spiritual sects often mortified and tortured the body to purify it of its wickedness. In modern society, the pendulum has swung back, and this negative attitude towards the body has now been replaced with an extreme infatuation with the body, expressing itself in pampering to any of its whims. Such infatuation with the body may stultify spiritual evolution as much as torturing the body previously did.

Unfortunately, the role of the bad kid on the block has now been conferred on the mind. Spiritual boilerplate arguments at nauseam blame the mind for all ailments of the individual and society. Contemporary spiritual culture now has accepted that the body is not the enemy on the spiritual path but an asset. I will argue here that the case is the same with the mind. Also, the mind is an asset on the spiritual path. It is not the mind that is bad, but what we do with it and how. The mind should thus have the same status as the body.

The *Bhagavata Purana* narrates how Lord Brahma (in Hinduism, the demiurge responsible for creating the world) had no idea how to start the creation process.[399] While contemplating this, he heard two letters from across the cosmic waters, the 16th and 21st consonants of the Sanskrit alphabet, respectively. These consonants, *ta* and *pa*, form together the word *tapa*, meaning to concentrate. Lord Brahma then practised concentration on the spirit for 1000 divine years and, through such concentration, managed to think the world into active existence.

Although in our personal lives, we don't get up to creating entire universes, nevertheless, in our small worlds, too, action follows thought. The reason why we often don't get to create something significant is that our thoughts are dispersed. Thus, our mind does not concentrate. Dispersion of thought in the *Yoga Sutra* is considered the cause of all

---

399 *Bhagavata Purana* II.9.5 -6

obstacles.[400] If we learn to concentrate our minds and turn our thoughts God-ward, our ability to create will be placed in the service of the Divine. Thoughts are concentrated through the discipline of *Raja* Yoga and turned God-ward through *Bhakti* Yoga.

In the *Bhagavata Purana*, the Supreme Being, in the form of Lord Vishnu, states that concentration is the core of His being and that the meaning of concentration is Himself.[401] He further states that in the beginning, He created everything by concentrating. Every highly creative person, whether an artist, scientist, etc., can confirm that creativity is powered by keeping the mind focused on the chosen subject. However, in our modern society, distraction is almost elevated to the status of a religion. I frequently see yoga students fail in their endeavour because they prefer to focus on something other than it. What is focus? It is the ability to let go of things that are not essential and, to some effect, sacrifice them.

With the vast array of distractions that social media and the internet offer, we need to be able to choose what is worth our attention and what isn't. The next stanza teaches us how to do this. Here, the *Bhagavata Purana* states that *maha-tattva* is what *prakriti* becomes first when stirred by divine will.[402] *Prakriti* is the divine process, the divine creative force, Shakti, the Mother of everything. The *tattvas* are evolutes or principles that She brings forth. If we wanted to take the anthropomorphism further, they would

---

400 *Yoga Sutra* I.32
401 *Bhagavata Purana* II.9.22
402 *Bhagavata Purana* III.10.14

be Her children. The first of all to emerge is called *mahat*, the Great One, because it leads to everything else. *Mahat* is Cosmic Intelligence; we could call it the intelligence of the Divine, which orders the entire universe and creation. It is akin to the cosmic *buddhi* (intellect), and the term *buddhi* is usually replaced by *mahat* (when talking of its cosmic function) because it is mainly used for the limited function intelligence has in a human.

The above stanza now reads as Shakti, stirred by divine will, first becomes cosmic intelligence. A crucial hint for us is buried here. There is only one true will, which is God's will. If we want to concentrate our mind and bring forth its capacity for intelligence, we need to surrender to the will of the Divine and ask for It to stir us so that we become capable of concentrating on the divine works that we are called to do, rather than whittling our life away with pointless pursuits.

In *Essays on the Gita*, Aurobindo says there must be a secret ideative capacity of the universal energy (which he calls *vijnana*), even if we suppose that energy and its instrumental idea, *buddhi*, are mechanical.[403] Let me unpack and deconstruct this statement. I mentioned above that the *mahat* or *buddhi* is an evolute of the *prakriti* or Shakti, which in some Indian schools of thought is considered mechanical, similarly as Western Science sees the laws of physics as mechanical. Aurobindo is prepared to accept that this intelligence is mechanical, but he says that behind it, there must be an unrecognised, unseen, ideative capacity, which we could call the Divine Idea-Being, which Itself

---

403 Sri Aurobindo, *Essays On The Gita*, p.426

must be sentient and conscious. Aurobindo suggests the name *vijnana* for the ideative capacity. It is what I have in my writing called the God immanent or cosmic intelligence and what Alfred North Whitehead has called process.

This means that even on the God immanent and Shakti-side of the Divine (the other side being the God transcendent and formless Absolute), there is sentience and an intelligent cosmic being that enacts Itself by becoming the world and all beings. While we can commune with the God transcendent through our consciousness (*atman, purusha*), we can commune with the God immanent by cultivating our mind to the point to which it becomes receptive to the descent of the mind of the Divine, which Aurobindo labels with the term supermind.

If you believe that your mind is wrong or something to be overcome, you cannot become a vehicle for the descent of the intelligence of God. Working for the descent of the supermind is the ultimate act of *bhakti*, love for the Divine and surrender to God. If, as a human collective, we cannot draw the mind of God down into us, we will fail as a species and make ourselves extinct through environmental holocaust and ecocide.

Aurobindo says that the world is not a figment in the universal mind but a conscious birth of that which is beyond the mind into the form itself.[404] Beyond the mind is the *vijnana*, the Divine becoming Itself by crystallising the world as Its divine body. This real body of the Divine is not a figment, not an illusion, but the divine process of God becoming Itself as the world. God has, therefore, two main

---

404 Sri Aurobindo, *The Life Divine*, p.125

aspects. On the one hand, there is the being aspect, the God transcendent, the infinite consciousness, and the formless Absolute. On the other hand, it is the becoming-aspect, the God immanent, the process, *prakriti* and Shakti. The drama of religion is that it has interpreted away this becoming aspect, the feminine aspect of God, the Mother and Shakti. The reason why religion failed to solve many of society's problems is because it reduced God to its supra- and extra-cosmic aspect, the God transcendent and Father, the male aspect of God. Mind and intelligence are aspects of the divine feminine but have become disconnected from the divine Shakti because male theologians have interpreted away the Mother, the process and God immanent, by declaring Her a figment of the mind, a mirage, an illusion. If we want to honour the Shakti, we need to cultivate, concentrate and open our minds to Her and make ourselves ready to download Her intelligence, a process that Aurobindo calls the descent of the supermind.

Aurobindo also talks of the real idea, the power of the conscious force that expresses real being, born out of real being and partaking in its nature, being neither emptiness nor illusion.[405] He wishes to express here a view of the Divine akin to that of Alfred North Whitehead, who also says that God is an entity that orders the world through real ideas. Professor Debashish Banerji comments on Aurobindo's passage above by saying that a real idea can be distinguished from a conceptual idea in that the former is reality itself embodied as the world and its forms.[406] That

---

405 Sri Aurobindo, *The Life Divine*, p.125
406 Debashish Banerji, *Seven Quartets of Becoming*, p. 267

CHAPTER 10

is what we must perceive and know: reality itself (i.e. the Divine) embodied as the world and its forms.

We find 'real idea as reality itself embodied as the world' challenging to understand because our language consists of conceptualisations. Our mind, untrained by yogic concentration and not yet cultivated through mystical insight, takes this to be just another nice-sounding or big-worded conceptualisation. It is anything but. The truth is that God has thought the world and all beings into existence by crystallising Herself as them. It isn't easy to express that in any human language. It is easier to understand it once one has seen it. However, whether we have seen it or not, the critical step is to place oneself into the service of this process. And the only way to do so is by utilising one's mind.

An essential category of real ideas is the initial aim, the complex of thoughts God had about each of us, which brought us into existence. The important thing here to understand is that we are God's real ideas, expressive of God's real being, rather than illusion or emptiness. We are of the substance of divine thought, of God, thinking an infinite number of permutations and computations of Itself into existence, which are neither empty nor illusory. Part of the agenda of the divine Shakti, the Mother, the God immanent, is to become Herself by expressing Herself through us, Her children. The key to consciously co-creating with the Mother is cultivating our mind so that we can receive Her descent. This is the discipline of *Bhakti* Yoga.

Banerji elaborates further that the very fact that the human mind can describe the natural universe in terms of laws is evidence of the presence of mind in the universe.[407] Let's recall that *Samkhya* philosophy, which is at the bedrock of yoga, posits that the reason why mind can understand the world is because the human mind is made up of the identical three elementary particles as the material world, i.e. the three *gunas*, *rajas* (energy), *tamas* (mass) and *sattva* (intelligence). On the same page, Banerji further develops Aurobindo's reasoning that we have inherited a conflicted mind of duality because duality is the instrument by which Brahman (infinite consciousness) produces through the cosmic mind (in which the human is embedded) multiple individualities. That puts a different spin on the so-often by new-age authors poo-pooed duality or dualistic mind.

The cosmic mind, and by extension our mind, is the device by which Being (i.e. God) experiences Itself as many separate and independent beings. The One has become the many, which is part of the agenda of the Divine. But the One cannot become the many unless It does so via the avenue of mind. It achieved this via the same mind, which now tells us that we are separate individuals, estranged from the One. That is so because the individual's mind has to identify itself with a body limited in time and space to take care of the body's survival. At first, it can do so only by de-identifying itself and separating itself from the One, the Brahman. With training (i.e. by making the mind *sattvic*, which is the subject of yoga), the mind can simultaneously see the individual, the One, and the One as the many.

We are now very close to what Krishna calls *vijnana* in stanza VII.2 of the *Bhagavad Gita*. Banerji further explains

---

407 Debashish Banerji, *Seven Quartets of Becoming*, p. 270

CHAPTER 10

that by the device of mind, the One has fragmented Itself so that It may exist in each of Its infinite portions or possibilities of being [capitalisations are mine for consistency].[408] As Krishna states in the *Gita*, this is an essential aspect of the Divine. In the meantime, it puts us into a difficult situation, where for some time, we experience ourselves as cut off from the well-spring of divine love. Only later, as we mature (through *Raja* Yoga), can we simultaneously be individuals separate from the One and still be capable of communion with It via *Bhakti*, *Jnana*, and *Karma* Yoga.

Swami Tyagisananda writes in his commentary on Narada's *Bhakti Sutra* that all Indian orthodox schools of philosophy (called *darshanas*), apart from that of ritualism (called *Purva Mimamsa*), state that spiritual liberation can be obtained only by those who first have a clear vision or image of the truth.[409] With image or vision, he means here that some form of intellectual inquiry has taken place by which the mind has identified:

- What exactly God or the Divine is?
- Which are Its aspects?
- What is It doing here, i.e. what is Its agenda?
- How are we related to It?
- How do we put ourselves into Its service?

Only then can the heart swing into action and undertake its endeavour of love of and surrender to the Divine. For if it takes action before, it probably does so believing that its religion, sect, or cult is better or more valid than others,

---
408 Debashish Banerji, *Seven Quartets of Becoming*, p. 271
409 Swami Tyagisananda, *Narada Bhakti Sutras*, p.125

which are practised by infidels at best and Satanists at worst. In other words, the heart easily falls prey to religious fundamentalism.

The tool by which we undertake the above intellectual inquiry is the often maligned and misunderstood mind. Because of this, Swami Tyagisananda says there is no reason to believe one should leave one's brain behind upon turning towards God. Thank you! It was precisely this that was asked of me by pretty much every spiritual movement, sect, or cult I joined in my younger years. I suspect now that if teachers suggest this fact, they often do so because they know that a student with an astute intellect would quickly notice that their approach to the Divine and their teachings about It are flawed. Therefore, be aware that if teachers advise you to leave your mind with your shoes at the entrance door.

Of course, using the mind to identify the goal does not mean that we are unaware of having to go at some point beyond the mind to attain mystical insight. But leaving the mind behind is not the task of the novice but that of the established mystic upon entering *nirbija samadhi* (*samadhi* on consciousness). Before we have reached that stage, we should even reject the words of Lord Brahma should they conflict with reason, so advises the Yoga Vasishta.

Another task for which the mind is advantageous is using heuristic shortcuts for the Divine, such as divine images or *mantras*. Swami Tyagisananda correctly writes that it is a psychological fact that thinking is possible only with the help of visual and auditory symbols. It is not feasible that whenever I think about the Divine or remind myself to surrender to, love and serve it, I embark on a full-fledged analysis of all aspects of the Divine. If I did, my service to the Divine would always be postponed, and a good part of each day would be taken up by re-establishing full *vijnana* (God-realisation). Therefore, heuristic shortcuts of visual (divine images) and audio (*mantras*) nature are recommended. Of course, as Aurobindo stated, we must regularly remind ourselves that the image (such as the deity or *avatar*) is not the Supreme Being (Purushottama) but only a stand-in. To use an IT metaphor, we click an icon to open an application. The icon, however, is not the application but only a practical path to access it, a heuristic shortcut.

Similarly, we use a divine image or form to access the Supreme Being. This is one of many valuable ways of using the mind on the path of *bhakti*. Therefore, we should not be afraid to use our minds but cultivate them to become the most helpful.

AVATARHOOD

For the human mind, it is almost impossible to think of the Divine without anthropomorphising it, and as previously noted, a human-like image of the Divine has its advantages as a heuristic shortcut. This is because it is not feasible to remind oneself of all its aspects every single time when invoking the Divine. Anthropomorphising the Divine, on the other hand, comes with dangers, and part of that is to mistake the deity or *avatar* for the totality of the Divine, thereby forgetting that the deity or *avatar* are only stand-ins for the entire vastness of the Supreme

Being (Purushottama). This often takes the form of simply believing in and worshipping a particular *avatar* rather than trying to follow their frequently complex and demanding teachings.

But what exactly is an *avatar*? It is often forgotten that the Divine does not have an ego from which to withhold sonship or *avatar*hood from any of its children. The only complete *avatar* in existence is the totality of the material universe with the entire community of sentient beings in it. But we know specific individuals have managed to call down much more of the Divine than others. How is it that the Divine is so much stronger and more apparent in some individuals than in others? How is it that Krishna and Jesus, to name two, spoke with such clarity, eloquence and authority of the Divine and reality that billions of people today worship them as God?

Nobody understood and explained this problem better than Shri Aurobindo, who also proclaimed himself an *avatar*. Aurobindo stated that it is forgivable and understandable that when Krishna in the *Gita* says "I, " the reader takes this to be the human-like charioteer of Arjuna, the godman Krishna, the embodied *avatar*. But Aurobindo exhorts us that this "I" in the *Gita* is the Purushottama, the Supreme Being.[410] Aurobindo reminds us that we must be devoted to the Supreme Being, which is nameless and simultaneously carries all names, not some sect or cult. The danger of being committed to some sect or cult (Aurobindo's own words) is that individuals and teachers outside the cult are usually labelled as inferior and non-divine. Such segregation,

---

410 Sri Aurobindo, *Essays on the Gita*, p. 433

however, is not in the spirit of the Supreme Being, which embodies Itself simultaneously through all religions, teachings, and individuals.

How is it, then, that an *avatar* can appear so powerful that it can be mistaken for the Supreme Being? Aurobindo explains that there are two aspects to divine birth: one is a descent of the Divine into humanity, and the other is the ascent, the birth of the human into the Divine, meaning a human rising into the divine nature and consciousness.[411] According to Aurobindo, *avatar*hood is the rising of the human into the Godhead, which is helped by God's descent into humanity. He points out that the descent of the Holy Spirit made Jesus an *avatar*.[412] This view is now held by some progressive Christian theologians such as Marcus J. Borg, a Lutheran theologian.[413] Borg admitted that if the orthodox view that Jesus was indeed the only begotten son of God was accurate, then what Jesus did on Earth was not extraordinary. Because, in that case, He should have had the power to vanquish all evil for once and all and establish the kingdom of God on Earth. If, however, the view is correct that Jesus transformed Himself and called down the Holy Spirit, then his transformation was extraordinary, and it was this view that Aurobindo held. About the *Gita*, Aurobindo says that although the *avatar* is here represented by the name Krishna, He lays no exclusive stress on this. The *Bhagavad Gita* emphasises what the *avatar* represents:

---

[411] Sri Aurobindo, *Essays on the Gita*, p. 148

[412] Sri Aurobindo, *Essays on the Gita*, p. 163

[413] Marcus J. Borg, *Meeting Jesus Again For The First Time*, Harper One, 1995

the Divine, the Purushottama, the Supreme Being, of whom all *avatars* are human births.[414] In its universality, the Divine takes up all *avatars*, teachings, and *dharmas*. For me, there is no doubt that the same Supreme Being spoke to us through Krishna, Jesus, St. Francis, Shri Ramakrishna, and Shri Aurobindo. But as Aurobindo said, it is important not to reduce the Supreme Being to any one of Its *avatars*.

Aurobindo teaches that the main thrust of all higher yoga is to call down the intelligence of the Divine, which he calls the supermind or the supra-mental. In an individual who practices with great intensity and integrity, this will seamlessly merge into calling down the *avatar*. This is the agenda of the Supreme Being, i.e. the divinisation of humanity and all life and matter. Judging by the numerous wars, atrocities, crimes against humanity, and millions of small-time cruelties and heartless acts that take place every day, it is apparent that humanity has integrated itself into this divine agenda only to a minimal extent. Only a few individuals, such as Krishna and Jesus, fulfilled human potential and followed the call of the Divine. That we all can do so becomes clear from the Nazarene's saying, "The things that I have done you shall also do and greater things you shall do".[415]

SHRADDHA

In the early years of translating Indian texts into Western languages, complex Sanskrit terms were often translated using Abrahamic terms that initially seemed suitable due

---

414 Sri Aurobindo, *Essays on the Gita*, p. 174
415 John 14:12

CHAPTER 10

to their commonality but ultimately revealed themselves as veiling the intent of the original Sanskrit term. One of the most damaging examples probably is replacing the Sanskrit *shraddha* with the English "faith". So writes Swami Medhananda that the untranslatable Sanskrit term *shraddha*, often rendered into English as "faith", encompasses a range of semantic connotations, including belief, reverence, humility, spiritual conviction, and the capacity and willingness to act following one's deepest convictions.[416]

As stated earlier, Aurobindo explains that *shraddha* has two main aspects: one focuses backwards, which is remembrance, and one focuses forwards, which is intuition.[417] Remembrance means that we have a form of memory that before we became these embodied beings estranged from our divine origin, we were, in fact, one with God. On the other hand, intuition in this context implies the knowledge that whatever happens, ultimately, we will go back home to God, even if possibly not on the straightest road.

It was my great fortune that I could be present at the time of the death of several wise and old people whose faces at the time of death radiated a tremendous and entirely unworldly happiness. When asked what they saw, they told me that they saw they were going home. Such vision is the intuition that is part of the meaning of *shraddha*. Of course, using the term intuition today is very difficult as it is often identified with the whims of the ego. The ego desires

---

[416] Swami Medhananda, *Why Sri Aurobindo's Hermeneutics Still Matter*, p. 11

[417] Debashish Banerji, *Seven Quartets of Becoming*, p.176

something but can't argue a proper case for why it should be allowed to indulge itself. It then rebrands its desire as intuition to achieve its aims still. Even so, it is helpful to translate the term *shraddha* as intuition-remembrance or, better, even to use the Sanskrit term without translating it. The problem with the term faith is that we all have an opinion of what it is, which belies the complexity of the term *shraddha*, which is neither reducible to the concept of good faith nor the one of blind faith.

In *Essays On The Gita*, Aurobindo gives a different formula for *shraddha*.[418] He says it consists of the three elements: assent of the mind, consent of the will, and the heart's delight. Assent of the mind means that we accept something, and it could also imply that our surface mind professes to accept something, even though we might reject it in the recesses of our subconscious. Consent of the will is something altogether much higher. Similar to the views of modern neuroscience, the mystics teach that we do not have free will. We only have some degree of choice based on how much our subconscious robotic programming controls us. Unlike neuroscience, the mystics teach that humans can develop will by aligning themselves with the will of the Divine. Because the will of the Divine is the only true free will in existence, it is our only avenue to freedom.

For the novice, this poses a paradox because how can we become free by submitting ourselves to the will of somebody more powerful? The answer to this is that it must be felt. Because the Divine is all-knowing, all-powerful, all-loving, and all-intelligent, by surrendering to It, we

---

418 Sri Aurobindo, *Essays on the Gita*, p.358

CHAPTER 10

become free. This attitude was beautifully expressed by St. Paul, who said, "For as in Adam we all die, in Christ we shall be all made alive".[419] Adam here stands for the human ego, and Christ for the immortal consciousness, the *purusha*. Because the Divine, the *purusha*, is beyond ego, surrendering to It does not mean we surrender to a more powerful ego. It means that we are surrendering to freedom and love itself.

We can only attain freedom by submitting to divine law, not rebelling against it. When we submit, we experience the delight (*ananda*) of the heart, which means we experience God's love, the third part of Aurobindo's formula for *shraddha*. This means that *shraddha* involves tasting at least some of the nectar that awaits us when entering into a love affair with the Divine. It is clear now that *shraddha* is a *sadhana* (spiritual practice and discipline) that goes far beyond the simple term faith.

Swami Tyagisananda states in his commentary on Narada's *Bhakti Sutra* that *shraddha* is conviction that has become dynamic, i.e. process-like.[420] It does not involve mere intellectual assent but readiness to realise the truth through the practice of the teachings when one is convinced of their rationality and utility. Tyagisananda points out that *shraddha* is etymologically connected to *satya*, i.e. truth. The Swami here clarifies crucial aspects of *shraddha*, i.e., its consistency with truth, rationality, and usefulness.

When I was a young seeker, I frequently found myself indoctrinated in what are today called high-demand

---

419 Corinthians 15:22
420 Swami Tyagisananda, *Narada Bhakti Sutras*, p.254

groups, i.e. sects and cults, not limited to any particular religion. Whenever I pointed out inconsistencies in their teachings or the behaviour of their authorities, I was either told to drop my mind, drop my ego, come into the present moment, or have faith. If you find yourself in a similar situation, remember that *shraddha* can never be inconsistent with rational and critical inquiry. That's why Krishna can say to Arjuna at the end of the *Gita*, "Now analyse everything that I have said to your best intellectual capacity and then do as you see fit".[421] Krishna understands that Arjuna, and by extension, all of us, can only act coherently and consistently if we have attained dynamic conviction of that action's truth. And we cannot be convicted of something unless we have proven it in the crucible of the intellect.

The *Bhagavad Gita* deals with *shraddha*, for example, in stanza XVII.3. Here, Krishna proclaims that the *shraddha* of every being is derived from their natural disposition due to past impressions. Krishna goes on to state that a person is primarily constituted by their *shraddha*, so that whatever one's *shraddha* is invested in, one verily becomes. In this context, *shraddha* could be translated as our system of values. Again, there is an emphasis on the process of *shraddha*. Of course, Krishna does not insinuate that our *shraddha* is permanently fixated due to our past live impressions, and we should accept it. He wishes to express that our *shraddha* is so crucial that we must wilfully create it through practice because our system of values will determine our life's direction.

---

421 *Bhagavad Gita* XVIII.63

CHAPTER 10

SHASTRA (SCRIPTURE)

Closely associated with the concept of *shraddha* is that of *shastra*. *Shastra* means 'path to truth,' but I conveniently use the shorthand 'scripture,' a term with its own associated problems. Swami Medhananda says that from an Aurobindonian standpoint, any inquiry into the meaning of scripture remains incomplete and sterile unless it is grounded in a fundamental attitude of *shraddha*.[422] Medhananda explains that in the context of hermeneutics, *shraddha* in scripture takes two primary forms: interpretive charity and spiritual receptivity. Interpretive charity means that we provisionally assume that the statements in a given scripture are consistent and internally coherent. According to this stance, we should resist the impulse to find contradictions or discrepancies in a scriptural text and then try to explain or resolve them by either claiming that some statements in the text are later interpolations or by appealing to some external framework. Such explanations are the common traps into which many Western Indologists fall. I'm not saying here that we should never explain texts by claiming passages are later interpolations or using frameworks external to a particular text. What I am saying is that these should only be used after we have made sincere and lengthy efforts to understand a *shastra* based on its own merit.

Medhananda clarifies that for Aurobindo, the proper reading of scripture requires patience, humility, and an openness to the possibility that our inability to reconcile

---
422 Swami Medhananda, *Why Sri Aurobindo's Hermeneutics Still Matter*, p. 11

certain statements in scripture may reflect not contradictions in the text but our own limitations as readers removed from the text by over a millennium. Medhananda points out that Aurobindo also repeatedly emphasised that Indian scriptures demand a commensurately spiritual receptivity and openness from the reader. This is a significant point. Aurobindo makes a strong case that the best scripture reader must have *shraddha* at their spiritual core; only then will scripture have the capacity to shape, surprise, transform, and enlighten us. This means interpretive *shraddha* involves a willingness to cede agency to scripture instead of arrogating agency exclusively to the reader. This is something that I felt very strongly throughout my whole life when studying Indian *shastras*; they came literally alive before my eyes and taught me. When I discovered the *Upanishad*s at age 15, I immediately noticed a living intelligence in the texts that far surpassed my own and that I needed to ask for their *darshan* to reveal their meaning and then wait patiently until I was addressed.

Medhananda explains further that ideally, when we read, interpret, and interrogate a scripture, we should also remain attentive to the various ways that the scripture can read, analyse, and even interrogate us—for instance, by calling into question our own unexamined presuppositions or by making available to us new perspectives from which we can reflect on, and potentially modify, our own entrenched modes of thinking and living. In other words, when we read a *shastra*, we cannot act as if it is the creation of some superstitious primitives living ages ago (a view that I sometimes seem to cognise in modern Indologists) but that the text is alive and communicates with us. If we are open, *shastra* can talk to us like a living teacher in front of us, and in most cases, better. Aurobindo managed to cultivate this attitude. From studying his commentaries on the *Vedas*, the *Upanishads* and the *Bhagavad Gita*, we can see that *shastra* revealed to him secrets that it hadn't revealed to anybody for centuries. It is because he was receptive and open; notably, he conceived of *shastra* as capable of giving such instruction. This is the secret to reading *shastra*. All the information is there if we are ready to listen.

Narada's *Bhakti Sutra* states that *bhakti* arises from studying scriptures describing the glory of the Divine.[423] This is consistent with the *Yoga Sutra*, which states that one's appropriate deity (*ishtadevata*) is revealed through the study of sacred treatises.[424] Knowing one's appropriate deity is necessary to develop *bhakti*. Madhusudana Sarasvati, the 16th-century philosopher who combined *bhakti* and *Advaita* philosophy, stated that today, the treatise for us needs to be the natural world. This is an important statement. I have met people who are not taken to books but can see and experience the Divine in the natural world. This tendency is also reflected in the fact that many mystics, even if they are scholars, often prefer to live in nature away from the cities. Many *shastras* give that very advice, i.e. to move out into nature to become able to listen.

In this context, Aurobindo observes that to understand scripture, it is not enough to be a scholar; one must be a

---

[423] Swami Tyagisananda, *Narada Bhakti Sutras*, p. 84
[424] *Yoga Sutra* II.24

soul.[425] To know what the seer saw, one must have sight and be a student, if not a master, of knowledge. Aurobindo here wishes to express that it is not enough to have a linguistic understanding of the letters and words on the page; it must be followed by mystical insight. In other words, we must do the practices that the texts suggest to derive knowledge. Only then can we come to know the meaning of the *shastras*.

YUGAS (WORLD AGES)

Both the *Mahabharata* and the *Puranas* subscribe to the *Yuga* doctrine, according to which there are four successive world ages (*Satya, Treta, Dvapara,* and *Kali Yugas*) during which human society is subject to entropy (i.e. gradual breakdown), successively degenerates and becomes more corrupt. According to this teaching, we are over 5000 years into the *Kali Yuga*, the age of darkness. There are different views on how long the *Kali Yuga* takes when it ends, and what comes after it. This teaching has, in recent decades, garnered more attention. This increase is due to the fact that the European-Enlightenment-inspired belief that we are entering a period of technological utopia in which science fixes all of our problems has gradually been replaced with the sobering realisation that most technologies we develop come with sinister side effects that take us decades or even centuries to understand by which time it is very late to rectify them.

---

425 Sri Aurobindo, *Collected Works of Sri Aurobindo*, Sri Aurobindo Ashram Trust, Pondicherry, 2003, Vol 12, p. 37

Another sobering realisation is that humanity does not seem capable of moving beyond permanent warfare. Geopolitical instability at the time of writing this book has been the highest since World War 2. The power of tyrannies and dictatorships in the world is increasing, corresponding with curtailing civil liberties and freedom of the press. While more and more wealth is concentrated in the hands of fewer people every year, the toiling masses are conversely working longer and more arduous hours by the year, and exploitation increases. Humanities mental health crisis is deepening with constant increases being reported of Autistic Spectrum Disorder, Borderline Personality Disorder, Bipolar Disorder and Anxiety and Depression. While the threat of Artificial Intelligence looms large, military expenditure is skyrocketing worldwide. The oceans are heating and acidifying, greenhouse gasses in the atmosphere are rising, the pole caps are melting, and typhoons, hurricanes, and cyclones are increasing in intensity. Desertification, acidification and salination of soil and its erosion are accelerating, leading to an accelerating decrease in arable land. This, combined with increasingly scarce water supplies, leads to accelerating refugee crises, which destabilises the coherence of the societies to which these climate- and economic refugees migrate. At the same time, habitat destruction, land clearing, overhunting, and climate change drive the 6th mass extinction of species. This mass extinction decreases biodiversity, the guarantor of homeostasis in the biosphere. The term homeostasis means that the bio-parameters (which guarantee life on Earth) oscillate only in a narrow bandwidth. Because of homeostasis, created by the symbiotic action of the entire biomass of the planet, the climate during the Holocene (the geological era comprising the last 10 Million years) was the most stable climate period in the planet's history. Without such a stable climate, the evolution of Homo Sapiens would have hit significant roadblocks. It is debated whether the coming Anthropocene, a new geological era marked by human-caused destabilisation of planetary homeostasis, will be hospitable to organisms more complex than even the single-cell varieties.

I am not saying that scientific and technological progress is all bad or could be rolled back. What I am saying is that the general *Sieg-Heil*-technology fanaticism[426] of the modernistic era has given way to a much more realistic and sober assessment of humanity's capacities. The *Yuga* doctrine conceived many thousand years ago, provides a surprisingly accurate report of where we are today. I am here only presenting a few of its snippets. They may help us come to terms with the fact that many things promised to us just a few decades ago have not only not materialised, but today, many people have a decidedly bleak outlook on our future. The *Puranas* and the *Mahabharata* have forecasted this development, explained the reasons, and taught solutions.

In the *Bhagavata Purana*, Krishna states that people will be unrighteous in their outlook in the age of *Kali*.[427] A later passage of the same text elaborates that many people's hobby is to chase after the wives and wealth of others and that material wealth takes the place of virtuous conduct

---

[426] I am using this term to draw attention to the fact that for a long time, this type of fanaticism was unquestioned and unquestionably similar to fascist ideology within a fascist society.

[427] *Bhagavata Purana* XI.7.5

CHAPTER 10

and character in estimating a person's worth.[428] I think nobody can dispute that this is our current state of affairs. A bit further down the track, the *Purana* adds that in the *Kali Yuga*, people tend to be miserly, merciless, greedy, luckless and vindictive on silly grounds.[429]

On the next page, the same *Bhagavata Purana* discusses a particularly worrisome tendency of the *Kali Yuga*: that spiritual teachings and teachers will become corrupted.[430] The *Bhagavata* states that teachers who are authorities in *adharma* (unrighteous conduct, corruption and vice) will begin to lecture on *dharma*, sitting in the sacred seats of respected teachers. The passage speaks for itself. In another passage, the *Bhagavata* supplies additional signs of the *Kali Yuga*, which are similarly unflattering, but again, it describes our age accurately.[431]

Early on in the *Bhagavata Purana*, it makes the initially surprising assertion that the Divine constituted of Sat-Chit-Ananda is suitable for worship during the *Krta Age*.[432] This requires explanation and analysis. *Krta Yuga* and *Satya Yuga* are synonyms and refer to the first age, variously called the Golden Age or Age of Truth. During this first of all *yugas* humanity presumably was spiritually more mature and more in tune with nature and the Divine. Sat-Chit-Ananda is the name of the Divine in the *Upanishads* and can be translated as Truth-Consciousness-Ecstasy. It is also the name Shri Aurobindo uses

---

428 *Bhagavata Purana* XII.2.40-42

429 *Bhagavata Purana* XII.3.25

430 *Bhagavata Purana* XII.3.38

431 *Bhagavata* Purana XII.2.1-16

432 *Bhagavata* Purana III.21.8

for the Divine but has been replaced in later ages by human-like deities. It is essential to understand that in a long bygone era, we were still spiritually mature enough to understand today's seemingly complex name of the Divine as Sat-Chit-Ananda or Truth-Consciousness-Ecstasy. In the present age, on the other hand, we seem to be deifying wealth, power, sexual prowess, violent entertainment, fame and the number of likes on social media. The *Purana* is, therefore, realistic in stating that humanity has lost Sat-Chit-Ananda out of sight.

Let's move forward to the solution that the *Puranas* and the *Mahabharata* have to offer for our predicament. This predicament was caused by humanity losing its footing in divine law and pursuing its own grandeur and ego. We can reverse this process by aligning ourselves again with the Divine, and a new Golden Age can dawn on us. The direction of humanity was always determined by a minority of bold, pioneering individuals, which drew the majority along with them. If enough individuals take up the challenge of the *Bhagavad Gita*, the *Bhagavata Purana* and other *shastras* to again align ourselves with the agenda of the Purushottama, the Supreme Being, through a convergence of *Raja*, *Karma*, *Jnana*, and *Bhakti* Yoga, the course of humanity will change.

CASTES AND VARNAS - ADDITIONAL NOTES AND REFERENCES

There is truth behind the *Gita's varna* system, which we need to understand as it is at the base of Krishna's call for finding our own personal destiny regarding how each individual must serve the Divine. In doing so, I am neither

CHAPTER 10

justifying the modern, hereditary Indian caste system nor its clones in Western society. In her book *Caste: The Origin of Our Discontents*, the American Pulitzer-Price-winning journalist Isabel Wilkerson describes that at the base of racism against African Americans in the United States lies a stratified caste system akin to that in India and Nazi Germany. As an Australian citizen, I am very well aware of the fact that the treatment of Australian Aborigines should be included in this list as well. When studying Australian history, I was struck by the fact that behind and underneath the categorisation of Australian Aborigines as subhuman (to be able to claim it for the British crown, Captain Cook declared Australia to be uninhabited by humans) was the systematic disowning and transfer of wealth from Aborigines to white colonialists over two centuries. Many fledgling Australian industries would not have survived, and its economy could only have developed into its current form with systematic land theft, and the supply of cheap or even free manual labour of a people subdued for 200 years. This means that although such societies look superficially racist, at the base of racism and similar systems of social stratification lies the systematic transfer of wealth and ownership. Although I cannot cover these themes adequately in this book on *Bhakti* Yoga, I feel it is necessary to mention them because I have frequently talked about caste and varnas. In addition to Wilkerson's book, I recommend Bill Gammage's *The Biggest Estate on Earth- How Aborigines Made Australia*.

The Sanskrit term underlying the English word caste is *varna*, which means colour. The idea here is that we are

319

coloured by the mental qualities of *tamas* (mass or inertia), *rajas* (frenzy or energy) and *sattva* (intelligence or wisdom). Based on that, our societal role should be in the spiritual profession, government and defence forces, business, or labour. According to the *Bhagavad Gita*, this distinction existed originally so that we could use our capacities and tendencies to serve the Divine and society. Initially, the castes were not hereditary, and it was possible to switch castes if the inherited situation did not suit one's actual constitution. Krishna frequently refers to the *varnas*, but Aurobindo, Swami Tapasyananda and others point out that he does not refer to the modern castes but mental qualities. Unfortunately, all medieval commentators read castes into Krishna's use of *varna*. They then interpreted his call to follow one's *svadharma* to mean to adhere to caste rules. I have quoted Swami Tapasyananda earlier, who argues that the medieval commentators did not do a great service to Lord Krishna with this line of reasoning. I will supply here more background information because unless we understand *varna* as a person's mental quality (rather than hereditary caste) and *svadharma* as an individual's inherent highest destiny (rather than the call to stick to one's caste rules), the philosophical depth of the *Bhagavad Gita* cannot be plumbed, nor can we yield to its call for an intimate, personal relationship with the Divine. Such was the view of Shri Aurobindo.

In the *Mahabharata*, Krishna says that devotees of the Lord are never *shudras* (the name of the lowest caste, supposedly dominated by tamas - inertia). Krishna here states that not birth makes one a *shudra*, but devotion to

CHAPTER 10

God or lack thereof, i.e. one's spiritual quality. The Krishna of the *Mahabharata, Gita* and *Bhagavata Purana* is familiar with the caste system. He argues, however, that hereditary caste does not matter; devotion to the Divine matters. He goes on to state that a wise person should not even slight an outcaste (who in the caste system are below the *shudras*) who is devoted to the Divine. Should he do so, he will fall into hell. Therefore, it does not behove us to distinguish between one devotee and another. Again, Krishna states here that the caste system is irrelevant, but what matters is one's level of realisation of the Divine and the service rendered to the Divine.

While many modern capitalist societies do not feature something as rigid as the Indian caste system, we should not be too smug. Realistically speaking, these societies have a caste system strictly oriented along the lines of a person's financial resources. If in capitalism you have no money, your situation is not much different from that of an Indian outcaste. If, on the other hand, you are a hereditary billionaire, you can do whatever you like. In between, there are graduations, again not so different from the caste system. The problem with wealth in the West is that it gives you access to expensive lawyers and, therefore, the ability to outspend lesser-funded opponents during legal proceedings. It would be essential to achieve a society in which a person's value is determined neither by the size of their asset portfolio nor by the family into which they are born.

Aurobindo, too, held that the injunction that *svadharma* (own duty) means adhering to one's caste is wrong.[433] He

---
433 Debashish Banerji, *Seven Quartets of Becoming*, p. 312

elaborates further that this wrong notion is informed by the erroneous teaching that the world is an illusion. If we believe that the world is an illusion, then, according to Aurobindo, adhering to caste rules is the next best thing for those unfit for spiritual liberation. Aurobindo says that if we admit that the world is real, finding one's *svadharma* means supporting God's work in the real world. It means to live for God in the world and help God lead the world towards a divine ideal, the divinisation of human society.

Epilogue

On a deeper level, our practice of *bhakti* creates an opening for the Divine to participate in the world more fully by individuating through us. There is indeed no difference between the Divine and the world. The world, the cosmos, is the body of the Divine. However, on a deeper level, because the Divine is a living intelligence, albeit a cosmic one, it requires for us limited embodied intelligences, to open ourselves to the frequencies of the Divine. Through that, the Divine can participate on a higher level in the world.

In Shri Aurobindo's own words, an avenue is created by realising that *ananda*, ecstasy, is the passive state of the Brahman and *prema*, love, is its active state. By tuning, through meditation and *sadhana*, into the ecstasy of the Brahman, we are ultimately filled with Its love and can carry this love out into the world. We will then experience that pure, divine love, *prema*, is not an emotion but a quality of the Divine bestowed on us.

As essential to this way of devotion, Aurobindo advises *manana* and *darshana*, which are the constant thinking of the Divine in all things and seeing of the Divine always and everywhere.[434] When doing so, communion with the Divine will come naturally. This communion, rather than union, should be our goal. Shri Ramakrishna expressed this beautifully when saying, "I want to taste sugar rather

---

434 Sri Aurobindo, *The Synthesis of Yoga*, p. 601

than becoming sugar", as the integrity of the devotee in such communion is sustained.

Adherence to *dharma* (right action) is essential on this path of *bhakti*, for Krishna exhorts us to see God in everything not contrary to *dharma*, strength uncorrupted by desire, and desire in alignment with *dharma*.[435] The *Gita* is not some ancient conversation that does not concern us. We must understand that Arjuna stands in here for all of us; he is asking the questions that baffle us all. On a metaphorical level, Arjuna stands for the surface self, or phenomenal self, and Krishna for the deep self, or true self.

Apart from understanding that Arjuna and Krishna represent aspects of our own psyche, we must also learn to cooperate more and feud less. The *Bhagavata Purana* says that living beings destroy each other and ultimately themselves through mutual feuds and prosper through mutual cooperation.[436] Beyond cooperating with each other, the *bhakta* partakes in the joys and sufferings of all beings. So says Krishna in the *Gita* that the greatest yogis are those who, seeing the *atman* in all others, feel their joy and suffering as they would their own.[437]

In order to truly understand the Divine, meditating on a deity or an *avatar* will ultimately not be enough. The *Bhagavata Purana* states that we need to meditate on each aspect of the Divine individually and, once we have achieved proficiency in that, on all parts together.[438] The

---

435 *Bhagavad Gita* VII.11
436 *Bhagavata Purana* I.15.24
437 *Bhagavad Gita* VI.32
438 *Bhagavata Purana* III.33.22

final master key to *Bhakti* Yoga is not having our own satisfaction in mind when performing actions but that of God. So states Shri Krishna, that we will gain devotion to Him by performing all our mundane efforts with His satisfaction in mind.[439] With all of these building blocks in place, we can create a divinised society guided by evolved, genuine love for the Divine, all beings, and the whole of the cosmos.

---

439 *Bhagavata Purana* XI.11.23-24

Bibliography

Aranya, Sw. H., *Yoga Philosophy of Patanjali with Bhasvati*, University of Calcutta, Kolkata, 2020.

Aurobindo, S., *Secret of the Veda*, Sri Aurobindo Ashram Trust, Pondicherry, 1995.

Aurobindo, S., *Essays on the Gita*, Sri Aurobindo Ashram Trust, Pondicherry, 1995.

Aurobindo, S., *Record of Yoga*, Vol. 2, Sri Aurobindo Ashram, Pondicherry, 2001.

Aurobindo, S., *The Life Divine*, Sri Aurobindo Ashram, Pondicherry, 1939-40.

Aurobindo, S., *Collected Works of Sri Aurobindo*, Sri Aurobindo Ashram Trust, Pondicherry, 2003.

Aurobindo, S., *Savitri – A Legend and a Symbol*, Sri Aurobindo Ashram Trust, Pondicherry, 1995.

Aurobindo, S., *The Integral Yoga*, Lotus Press, Twin Lakes, 1993.

Aurobindo, S., *The Synthesis of Yoga*, Sri Aurobindo Ashram, Pondicherry, 1948.

Aurobindo, S., *The Upanishads*, Sri Aurobindo Ashram Trust, Pondicherry, 1996.

Bader, J., *Meditation in Sankara's Vedanta*, Aditya Prakashan, New Delhi, 2010.

Banerji, D., *Seven Quartets of Becoming- A Transformative Yoga Psychology Based on the Diaries of Sri Aurobindo*, Nalanda International, Los Angeles, 2012.

Bhattacharya, V., editor and translator, *The Agamasastra of Gaudapada*, Motilal Banarsidass, Delhi, 1963.

Borg, M.J., *Meeting Jesus Again For The First Time*, Harper One,1995.

Chandra Vasu, R.B.S., translator, *The Gheranda Samhita*, Sri Satguru Publications, Delhi, 2006.

Chapple, C., translator, *The Yoga Sutras of Patanjali*, Sri Satguru Publications, Delhi, 2010.

Cobb, J.B., *A Christian Natural Theology*, Westminster John Knox Press, 2007.

Cole, C.A., Asparsa Yoga – *A Study of Gaudapada's Mandukya Karika*, Motilal Banarsidass, Delhi, 2002.

Dasgupta, S., *A History of Indian Philosophy*, 1st Indian edn, 5 vols, Motilal Banarsidass, Delhi, 1995.

Easwaran, E., *The Bhagavad Gita For Daily Living*, 3 vols, Nilgiri Press, 1975.

Eliade, M., Yoga – *Immortality and Freedom*, 2nd edn, Princeton University Press, Princeton, New Jersey, 1989.

Gambhirananda, Sw., *Bhagavad Gita with Commentary of Sankaracarya*, Advaita Ashrama, Kolkata, 2017.

Gambhirananda, Sw., translator, *Brahma Sutra Bhasya of Sri Sankaracarya*, Advaita Ashrama, Kolkata, 1985.

Gambhirananda, Sw., translator, *Eight Upanisads*, Advaita Ashrama, Kolkata, 2016.

Ganguli, K.M., translator, *The Mahabharata*, 12 vols, Munshiram Manoharlal, New Delhi, 2018.

Godman, D. (ed.), *Be As You Are – The Teachings of Ramana Maharshi*, Penguin Books India, New Delhi, 2005.

Gurdjieff, G.I., *Beelzebub's Tales To His Grandson*, Penguin Books, 1999.

Jagadananda, Sw., translator, *Upadesa Sahasri of Sri Sankaracarya*, Sri Ramakrishna Math, Madras.

Jagadananda, Sw., translator, *Vakyavrtti of Sri Sankaracarya*, Sri Ramakrishna Math, Madras.

Johnson, R.A., *We: Understanding the Psychology of Romantic Love*, Harper One, 2009.

Krishna, G,. *Kundalini – Evolutionary Energy in Man*, Shambala, 1997.

Krishnamurti, J., *Krishnamurti to Himself*, HarperCollins, San Francisco, 2013.

Krishnamurti, J., *Krishnamurti's Journal*, 2nd rev. edn, Krishnamurti Foundation Trust India, Chennai, 2023.

Krishnamurti, J., *The Awakening of Intelligence*, HarperCollins, San Francisco, 2007.

Krishnamurti, J., *The First and Last Freedom*, HarperCollins, San Francisco, 1995.

Kunjunni Raja, K., editor, *Hathayogapradipika of Swatmarama*, The Adyar Library and Research Centre, Madras, 1992.

Leggett, T., *Realization of the Supreme Self*, New Age Books, New Delhi, 1995.

Leggett, T., translator, *Sankara on the Yoga Sutras*, 1st Indian edn, Motilal Banarsidass, Delhi, 2012.

Lester, R.C., *Ramanuja on the Yoga*, Adyar Library and Research Centre, Madras, 1996.

Madgula, I.S., *The Acarya*, 2nd rev. edn, Motilal Banarsidass, Delhi, 2021.

Madhavananda, Sw., translator, *The Brhadaranyaka Upanisad*, Advaita Ashrama, Kolkata, 2017.

Mani, V., *Puranic Encyclopedia*, 1st English edn, Motilal Banarsidass, Delhi, 1995.

Medhananda, Sw., *Why Sri Aurobindo's Hermeneutics Still Matter*, Ramakrishna Institute of Moral and Spiritual Education, Mysore.

Mueller, M., editor, *The Sacred Books of the East*, vol. 38, *Vedanta Sutras*, trans. G. Thibault, Motilal Banarsidass, Delhi, 1982.

Natarajan, A.R., *Ramana Maharshi – The Living Guru*, Ramana Maharshi Centre for Learning, Bangalore, 2016.

Natarajan, A.R., *Timeless in Time – A Biography of Sri Ramana Maharshi*, 2nd edn, Ramana Maharshi Centre for Learning, Bangalore, 2020.

BIBLIOGRAPHY

Nikhilananda, Sw., translator, *The Mandukya Upanishad with Gaudapada's Karika and Sankara's Commentary*, Advaita Ashrama, Kolkata, 2007.

Panoli, V., translator and commentator, *Gita in Shankara's Own Words*, Shri Paramasivan, Madras, 2000.

Prabhavananda, Sw., *Bhagavad Gita*, Vedanta Press, Hollywood, 1944.

Prabhupada, B. Sw., *Bhagavad Gita As It Is*, The Bhaktivedanta Book Trust, New York, 1968.

Radhakrishnan, S., editor, *The Principal Upanisads*, HarperCollins Publishers India, New Delhi, 2014.

Radhakrishnan, S., *Indian Philosophy*, Indian edn, 2 vols, Oxford University Press, New Delhi, 1960.

Radhakrishnan, S., translator and commentator, *The Bhagavad Gita*, HarperCollins Publishers India, New Delhi, 2022.

Ramakrishnananda, Sw., *Life of Sri Ramanuja*, Sri Ramakrishna Math, Madras.

Ramanujacharya, S., *Gita Bhasya*, transl. Svami Adidevananda, Sri Ramakrishna Math, Madras, 1991.

Sapolsky, R. M., *Behave: The Biology of Humans at Our Best and Worst*, Penguin Press, 2017.

Shankaracharya, S., *Bhagavad Gita with Commentary*, transl. Swami Gambhirananda, Advaita Ashrama, Calcutta, 1997.

Stoler Miller, B., *The Bhagavad Gita*, Bantam Books, New York, 1986.

Subramaniam, K., translator, *Mahabharata*, Bharatiya Vidya Bhavan, Mumbai, 2019.

Subramaniam, K., translator, *Srimad Bhagavatam*, 7th edn, Bharatiya Vidya Bhavan, Mumbai, 2017.

Swahananda, Sw., translator, *Chandogya Upanisad*, Sri Ramakrishna Math, Madras, 1976.

Tapasyananda, Sw., *Srimad Bhagavad Gita*, Sri Ramakrishna Math, Chennai, 1984,

Tapasyananda, Sw., *Srimad Bhagavata*, Sri Ramakrishna Math, Chennai, 1981.

Tapasyananda, Sw., translator, *Sankara-Dig-Vijaya*, Sri Ramakrishna Math, Chennai.

Tapasyananda, Sw., translator, *Sivanandalahari of Sri Sankaracarya*, Sri Ramakrishna Math, Madras.

Torwesten, H., Ramakrishna – *Schauspieler Gottes*, Fischer Taschenbuch Verlag, Frankfurt, 2001.

Tyagisananda, Sw., *Narada Bhakti Sutras*, Sri Ramakrishna Math, Chennai, 2001,

Vireswarananda, Sw., translator, *Srimad Bhagavad Gita*, Sri Ramakrishna Math, Madras.

Whitehead, A.N., *Adventure of Ideas*, Free Press, 1967.

Whitehead, A.N., *Process and Reality*, Free Press, 1979.

Whitehead, A.N., *Religion in the Making*, Fordham University Press, 1996.

Wilkerson, I., *Caste: The Origin of Our Discontents*, Random House, 2020.

Yogananda, P., *God Talks with Arjuna*, 3 vols, Motilal Banarsidass, 1999.

Author Information

Gregor began *Raja* Yoga in the late 1970s and added *Hatha* Yoga in the early 1980s. Shortly after that, he began yearly travels to India, where he learned from various yogic and tantric masters, traditional Indian *sadhus,* and ascetics. He lived many years as a recluse, studying Sanskrit and yogic scripture and practising yogic techniques.

Gregor's textbook series, consisting of *Ashtanga Yoga: Practice and Philosophy, Ashtanga Yoga: The Intermediate Series, Pranayama: The Breath of Yoga, Yoga Meditation: Through Mantra, Chakras and Kundalini to Spiritual Freedom, Samadhi: The Great Freedom, How to Find Your Life's Divine Purpose, Chakras, Drugs and Evolution,* and *Mudras: Seals of Yoga,* has sold over 100,000 copies *worldwide and* been translated into eight languages. His blog articles can be found at www.chintamaniyoga.com.

Today Gregor integrates all aspects of yoga into his teaching in the spirit of Patanjali and T. Krishnamacharya. His zany sense of humour, manifold personal experiences, vast and in-depth knowledge of scripture, Indian philosophies, and yogic techniques combine to make Gregor's teachings easily applicable, relevant, and accessible to his students. He offers workshops, retreats and teacher trainings worldwide.

Contact Gregor via:
www.chintamaniyoga.com
www.8limbs.com
https://www.facebook.com/gregor.maehle

Made in the USA
Middletown, DE
02 November 2024